D1271187

Love's Enlightenment

A number of prominent moral philosophers and political theorists have recently called for a recovery of love. But what do we mean when we speak of love today? *Love's Enlightenment* examines four key conceptions of other-directedness that transformed the meaning of love and helped to shape the way we understand love today: Hume's theory of humanity, Rousseau's theory of pity, Smith's theory of sympathy, and Kant's theory of love. It argues that these four Enlightenment theories are united by a shared effort to develop a moral psychology that can provide both justificatory and motivational grounds for concern for others in the absence of recourse to theological or transcendental categories. In this sense, each theory represents an effort to redefine the love of others that used to be known as *caritas* or *agape* – a redefinition that came with benefits and costs that have yet to be fully appreciated.

Ryan Patrick Hanley holds the Mellon Distinguished Professorship in Political Science at Marquette University. He is the author of *Adam Smith and the Character of Virtue* (Cambridge, 2009), and the editor of *Adam Smith: His Life, Thought, and Legacy* (2016), and the Penguin Classics edition of Adam Smith's *Theory of Moral Sentiments* (2010). His articles on eighteenth-century philosophy have recently appeared or are forthcoming in the *American Political Science Review*, the *Archiv für Geschichte der Philosophie*, the *Journal of Politics*, and the *Journal of the History of Philosophy*, among others. He is also the recipient of fellowships from the Arete Initiative, the Earhart Foundation, and the National Endowment for the Humanities.

Love's Enlightenment

Rethinking Charity in Modernity

RYAN PATRICK HANLEY

Marquette University

CAMBRIDGE
UNIVERSITY PRESS

CAMBRIDGE
UNIVERSITY PRESS

One Liberty Plaza, 20th Floor, New York, NY 10006, USA

Cambridge University Press is part of the University of Cambridge.

It furthers the University's mission by disseminating knowledge in the pursuit of education, learning, and research at the highest international levels of excellence.

www.cambridge.org
Information on this title: www.cambridge.org/9781107105225

© Ryan Patrick Hanley 2017

First published 2017

A catalogue record for this publication is available from the British Library.

Library of Congress Cataloging-in-Publication Data
Names: Hanley, Ryan Patrick, 1974– author.
Title: Love's enlightenment: rethinking charity in modernity /
Ryan Patrick Hanley, Marquette University.
Description: New York: Cambridge University Press, 2017.
Identifiers: LCCN 2016016147 | ISBN 9781107105225 (hardback)
Subjects: LCSH: Love – Philosophy. | Empathy. | Attitude (Psychology) | Altruism.
Classification: LCC BD436.H265 2016 | DDC 177/.7–dc23
LC record available at https://lccn.loc.gov/2016016147

ISBN 978-1-107-10522-5 Hardback

For my father

Contents

Acknowledgments

I am deeply grateful to a number of institutions and individuals for their help with this project. A "Defining Wisdom" Fellowship from the University of Chicago's Arete Initiative enabled me to begin the project in earnest. As it began to take form, I was fortunate to receive helpful feedback from fellow participants and audiences at presentations and workshops at the University of Antwerp, the University of Arizona, the University of Chicago, the École Normale Supérieure-Lyon, Harvard University, the University of Illinois-Chicago, Northern Illinois University, and the University of Notre Dame. Parts of the project were also presented at annual meetings of the American Society for Eighteenth-Century Studies and the Association for Political Theory. At these events and in correspondence and discussion, several scholars generously shared their wisdom and insight with me. For engaging my work and challenging me to develop my arguments further, I am deeply grateful to, among others, Ruth Abbey, Larry Arnhart, Derek Barker, Kate Bermingham, Bruno Bernardi, Richard Boyd, Lauren Brubaker, Paddy Bullard, Maria Carrasco, Josh Cherniss, Susan Collins, Remy Debes, Patrick Deneen, Sam Fleischacker, Fonna Forman, Michael Frazer, Christel Fricke, Michael Gill, Charles Griswold, James Harris, Warren Herrold, Sharon Krause, Jonathan Lear, Wim Lemmens, Harvey Mansfield, Philip Muñoz, Clifford Orwin, Jennifer Pitts, Andrea Radesanu, Santi Sanchez, Eric Schliesser, Claudia Schmidt, Dave Schmidtz, Michelle Schwarze, John Scott, Houston Smit, Alexis Tadié, Jacqueline Taylor, Mark Timmons, Helga Varden, David Williams, Nick Wolterstorff, Mark Yellin, Scott Yenor, Catherine Zuckert, and Michael Zuckert. Three anonymous reviewers at Cambridge University Press also provided helpful comments and suggestions. My work on this project was also greatly aided by the contributions of several excellent research assistants: Brittany Hickman, Anthony Lanz, Christy Lennon, Darren Nah, Shana Scogin, and Lilya Yakova.

I am also grateful for permission to reprint material that previously appeared elsewhere in different forms. An earlier version of the Hume chapter was published as "David Hume and the 'Politics of Humanity'," *Political Theory* 39 (2011): 205–233. An earlier version of the Smith chapter was published as "Adam Smith: From Love to Sympathy," *Revue Internationale de Philosophie* 68 (2014): 251–273. And some material in the Rousseau chapter first appeared in French in "Pitié développée: Aspects éthiques et épistémiques," in *Philosophie de Rousseau*, ed. Blaise Bachofen, Bruno Bernardi, André Charrak, and Florent Guénard (Paris: Classiques Garnier, 2014), 305–318.

This work on love owes to those I love – and especially my mother, my sister, my daughter, and my wife – more than I know how to say. I dedicate it to my late father, whose love and support made it, and so much else, possible.

Texts and Abbreviations

Citations to the works of Hume, Rousseau, Smith, and Kant are, wherever possible, to the standard English-language scholarly versions of their collected works: the *Clarendon Edition of the Works of David Hume*; the *Collected Writings of Jean-Jacques Rousseau*; the *Glasgow Edition of the Works and Correspondence of Adam Smith*; and *the Cambridge Edition of the Works of Immanuel Kant*. For Rousseau and Kant, citations are also given to the standard editions of the French and German originals, the *Oeuvres complètes* and the *Akademie Ausgabe*. Passages in those texts of Hume and Smith for which there exist standard systems of paragraph numbering are cited using these numbers; all other passages are cited by page number (and series volume number, when available), with individual titles abbreviated as below.

HUME

Abstract	Abstract of the *Treatise*, in T.
DCNR	*Dialogues Concerning Natural Religion*, ed. Richard H. Popkin (Indianapolis, IN: Hackett, 1980).
DP	*Dissertation on the Passions*, ed. Tom L. Beauchamp (Oxford: Clarendon Press, 2007).
EMPL	*Essays, Moral, Political, and Literary*, ed. Eugene F. Miller (Indianapolis, IN: Liberty Fund, 1985).
EHU	*An Enquiry Concerning Human Understanding*, ed. Tom L. Beauchamp (Oxford: Clarendon Press, 2000).
EPM	*An Enquiry Concerning the Principles of Morals*, ed. Tom L. Beauchamp (Oxford: Clarendon Press, 1998).

H   *The History of England*, ed. William B. Todd, 6 vols.
            (Indianapolis, IN: Liberty Fund, 1983).
NHR   *Natural History of Religion*, ed. Tom L. Beauchamp
            (Oxford: Clarendon Press, 2007).
T   *A Treatise of Human Nature*, ed. David F. Norton and
            Mary J. Norton (Oxford: Clarendon Press, 2007).

ROUSSEAU

C   *The Confessions*, trans. Christopher Kelly, in *The*
            Confessions and Correspondence, Including the Letters to
            Malesherbes, ed. Christopher Kelly, Roger D. Masters, and
            Peter G. Stillman (Hanover, NH: University Press of New
            England, 1995).
DPE   *Discourse on Political Economy*, trans. Judith R. Bush,
            in *Discourse on the Origins of Inequality, Polemics,*
            and Political Economy, ed. Roger D. Masters and
            Christopher Kelly (Hanover, NH: University Press of
            New England, 1992).
E   *Emile, or On Education*, trans. Allan Bloom, in *Emile,*
            or On Education, includes Emile and Sophie, or The
            Solitaries, ed. Christopher Kelly (Hanover, NH: University
            Press of New England, 2010).
EL   *Essay on the Origin of Languages*, trans. John T. Scott, in
            Essay on the Origins of Languages and Writings Related
            to Music, ed. John T. Scott (Hanover, NH: University Press
            of New England, 1998).
ES   *Emile and Sophie; or, The Solitaries*, trans. Christopher
            Kelly, in *Emile, or On Education, includes Emile and*
            Sophie, or The Solitaries, ed. Christopher Kelly (Hanover,
            NH: University Press of New England, 2010).
FD   *Discourse on the Sciences and Arts* (First *Discourse*),
            trans. Judith R. Bush, in *Discourse on the Sciences*
            and Arts and Polemics, ed. Roger D. Masters and
            Christopher Kelly (Hanover, NH: University Press of
            New England, 1992).
FG   "Fragments on God and Revelation," trans. Christopher
            Kelly, in *Autobiographical, Scientific, Religious, Moral,*
            and Literary Writings, ed. Christopher Kelly (Hanover,
            NH: University Press of New England, 2006).
J   *Julie, or the New Heloise*, trans. Philip Stewart
            and Jean Vaché (Hanover, NH: University Press of
            New England, 1997).

LB   *Letter to Beaumont*, trans. Judith R. Bush and Christopher Kelly, in *Letter to Beaumont, Letters Written from the Mountain, and Related Writings*, ed. Christopher Kelly and Eve Grace (Hanover, NH: University Press of New England, 2001).

LdA   *Letter to d'Alembert*, trans. Allan Bloom, in *Letter to d'Alembert and Writings for the Theater*, ed. Christopher Kelly (Hanover, NH: University of New England Press, 2004).

LF   *Letter to Franquières*, trans. Terence E. Marshall, in *The Reveries of the Solitary Walker, Botanical Writings, and Letter to Franquières*, ed. Christopher Kelly (Hanover, NH: University Press of New England, 2000).

LP   *Letter to Philopolis*, trans. Christopher Kelly and Roger D. Masters, in *Discourse on the Origins of Inequality, Polemics, and Political Economy*, ed. Roger D. Masters and Christopher Kelly (Hanover, NH: University Press of New England, 1992).

LS   *Letters to Sara*, trans. Christopher Kelly, in *Autobiographical, Scientific, Religious, Moral, and Literary Writings*, ed. Christopher Kelly (Hanover, NH: University Press of New England, 2006).

ML   *Moral Letters*, trans. Christopher Kelly, in *Autobiographical, Scientific, Religious, Moral, and Literary Writings*, ed. Christopher Kelly (Hanover, NH: University Press of New England, 2006).

OC   *Oeuvres complètes*, ed. Bernard Gagnebin and Marcel Raymond, 5 vols. (Paris: Gallimard, 1959–1995).

RSW   *Reveries of the Solitary Walker*, trans. Charles E. Butterworth, in *The Reveries of the Solitary Walker, Botanical Writings, and Letter to Franquières*, ed. Christopher Kelly (Hanover, NH: University Press of New England, 2000).

SD   *Discourse on the Origins of Inequality* (Second Discourse), trans. Judith R. Bush, in *Discourse on the Origins of Inequality, Polemics, and Political Economy*, ed. Roger D. Masters and Christopher Kelly (Hanover, NH: University Press of New England, 1992).

SMITH

CAS   *Correspondence of Adam Smith*, ed. E. C. Mossner and I. S. Ross (Indianapolis, IN: Liberty Fund, 1987).

ED   "Early Draft" of the *Wealth of Nations*, in LJ.
EPS   *Essays on Philosophical Subjects*, ed. W. P. D. Wightman
            and J. C. Bryce (Indianapolis, IN: Liberty Fund, 1982).
LER   "Letter to the *Edinburgh Review*," in EPS.
LJ   *Lectures on Jurisprudence*, ed. R. L. Meek, D. D.
            Raphael, and P. G. Stein (Indianapolis: Liberty Fund,
            1982) [LJA = "Report of 1762–63" and LJB = "Report
            dated 1766"].
LRBL   *Lectures on Rhetoric and Belles-Lettres*, ed. J. C. Bryce
            (Indianapolis, IN: Liberty Fund, 1985).
TMS   *The Theory of Moral Sentiments*, ed. D. D. Raphael and
            A. L. Macfie (Indianapolis, IN: Liberty Fund, 1982).
WN   *An Inquiry into the Nature and Causes of the Wealth
            of Nations*, ed. R. H. Campbell, A. S. Skinner, and
            W. B. Todd (Indianapolis, IN: Liberty Fund, 1981).

                            KANT

A   *Anthropology from a Pragmatic Point of View*, trans.
            Louden, in *Anthropology, History, and Education*, ed.
            Günter Zöller and Louden (Cambridge: Cambridge
            University Press, 2007).
AA   *Kants gesammelte Schriften* (*Akademie Ausgabe*), ed.
            Royal Prussian Academy of Sciences, 29 vols. (Berlin:
            Walter de Gruyter, 1900–).
CPrR   *Critique of Practical Reason*, trans. Mary J. Gregor, in
            Practical Philosophy, ed. Mary J. Gregor (Cambridge:
            Cambridge University Press, 1999).
G   *Groundwork of The Metaphysics of Morals*, trans. Mary
            J. Gregor, in *Practical Philosophy*, ed. Mary J. Gregor
            (Cambridge: Cambridge University Press, 1999).
LE   *Lectures on Ethics*, trans. Peter Heath
            (Cambridge: Cambridge University Press, 2001).
LoP   *Lectures on Pedagogy*, trans. Robert B. Louden, in
            Anthropology, History, and Education, ed. Günter Zöller
            and Louden (Cambridge: Cambridge University Press,
            2007).
MM   *The Metaphysics of Morals*, trans. Mary J. Gregor, in
            Practical Philosophy, ed. Mary J. Gregor (Cambridge:
            Cambridge University Press, 1999).
O   *Observations on the Feeling of the Beautiful and
            Sublime*, trans. Paul Guyer, in *Anthropology, History,*

	and Education, ed. Günter Zöller and Robert B. Louden (Cambridge: Cambridge University Press, 2007).
RWL	*Religion within the Boundaries of Mere Reason*, trans. George di Giovanni, in *Religion and Rational Theology*, ed. Allen W. Wood (Cambridge: Cambridge University Press, 2001).
R	"Remarks in the *Observations on the Beautiful and Sublime*," trans. Patrick Frierson and Paul Guyer et al. in *Observations on the Feeling of the Beautiful and Sublime and Other Writings*, ed. Patrick Frierson and Paul Guyer (Cambridge: Cambridge University Press, 2011).

I

Introduction

TODAY'S CHALLENGE

Love is in the air. The past several years have seen a flurry of new books on love across a broad range of academic disciplines. From a historian we thus have a major new intellectual history of love, from philosophers we have important new studies of love's "vision" and love's "paradox," and from a psychologist we have a new theory of how love "affects everything we feel, think, do and become."[1] All of this might lead us to wonder: why now? Why, that is, is love presently so ascendant as a topic of popular and academic inquiry?

The reasons are surely many and complex. But at least one of them is likely political. That is, there seems to be – at least in the opinions of several of the most important recent theorists of love – something about our present political state that makes desirable, and perhaps even demands, a recovery of the primacy of love. This at any rate has been explicitly and recently suggested by several prominent political thinkers who ring changes on a common theme: namely the need to recover love to offset the egocentrism and individualism that capitalism and liberalism encourage.

This theme has been especially prominent in recent French thought. Alain Badiou has argued in his "praise of love" that while "in today's world, it is generally thought that individuals only pursue their own self-interest," love yet stands as "an antidote to that." In his view, "the re-invention of love" emerges as a "possible point of resistance against the obscenity of the market."[2] Luc Ferry has recently advanced a similar claim. Ferry and Badiou differ considerably on the questions of

I

whether a "politics of love" is either desirable or possible, and whether our current moment is one of decline or progress.[3] Yet such differences are perhaps less crucial than their agreement that (in Ferry's words) "our societies have become societies of hyper-consumption" which prize self-gratification, a direct consequence of the so-called "*marchandisation du monde*."[4] And so too Jean-Claude Kaufmann, whose study of love begins by announcing that "the accumulation of wealth and facile consumerism are nothing more than screens that cover up a great psychological poverty" and goes on to argue that in fact "all this could have been completely different if history had taken a different direction and if love had been able to establish itself as a political principle."[5]

Yet recent interest in love is hardly limited to France. A similar focus on love has also, perhaps surprisingly, emerged of late in the seemingly less auspicious field of Anglo-American liberal theory. In this vein, several studies, and especially those of Nicholas Wolterstorff and Martha Nussbaum, have taken aim at the long-standing assumption that liberalism is properly founded on a strict line of demarcation that separates justice from love. Wolterstorff and Nussbaum each – albeit in their own different ways – question the notion that the principal responsibility of liberalism is merely to secure the conditions for justice and negative liberty, and that as such the claims of love are best relegated to the realm of the supererogatory. To attempt to separate justice from love in this manner, they insist, would in fact serve merely to condemn both justice and love to irrelevance; what is needed, and what each seeks to provide, is rather a way by which love and justice can be reintegrated in such a way that modern liberalism might be furnished with the moral psychology that has been thus far left unarticulated.[6]

Nussbaum makes especially explicit why this task is particularly critical at the present moment. Our world, she explains, is one "in which the most intransigent obstacle to concern for others is egoistic immersion in personal and local projects." Part of her interest in recovering love thus emerges from her concern to diffuse that "narrowness, partiality, and narcissism" endemic to our world, and with which love is necessarily in "continual struggle."[7] Indeed one of her main aims is to recover the other-directedness that defines love as a means of mitigating the self-centeredness that defines our world. Noting that "most people tend toward narrowness of sympathy" and "can easily become immured in narcissistic projects and forget about the needs of those outside their narrow circle," Nussbaum praises other-directed love as the best means of "getting people to think larger thoughts and recommit themselves to a larger common good" and thereby overcome what, following Kant, she calls "radical evil" – those "forces that lurk in all societies and, ultimately, in all of us: tendencies to protect the fragile self by denigrating and subordinating others," which incapacitate us "to see full and equal humanity in another person."[8]

Nussbaum's worries likely resonate with many of us. That the conditions of our political and economic life privilege self-centeredness over concern for others is a worry that has troubled political thinkers at least since the Enlightenment; indeed just as Ferry and Nussbaum and others today worry about the narcissism and the egocentrism encouraged by capitalism, many prominent eighteenth-century voices anticipated just this worry in calling prominent attention to the celebration of self-love and egocentrism that they took Hobbes and Mandeville and others to have been encouraging. And it is a worry that also seems unlikely to abate anytime soon; that individualism has supplanted community and social atomism has supplanted social connection are among the most familiar features of the debate over the benefits and challenges of our globalized capitalist world. Now, a very different book would be necessary to diagnose all the sources of this concern and indeed to assess its legitimacy. What follows simply assumes that this worry, so powerfully expressed by Nussbaum, is in fact legitimate and worthy of our attention. And if so, a new challenge demands our attention, and it is on this challenge that this book focuses. Put bluntly: even if we agree with Nussbaum that egocentrism is a problem – and perhaps even a primary ethical problem in the modern world – what reason is there to think that love is the answer? Put differently: even if egocentrism demands a response, what reason is there to think that love is capable of providing it? Can love alone pull this tall task off? And if so, what kind of love exactly do we need for the job?

The last question is easier to answer than the others. If the main problem to be combated is selfishness and egocentrism, then the love we must recover will be that capable of lifting us out of our individual selves and enabling us to establish a substantial bond with others that can trump or at least mitigate the exclusivity of self-concern.[9] Today we sometimes identify this disposition in terms that are more generically associated with other-directedness rather than with love per se; in this vein, social scientists of course often speak of "altruism" in contrast with "egoism." Yet in some deep sense, this simply won't do if altruism connotes an absence of self-preference and perhaps at best a positive but dispassionate preference for others.[10]

What today's theorists of love are instead after – and in their wake, a number of other thinkers concerned to defend additional forms of other-directed obligations variously associated with philanthropy and humanitarian action and global justice – is a considerably warmer and more affective disposition than altruism. To fill this void, they invoke the practical utility of other-directed sentiments that, like altruism, push back against the selfishness of egocentrism, but unlike altruism, do so in ways that draw on and encourage deeper affective commitment: sentiments such as compassion, pity, and sympathy.[11] The advantage of these dispositions is that they encourage us not merely to feel for others, as affect alone would have us do, but also encourage us to recognize others as beings fundamentally equal to ourselves and who demand and deserve not just our recognition and our respect but also our care and concern – beings who possess a unique dignity, and whose welfare exerts legitimate claims on us.[12] In large part, it is these notions of sentimentalized other-directedness, such as pity and compassion and sympathy, that those who today call for a resuscitation of love have in mind in their efforts to combat egocentrism.

In this sense, sentimentalized other-directedness does the work that an older tradition invoked a specific concept of love to do – namely the concept of love that in ancient Greek was called *agape* and in Latin, *caritas*. This sort of love – a love that is perhaps best rendered in English as "neighbor-love," if only to distinguish it from the many other forms of love that are perhaps more familiar to us today – shared an end common to modern sentimentalized other-directedness: namely to minimize, if not eliminate, self-preference and to encourage a substantial and indeed transformative concern with the well-being of others. This concern is perhaps best known today in the form of the Christian command to love one's neighbor, though this of course was hardly a concern exclusive to Christianity, as several studies of the theological ethics that emerge from the Jewish, Islamic, Buddhist, and Hindu traditions have helpfully emphasized.[13] Yet, it is, of course, the Christian concept that is most proximate for the early modern and modern thinkers who developed the theory of other-directedness that is our focus here. And this modern theory of other-directedness of course finds much to admire in the Christian conception of *agape*. At the same time, it also finds much to which it must necessarily object. Most crucially: the traditional conception of love of one's neighbor was founded on a belief that human beings were capable of transcendence. Yet it is part and parcel of our theoretical landscape today to regard such foundations suspect as grounds for universal ethical claims. In this sense, the shift from transcendental love to sentimentalized other-directedness is a clear step forward. At the same time, it may be that something important has been lost in this shift.

What follows is an effort to make sense of this shift by tallying both the costs and the benefits of this transformation of *agape* or *caritas* into pity, compassion, and sympathy. If it does its job well, such an enquiry may help us to gain clarity on what has been gained as well as what may have been lost in the shift from the traditional vision of love to our contemporary vision. It may also help those of us committed to advancing the political task described by Nussbaum to understand how we might best move forward and advance this vision in practice. But in order to see clearly love's present dilemmas and its possible future, we need to begin by taking a brief look at its past, and specifically at its classical origins and modern enlightenment.

LOVE'S TRADITION

The history of love poses several challenges for us today. First and foremost, when we talk of love today, we tend to talk principally, if not exclusively, about what is often called romantic love. Yet this love, so familiar to us today, is itself largely the product of a specific revolution in the history of thinking about love, and even while scholars will continue to debate the degree to which the idea of romantic love could be said to have existed prior to Romanticism, it remains the case that the Romantic Revolution not only rendered the concept of romantic love commonplace but also served to displace the primacy of certain traditional conceptions of love.[14] Yet it is to these traditional conceptions that we must turn if we are to appreciate the nature of the Enlightenment's own revolutionary reconsideration of the forms of love that were conceptually dominant prior to the advent of Romanticism. And herein lies a second challenge for our efforts to recover the history of love today. The tradition of thinking about love prior to Romanticism in fact embraced several distinct concepts that received their most powerful articulations from a number of different thinkers. Foremost among these, three tend to be emphasized: love as longing for possession, whose conceptual roots lie in the *eros* described by Plato; love of friends and family, whose conceptual roots are perhaps best traced to the *philia* described by Aristotle; and neighbor love, the conceptual roots of which lie in the *agape* described in the New Testament.[15] Each of these connotes a substantively independent conception of love, and the question of the degree to which they can be synthesized in a manner capable of resolving their seeming contradictions remains a matter of great concern to love's most careful modern scholars. Yet what distinguishes these three principal traditional concepts of love is less important for our inquiry than what binds them to each other and also sets them apart from the sorts of sentimental other-directedness that is the focus of what follows. This difference concerns their orientation to transcendence.

What then is transcendence? For our purposes, transcendence represents an attempt to go beyond the limits of the self, and thereby to gain access to a realm that is dedicated to or oriented around certain goods recognizably superior to the goods of basic self-interest. Within recent political theory, likely the most comprehensive and insightful treatment of the concept of transcendence and its significance is to be found in the work of Charles Taylor. Taylor structures much of his narrative of the emergence of the secular age in terms of modernity's rejection of transcendence in favor of immanence; indeed the historical conflict between "transcendent religion" and "its frontal denial" is, on his account, what makes possible a contemporary world in which for many, quite simply, "the transcendent is off their map."[16] A very similar notion has been recently expressed by Robert Spaemann. Glossing Hume's claim that however far our imagination travels, we yet "never really advance a step beyond ourselves," Spaemann interprets this to mean "that the subject remains in itself and that every notion of self-transcendence or being-outside-of-oneself is an illusion" – a position he calls "the heart of the modern worldview" and indeed "the mainstream of modern consciousness."[17] But what is important for present purposes is not only the insistence on the modern antipathy to transcendence emphasized by Spaemann and Taylor alike, but even more importantly, Taylor's articulation of the substantive tension of the commitment to or longing for transcendence with the commitment to or longing for human flourishing; indeed Taylor himself often describes aspirations to transcendence in terms of the "call to live beyond" and specifically "a beyond of human flourishing."[18] This is crucial for our study of the evolution of the traditional understanding of love, and especially for our contrast of traditional and enlightened theories of love. In short: for all of their many other undeniable differences, the old concepts of *eros* and *philia* and *agape* each depend upon a concept of transcendence from which the modern concepts of sympathy, compassion, and pity seek to declare independence.

This claim is central to much of what follows, and as such it is important to be as clear as possible about what does and does not follow from it. In the first place, to say that *eros* and *philia* and *agape* all depend upon a concept of transcendence is not to say that they ought to be *reduced* to concepts of transcendence; clearly central to our experiences of all three concepts (and most especially and obviously to *eros*) are the ways in which our experiences are shaped by the conditions of our embodiment. Further, to say that *eros* and *philia* and *agape* are united in depending on a concept of transcendence is not to say anything about the possible differences in the ways each of these seeks to realize transcendence; indeed, as will be argued subsequently, one of the key differences that separates *eros* and *philia* on the one hand from *agape* on the other is that where the former take the realization of transcendence as their end, the latter takes the condition of transcendence as its point of departure. This inversion of causal direction represents an extremely significant difference among these ideas – a difference I think is at least, if not more, foundational than those clear and obvious differences in the ways in which they are felt, and by whom and toward whom they are felt. But for all these differences, it remains the case that – and this is the claim for which I want to argue here – *eros* and *philia* and *agape* are all inconceivable and indeed nonsensical if the very concept of transcendence is precluded. This fact not only unites these concepts of love together but also suggests why they cannot be at home in an age skeptical of transcendence – and in turn suggests why a search for a substitute might have been seen as so pressing at the advent of this age.[19]

To begin with the two ancient Greek philosophical concepts: *eros* and *philia*, while directed to different ends, each share a common ambition of transcendence of the limitations of the self culminating in access to a higher and more perfect realm. The key text for the Platonic conception of *eros* on this front is Diotima's speech on the ascent or ladder of love in *Symposium*. Diotima's famous speech in many ways represents the highwater mark of *eros*, for it is in her speech that the dialogue's interlocutors come to see the ways in which erotic longings – which to that point in the discussion had been associated largely with the sexual desires of one person for one specific other – can lead their possessor to seek something infinitely greater and more beautiful than physical gratification or possession of another individual. *Eros* properly understood, she explains, has the potential to encourage in its possessor "a permanent turn to the vast open sea of the beautiful," culminating in the knowledge of "what is beauty itself."[20] Here and elsewhere, Diotima makes clear that this turn itself depends on a specifically upward movement toward the transcendent sphere – hence her claim that "erotics" begins with apprehension of beautiful things before us, but then seeks "always to proceed on up for the sake of that beauty, using these beautiful things here as steps: from one to two, and from two to all beautiful bodies; and from beautiful bodies to beautiful pursuits; and from pursuits to beautiful lessons; and from lessons to end at that lesson, which is the lesson of nothing else than the beautiful itself."[21] The significance of *eros* thus lies in its capacity to lead us up from a lower realm of selfish desires for the possession of particular beauties to the transcendent realm of absolute beauty culminating in an acquisition and eternal possession of the beautiful, and "the good's being one's own always."[22]

Diotima's conspicuous emphasis on the ways in which *eros* encourages our desires for possessing the good and making it our own has often led commentators to speculate about the degree to which *eros* should be fundamentally understood as selfish.[23] Yet this association of possession with selfishness, however familiar it may be to us in our age of acquisitiveness, maps uneasily onto Plato's characterization of *eros* in the speech given by Diotima. Clearly Plato is invested in the claim that *eros* is born in need and longs to possess the beautiful. But his focus here seems to be less to denigrate *eros* as an exacerbation of self-love than to show how it might serve to bind the self to the transcendent, and indeed elevate the self above the self. Indeed part of what makes Plato's vision of *eros* so powerful is the promise that it extends to us that we need not be imprisoned by our self-love, and that the longing born in self-love can lead us outside of ourselves to others, and ultimately beyond others to transcendent beauty. In this way, Plato's vision of *eros* points to a way in which self-love, the love of others, and the love of what is best and most beautiful can be seen as connected.[24]

Aristotle's concept of *philia* of course deals with a different sort of disposition altogether. His aim is to define the sort of disposition that binds friends rather than sexual partners together, and on such grounds the differences between his theory of love and Plato's have been often emphasized. Yet emphasizing these differences can run the risk of blinding us to the similarities that tie his concept of love to Plato's as well as to the Christian conception of love, and distance it from modern conceptions of sentimental other-directedness. Two similarities are especially important: the orientation of *philia* to the self and the orientation of *philia* to the transcendent.

On the former front, Aristotle introduces a key element of his treatment of *philia* in his effort to resolve an impasse over whether it is good for a friend to love himself more than he loves others. Aristotle's answer rests on a distinction between two types of self-love. He admits that the former, familiar type of self-love is hardly admirable – the sort exhibited by those who "crave" and "zealously chase after" and fight over such goods as "money, honors, and bodily pleasures."[25] But against this he sets another self-love, that of the one who "takes for himself the things that are most beautiful and most good" and claims for himself "the greater share of the beautiful" – a view that suggests that what the self-lover loves is not only, or not simply, what is best within him (in Aristotelian terms, *nous* or intellect), but also the beautiful and noble that is best absolutely.[26] In this sense Aristotle's self-loving friend seeking always to claim the beautiful shares much in common with Diotima's lover who also aims to possess beauty for himself and "come close to touching the perfect end."[27]

The self-love that animates *philia* is then guided by a specific orientation to the transcendent category of the beautiful and noble, and particularly by the desire to possess it. But Aristotle also goes a further step, and in so doing he makes clear that the self-love of *philia* not only orients its possessor to the transcendent, but also encourages a reorientation of his relations with others:

Hence such a person would be a lover of self most of all, though in a different form from the one that is reproached, differing as much as living by reason does from living by passion, and as much as desiring either the beautiful or what seems advantageous. Everyone, then, approves of and praises those who are exceptionally zealous about beautiful actions, and if they all competed for the beautiful, and strained to the utmost to perform the most beautiful actions, then for all in common there would be what is needful, and for each in particular there would be the greatest of goods, if indeed virtue is that. Therefore, a good person ought to be a lover of self, since he will both profit himself and benefit the others by performing beautiful actions.[28]

Philia properly understood is thus transformative on multiple levels. In the first place it represents a new orientation to the self and specifically a willing and even conscious preference for the transcendent goods of beauty and nobility over those more common external goods desired by the vulgarly selfish. In the second place, and perhaps more importantly, it is precisely this longing for transcendent nobility that leads one animated by it to perform the "beautiful actions" that Aristotle says are of such explicit benefit to others.[29] It is precisely this concern with the beautiful and noble in its transcendent sense that Aristotle thinks distinguishes the best and highest forms of *philia* from other, lesser forms of friendship based on pleasure or convenience or utility, and distinguishes the philanthropy that is the product of this peak *philia* from the comparatively weak "goodwill" that we feel for strangers.[30]

For all their differences, *eros* and *philia* thus share a concern to elevate their possessors from conventional self-concern to a concern with the transcendent. And at least in the case of *philia* (though perhaps also in the case of *eros*) the experience of the transcendent itself leads to a new, more beneficent relationship with others.[31] In any case, what seems clear is that *eros* and *philia* are both concerned with establishing a proper ordering of three categories: self-love, other-love, and love of the beautiful. And this, in turn, brings us to *agape*. The question of the compatibility of *agape* and *eros* has long exercised scholars, and we would be remiss were we to fail to note at the outset the extensive debate on this front; where many of the most respected and careful students of *eros* and *agape* have judged them incompatible on the grounds of their differing views on the self, a diverse set of prominent voices has been equally insistent that separating *eros* from *agape* only reduces each to "caricature."[32] Yet when examined from the perspective of the ways in which the original concept of *agape* evolved into the sentimentalized form that is our main focus in what follows, we may in fact be more inclined to emphasize its similarities to the two classical conceptions of love, as well as its distance from modern sentimental conceptions. The fault lines for both comparisons concern the way in which *agape* conceives its relationship to self-love on the one hand, and to the transcendent on the other.

A comprehensive review of the sources of *agape* as a concept would require a wide-ranging study of Biblical texts, Hellenistic Neoplatonic philosophical sources, and the extensive commentaries of the Church Fathers, especially Augustine.[33] Yet clearly the fundamental text, all agree, is Jesus's response to the lawyer who wants to hear him explain "which is the great commandment in the law." Jesus replies:

Thou shalt love the Lord thy God with all thy heart, and with all thy soul, and with all thy mind. This is the first and great commandment. And the second is like unto it, Thou shalt love thy neighbour as thyself. On these two commandments hang all the law and the prophets.[34]

Of all that could be said about these words, two points seem relevant in the present context. The first concerns the first commandment. In commanding his audience to love God first, Jesus makes clear that *agape* is founded on love of the transcendent. And indeed when we say today, as does Badiou, that "Christianity itself is the finest example of love's intensity towards a transcendental conception of the universal," it is this insistence on the primacy of the love of God that we have in mind.[35] Now, for what it might be worth, it should be said again, *pace* Badiou, that among the world's religions Christianity has hardly cornered the market on the concept of the primacy of love of the transcendent and universal; as is generally appreciated, this is a core principle of theological ethics in several other world traditions as well.[36] But even if we take Christianity to be the "finest example" of this conception of love, it is crucial not to lose sight of the way in which its commitment to the transcendent binds it to both *eros* and *philia*. For while it would be a grave substantive error to equate God with the beautiful, it is yet true and key that *agape* and *eros* and *philia* have come in our tradition to be associated with an orientation toward transcendence, without which each concept would be unintelligible.[37] Furthermore, the transcendent God who is both the beginning and the end of *agape* reveals the degree to which *agape* is oriented around transcendence, and privileges this orientation even above practical restraint of self-love.

A second point relates to the second commandment. In commanding a love of neighbors in the same manner as love of self – a commandment that is said to be "like unto" the first – Jesus suggests that the experience of transcendent love that comes from obedience to the first commandment transforms our orientation to both ourselves and to others. Here again *agape* reveals the depth of what it shares with *eros* and *philia*. In the first place, even as *agape* aspires to the transcendence of the self, it resists the renunciation of the self. As many have noted, to suggest that Jesus calls for abnegation of self-love is seriously to misconstrue his explicit invocation of self-love as a part of our created natures as well the proper measure of our love for our neighbors.[38] In this *agape* shares something particularly important with *eros* and *philia*, for like them it aims at a transcendence of the most vulgar forms of self-love, but this transcendence is itself driven by what might be called self-love rightly understood: a self-love that orients us by the transcendent categories most needed for our genuine health and happiness, and not merely the satisfaction of those more basic desires that we conventionally associate with self-interest.[39] Thus while the term "neighbor-love" can serve as a useful shorthand for *agape*, we miss much of what is essential to it if we define *agape* simply as neighbor-love, independent of reference to the specific types of self-love and divine love that in fact distinguish it.[40]

Relatedly, and perhaps most importantly, *agape*, like *eros* and *philia*, reaches its end not simply in an experiencing of the transcendent, but in the way in which a lexically prior love of the transcendent transforms its possessor's relationship with both self and with others. In this sense, *agape* represents an innovation on *eros* and *philia*, in the way suggested briefly earlier. For where *eros* seeks transcendence via its ascent and *philia* discriminates between a selfish self-love and a self-love aiming for the beautiful and noble, *agape* requires first a love of God and only then a love of neighbor – an ordering that is of the greatest significance. A gloss by Kierkegaard, one of the most important post-Enlightenment theorists of love, is helpful here:

Love God above all else and then love your neighbor and in your neighbor every man. Only by loving God above all else can one love his neighbor in the next human being. The next human being – he is one's neighbor – this the next human being in the sense that the next human being is every other human being.[41]

Agape thus conceived ultimately represents an ascent from the self, but in terms of its causality it is an ascent that begins as an ascent to God, and only afterward will come to establish new relations with others. This in some sense marks a reordering of the causality of *eros*, which ends with the transcendent, even if it replicates that movement first to the noble and only afterward toward others that characterizes the *philia* described by Aristotle. But this difference, however significant, should not lead us to lose sight of the specific way in which *agape* and *eros* and *philia* are in fact united on this front. For all three are misunderstood if they are regarded as aiming at or encouraging the love of one specific object. Rather, what defines each of them and indeed binds them together is that each encourages a new disposition that aims to balance three seemingly discrete categories: love of self, love of others, and love of the divine or transcendent. In this sense, *eros* and *agape* and *philia*, for all their clear differences, each describe a triangle, the ultimate aim of which is to define the proper balance between the sometimes competing but ultimately complementary ends mandated by the love of self, the love of others, and the love of the divine.

This idea, I recently discovered, was rendered in an especially powerful way by Martin Luther King, Jr. In a sermon published under the title "Three Dimensions of a Complete Life," King explains that

any complete life has the three dimensions suggested in our text – length, breadth, and height. The length of life is the inward drive to achieve one's personal ends and ambitions, an inward concern for one's own welfare and achievements. The breadth of life is the outward concern for the welfare of others. The height of life is the upward reach for God. Life is at its best a coherent triangle. At one angle is the individual person. At the other angle are other persons. At the tiptop is the Infinite Person, God. Without the due development of each part of the triangle, no life can be complete.[42]

King here not only provides a beautifully rendered version of the metaphor that I want to employ, but he also introduces the claim that it is impossible to realize the "completeness" of a life without the requisite cultivation of each of the three loves: love of self, love of others, and love of God. Any limitation of our ambitions to only one or two of the three risks imbalance; our full development demands a conscious effort on our parts to attain what King calls "height" as well as length and breadth.

LOVE'S ENLIGHTENMENT

The classical conceptions of love are thus united by their shared commitment to transcendence, whatever else we might and should say about their differences. In this they are also radically distinct from the sorts of sentimental other-directedness that serve as their proxy today. But what explains this shift? Or put differently, how exactly did the traditional conceptions of other-directed love that emerged from the ancient Greek and Christian ethical traditions – that is, from what Ferry has called "*le cosmologico-éthique*" and "*le théologico-éthique*" – come to be translated into the forms in which we know them today?[43]

Clearly the full answer is complex. One could not hope to do full justice to this question without detailed study of the many revolutions that the concept of love has experienced in the course of its long history in the West – thus the emphasis that the authors of the major synoptic histories of love have placed on such moments as the early Christian encounter with Neoplatonism, the incipient romanticism of the troubadours and the Renaissance, and the challenges posed by the Reformation and by the early modern scientific revolution.[44] Yet for all of the contributions of each of these stages in the evolution of love to the emergence of our modern concept, one of the most important stages in the evolution of the charitable love that is our primary focus here is the stage in which the appeal to transcendence was dethroned from its traditional primacy. And this stage we can locate squarely in the Enlightenment. On some level one hesitates to put it this way; for more than a century the Enlightenment has been so often invoked as the source of both all that is good and all that is bad in modern life that recurring back to it in almost any context runs the risk of banality.[45] Yet in this case the risk is worth it. We are right to be skeptical of certain hyperbolic assertions that wish to find everything in the Enlightenment. But in the case of love, several specific eighteenth-century moral thinkers deserve credit for inaugurating a genuine revolution of thinking about love – a revolution that both marked a decisive break with traditional conceptions and also laid a foundation for our contemporary understanding of other-directedness.

Today we appreciate better than ever before, and especially within political theory, the significance of the Enlightenment on this front. As three excellent recent books have demonstrated, the eighteenth century introduced a host of substantive concepts and indeed a new way of thinking about the place of affect or sentiment in practical life, a new way of thinking that continues to shape in fruitful ways how we think about the possibilities (and limits) of affect in politics today.[46] In what follows I want to extend this line of reflection to focus specifically on the question of love as a preeminent form of other-directed sentiment and in so doing suggest that not only did the Enlightenment lay the foundations for how we understand love today, but it also specifically did so by compelling a rejection of the traditional conceptions of love on quite specific grounds. In so doing I want to extend further an observation made by Carl Becker, one of the great historians of the Enlightenment, who observed of the eighteenth-century concepts of *bienfaisance* and *humanité* that these were "coined by the Philosophers to express in secular terms the Christian ideal of service."[47] In some sense this seems right; that the Enlightenment concept of other-directedness aimed to reestablish on secular foundations a category it inherited from Christian (and classical) sources is a foundational principle of the story that this book means to tell. At the same time, this regrounding, I think, represents a much more radical and revolutionary and simply remarkable move than Becker's formulation would seem to suggest. To demonstrate this, we need to focus on two specific sides of the Enlightenment: the revolution that it brought in epistemology, and the revolution that it brought in ethics.

On the former front, and especially crucial for the present project, is the way in which the Enlightenment compelled a reconsideration of our epistemic capacities and limits. Much attention of course has been given to the most dramatic elements of this revolution, including most obviously the ways in which the Enlightenment, as has been traditionally emphasized, celebrated reason's potential and its capacity to promote scientific and technological progress. Yet, alongside this maybe too familiar story lies another side of the Enlightenment's epistemic revolution, namely its more skeptical side. This side tends to be the less celebrated, perhaps because its aims are more deflationary and critical rather than positive and progressive. But the key claim on this side is of paramount significance for the study of love in which we are engaged. It is specifically that a prominent strain of Enlightenment sought to render illegitimate the appeal to transcendence as a legitimate category on which to found practical claims.

This claim is somewhat more subtle than a much more familiar and certainly related claim: namely that the primary epistemic legacy of the Enlightenment lies in its challenge to religion, and especially in its efforts to demonstrate the superiority of reason to revealed religion. As a generalization about the aims of Enlightenment, this claim seems to me almost certainly false; however convenient it might be for us to think of the Enlightenment in terms of "atheism," the truth is that with very few exceptions even the most skeptical of Enlightenment philosophers tended to regard themselves less as enemies of religion than as champions of what they tended to call "true religion," an understudied category in the intellectual history of the eighteenth century. Here again another very different book would be necessary to demonstrate this.[48] For our present purposes, what matters is that the Enlightenment sought less simply to debunk religion than to achieve what may appear a more modest goal, but one whose long-term implications were of great significance: namely the effort to demonstrate the illegitimacy of transcendence as an ethical category. The clearest example of this may be Hume. Hume's contribution to secularization was not so much any demonstration of the irrationality of belief or the nonexistence of God, but rather his insistence that our basic incapacity to know the will of God with any universal assurance must necessarily render suspect any appeal to God or any other similar transcendent category as the grounds for ethics or politics. Hume's key contribution thus was less to disprove the existence of God than to dethrone the idea of God from its traditional primacy as a foundation for normative ethics and for ethical inquiry.[49] It is in this sense then that we properly credit Hume – along with, of course, other Enlightenment thinkers – as inaugurating the "secular age" in which we now live: an age that, as Hume would no doubt have approved, demands that we ground our ethical commitments in categories and claims that are available to and apparent to all, independent of faith or other belief commitments.

This in turn leads to the second revolution of the Enlightenment that bears on our inquiry into the modern transvaluation of love. The Enlightenment, seen in terms of its contributions to practical ethics, was itself animated by a sustained and deep concern to mitigate egocentrism and encourage other-directedness, a concern it of course shared with both the classical and the contemporary thinkers profiled in this chapter's opening section. That the Enlightenment would have been drawn to this concern is hardly surprising; the eighteenth century was itself defined by a striking movement toward the liberalization of economic and political life, and as its moral and political thinkers were the first to realize, this shift demanded a particular focus on developing moral psychologies capable of managing these challenges.[50] Yet even as the eighteenth century inherited from its predecessors the traditional concern to mitigate self-preference, the remedies available to Enlightenment thinkers were not those available to love's traditional defenders – and this largely (but not exclusively by any means) because of the epistemic revolution described earlier. By precluding transcendence as a legitimate ground for ethical speculation, *agape* and other such traditional conceptions of transcendent love were in some sense taken off the table. An alternative was needed, specifically one capable of responding to the practical challenges of egocentrism in a manner consistent with an epistemic consensus that our foundational commitments remain readily available and accessible to all.

Ultimately this concern to save other-directedness in a world that precludes recourse to transcendence I think best explains the Enlightenment's turn away from the love familiar from traditional conceptions to the sentimental other-directedness that we today recognize as one of its primary legacies for practical ethics. Whether we identify this category as sympathy or compassion or pity or humanity, what all of the iterations of this phenomenon share is that they recognizably work to encourage other-directedness and mitigate self-preference, and the means by which they do so depend not on faith in an unseen transcendent but on the more immediate and palpable sensations or sentiments available to all human beings as a simple condition of their natural physical constitution. In this sense, the concept of other-directedness developed in the Enlightenment is especially remarkable insofar as it is at once both critical and constructive: critical insofar as it seeks to provide an alternative to traditional concepts of *agape* or *caritas* that were judged insufficient, constructive insofar as it aims to set forth a new remedy for the unique challenges of modern self-love. In some obvious sense of course, the constructive project formed a more explicit focus than the critical project; clearly the Enlightenment figures that will be our focus here were more worried by the immediate practical threats posed by the conceptions of self-love notoriously championed by Hobbes and Mandeville than by any direct damage that the theories of love defended by Plato or Augustine were likely to do in the world. Yet as I hope to show in the text that follows, full appreciation of the constructive side of the project requires due attention to the way in which this side itself emerged from certain elements in the critical side of their projects.

On the whole, the theory of other-directedness that emerges from this both critical and constructive project constitutes a striking and undeniable achievement. Not only did the eighteenth century lay the foundation for how we think about affect today, but it also furnished us the resources necessary to respond to one of the most challenging practical questions in modern ethics in a manner that demands recourse only to categories readily available to us. Thanks to its innovations, it is now indeed possible to argue for the priority and even the superiority of other-directedness to self-preference without having to recur to the transcendent categories on which the traditional conception of love was based. At the same time, this advance comes with a new challenge of its own – a challenge perhaps most easily conceived by extending the image used earlier. The traditional conception of love, described previously, formed a triangle in which three distinct types of love – self-love, other-love, divine love – each played a role in supporting the balance of the whole. But the Enlightenment conception of love, in precluding the transcendent category of the beautiful or the divine, reduced this triangle to a line. As a result, after the Enlightenment, love of others came to be conceived not as a triangulated balance of self-love and other-love and divine love, but as the occupation of a proper point on a flat continuum defined by the two poles of love of self and love of others. In the terms of King's metaphor, modern sentimental other-directedness preserves only length and breadth without height. In what follows I try to show what we gain in reconceiving love this way, as well as what we have lost and would do well to recover, as best we can, within the context of our present moment.

FOUR CONCEPTS AND A CHALLENGE

So far our focus has been on explaining why the Enlightenment conception of love deserves our attention. But now we need to be clear about exactly what part or parts of this conception will be our focus here. What follows offers less a survey of eighteenth-century views on love (a project that would require wide investigation of a dazzlingly broad range of literary and philosophical texts as well as social practices and institutions) than focused and detailed examination of the most significant philosophical conceptions of other-directedness that emerged in the course of the Enlightenment. And even these are perilous waters. Early modern moral philosophy is suffused with attempts to define other-directedness: one thinks immediately of Descartes on generosity, of Leibniz and Spinoza on charity, of Shaftesbury and Hutcheson on benevolence, of Butler on compassion – theories all deserving of (and indeed that have received) scholarly attention.[51] But what follows focuses on another set of thinkers and doctrines, and four in particular: Hume's concept of humanity, Rousseau's concept of pity, Adam Smith's concept of sympathy, and Kant's concept of love.

Why then these four and not those others mentioned earlier – or indeed those many others not mentioned but also deserving of attention? Three reasons might be given. The first concerns the simple stature and influence of these four thinkers and concepts. On some basic level, while the ideas of Leibniz and Shaftesbury and Butler deservedly remain of tremendous interest to historians of philosophy (among whom I count myself), the ideas of Hume, Rousseau, Smith, and Kant – and specifically their concepts of other-directedness – continue to be invoked in contemporary debate.[52] As such we owe it to ourselves to try to understand their concepts as well as we can, even if only for the sake of better understanding what we ourselves mean when we invoke their terms. Secondly and more substantively, each of our four thinkers not only speaks insightfully about other-directedness, but also renders their particular theory of other-directedness central and indeed foundational to their larger moral and political systems. As I argue in what follows, for each one of our four thinkers there is a sense in which the theory of other-directedness that the thinkers defend can be seen as in itself suggestive or representative of the core (if not the whole) of their practical philosophy. Third and most importantly, Hume and Rousseau and Smith and Kant share a crucial commonality: each presents his concept of other-directedness as at once a response to the chief ethical question with which we are engaged – namely the mitigation of self-love – and as the product of his sustained reflections on the ways in which this particular concept emerges as the best available practical means of reaching these other-directed normative ends. This is not to say that all four of these theories are in lock-step with each other; as we shall see, there are significant differences that distinguish these theories from each other, and indeed render some more viable today than others – a point to which we will return in the epilogue. But for now what needs emphasis is that for all of these clear and crucial differences, each of the four theories to be examined here emerges as an attempt to provide a constructive response to the unique challenges posed by self-love in modernity, and specifically as a response that can improve on the response to this challenge given by the traditional conceptions of love.

The studies of these four concepts that occupy the four chapters that follow will not be for the faint of heart. The aim of each study is twofold: first, to show how each of these concepts can illuminate our master question about love and its modern transformation; and second, to show how each of these concepts emerges from and further develops key core commitments specific to the thinker in question. This second aim demands a fair amount of technical discussion that will sometimes be of greater interest to specialists on these four thinkers than to students of love more generally; conscious of this, I have largely relegated to endnotes my efforts to cut new edges in the specialized scholarship. My hope is that by so doing the book may be of service both to students of love more generally and to more specialized students of the history of philosophy.

Yet it is for the former audience in particular that I want to sound the note on which this introduction will conclude. One of my key questions in what follows is a very basic one – but still, I think, by far the most important. That question, quite simply, is: does all this work? Can the sentimentalized other-directedness that the Enlightenment conceived and its successors have championed respond adequately to the task for which it was originally developed, namely that of restraining self-love and egocentrism? Answering this question will require careful study of what in fact the Enlightenment thinkers sought to achieve through their conceptions, as well as an effort to appreciate the degree to which their concerns may differ from our own.

To give away the game at the outset, at least in part: what follows argues that the Enlightenment thinkers were right to be optimistic about the capacity of their invention to do the job for which it was intended. This invention, sentimental other-directedness, was specifically set forth as a means of mitigating the most destructive practical effects of egocentrism and individualism and selfishness in both the public and the private spheres. But that job, as envisioned by the Enlightenment thinkers, differs in a subtle but key way from the job envisioned by today's theorists of other-directedness. For insofar as they turn to the Enlightenment concepts of humanity or sympathy or pity not merely as means of curbing egocentrism but also as grounds for establishing a warm and positive attachment of self to others – and especially an attachment capable of restoring the bonds of unity and community that capitalism and liberalism are so often said to attenuate – it seems to me that they might well be (forgive me) looking for love in all the wrong places.

As I hope to show, the very aspect of the Enlightenment conception of other-directedness that rendered it successful at achieving its envisioned ends is precisely what renders it unable to carry the weight that its contemporary revivers want it to bear. This specific aspect concerns the Enlightenment's conceptualization of other-directedness as a sentiment at once both *wide* and *weak*. This dual emphasis unites all four of our thinkers' accounts of other-directedness. Thus in the first place, they each explicitly claim that the specific advantage of the concept of other-directedness that they mean to develop is its wideness, or universality – and specifically that it is capable of being felt at once *by* every human being, and *toward* every human being. And in the second place, all four thinkers also explicitly claim that one advantage of their form of other-directedness is that it is not strong, but weak – and specifically that it demands of us not the sort of all-encompassing love toward all others that would exhaust individuals of such limited energies and capacities as ourselves, but rather asks us only to exert that degree of minimal restraint necessary to check or restrain our self-love.

So to the basic question of "will it work?" I want to argue that the eighteenth-century concept of other-directedness can in fact work well for the problem it was intended to solve, but that this problem is something quite different than the one for which this same concept is often employed today. One reason why it is important to emphasize this is that the attempt to employ the Enlightenment's remedy for today's problems may well have as a perverse unintended consequence the encouragement of the very sorts of egocentrism that the Enlightenment conception originally aimed to mitigate. As we shall see, compassion and sympathy and pity can all be pleasant feelings, and as such it is not unreasonable for us to ask ourselves whether we value them for the ways in which they gratify our selfishness rather than for the ways in which they benefit others. If so, sentimental other-directedness, though intended as a means of establishing a stable balance point on the binary continuum of self-love and other-love, may by its very nature upset this balance and incline us toward the selfish side. The issue essentially concerns whether, in flattening the triangle to a line, the other-directed sentiments can resist degeneration into a deeper self-centeredness that preclusion of access to a transcendent sphere perhaps invites.

Seen in one light, the answer must be no. The love of others, and especially the love of strangers, will seem to more orthodox minds simply incomprehensible in the absence of a prior love of God. Thus, echoing the lines from Kierkegaard quoted previously, the distinguished theologian Paul Tillich insists that "the dependence of the whole realm of moral action on the presence of the Spiritual power" is particularly evident in *agape*, which challenges us to see others not simply as bundles of needs or desires demanding fulfillment, but which enables us to see the other "as God sees him."[53] More recently, it has been similarly insisted that it is only once we have "an intimate encounter with God" that we can come to truly love the stranger, and thus become a practitioner in our own right of the true humanitarianism that demands to be distinguished from more common forms of "welfare activity" and mere "social assistance."[54]

But others of course are more hopeful. Two distinct lines of argument push back against the orthodox conclusions on this front. The first suggests that it may well be possible, and indeed desirable, for us to realize a self-consciously secular or anti-transcendent conception of other-directed love. Sometimes this hopefulness takes an aggressive form. In a recent effort to develop a "secular" theory of human dignity, George Kateb suggests that all foundational invocations of God ought to be regarded as "the fault of our tiredness, confusion, or longing," insisting that we do better as theorists to "try to do without such props," which can "always give way to enlightenment."[55] So too, and indeed with specific reference to the concepts of love and transcendence, Irving Singer declares himself "an opponent" and "an enemy" of the concepts of transcendence and merging, and encourages us to regard attempts to apply these concepts to love as akin to political totalitarianism.[56] And Nussbaum perhaps most prominently has called "the yearning for the transcendent" merely a "first cousin to cynicism," and argues that we would do better to trade the "love that seeks transcendence" for "a love that repudiates that aspiration as immature and a precursor of disillusionment" – a sort of reprise of Freud's notorious excoriation of what he called "the oceanic feeling" that seeks "something like the restoration of limitless narcissism."[57]

Yet others want to push back against the effort to transcend transcendence. Agreeing with those thinkers who regard it as desirable and necessary to reground our core concepts in secular or immanent terms, such voices counter that it remains necessary for us to attempt to recover within this secular idiom certain key features of the concepts being replaced. Two key voices on this front are those of Ferry and Irigaray. Ferry welcomes and celebrates modern humanitarianism as "a particularly clear example of the shift from the love of one's nearest and dearest to the love of one's neighbour."[58] But not only does he regard modern humanitarianism as noble in itself, he also seeks to discover resources within the binary of self and other capable of reproducing within the binary itself the transcendence that distinguished earlier concepts of love. In this vein, one of his key claims is that for us living today, the old sort of transcendence is simply unavailable: "salvation is found in imminence, not in transcendence." At the same time, we cannot do without transcendence altogether, he thinks; what is needed, he argues, is not transcendence of the sacred, but rather what he calls "*la sacralisation d'autrui*" – "a making sacred of the other, a transcendence of the beloved, which nonetheless remains completely circumscribed within the sphere of immanence to humanity." Ferry calls this "the foundation for a new form of transcendence, a new way of thinking about the meaning that we give to life." And this leads to perhaps his most striking claim:

Love, like beauty, grasps us as a sort of transcendence, and yet this transcendence, which can at times make me "come out of myself," from my egocentricity, is most directly demonstrated in the most secret intimacy, in the most radical imminence to my subjective awareness. We do experience the transcendence of the other, of his otherness, but this transcendence does not come down from on high, from the cosmos or from God, or even from practical reason and the simple "respect" that is rationally owed to others. This transcendence is experienced nowhere else – to use the cardinal formula of Husserl's phenomenology – than in the most intimate immanence there is, the one expressed in every language by the universal metaphor of the "heart."[59]

And Ferry is not alone in so hoping. Irigaray, in her own penetrating study of love, similarly welcomes the discovery of an immanent divine: "the unveiling of another relation with the divine than the one that we already know, a divine not only living with humans but in them, and to be greeted and listened to between us."[60]

Taken altogether, we can thus identify three broad ways of thinking about love today. One strain, that of religious orthodoxy, seeks to keep alive a traditional conception grounded in transcendence. A second strain, that of Ferry and Irigaray, also seeks to preserve transcendence, but on secular and specifically intersubjective grounds. A third strain, represented here by Nussbaum, aims to liberate us from the concept of transcendence altogether. In the face of such different possible paths, we will of course want to know which is likely to be most promising as we seek to move forward today. My own sense is that none of these three available strands are likely to be successful taken alone. The orthodox position, however attractive to some, is not available to many today. This is not to say that it is dead. As the lines from King quoted previously suggest, for religious believers this view remains alive for them even in a secular world. But the key point here is that it is a view that is available only to religious believers, and one that necessarily excludes all those whose understanding of ethical phenomena is grounded in commitments independent of religion. This is important because it suggests the limits of the aggressively secular position as well. This position likewise leaves many – most obviously, religious believers – out in the cold. But not only religious believers: insofar as the aggressively secular conception rejects all forms of transcendence, not only must it alienate religious believers who necessarily see love through the lens of transcendence, but it must also alienate those many others who may have little use for religious notions of transcendence but who still experience love in some very basic sense as a going out to another in a way that lifts them above and beyond themselves. And if the other position defined by Ferry and Irigaray may allay this particular worry insofar as it restores a commitment to self-transcendence, it yet remains the case that its attempt to render transcendence immanent invites a propensity to the deification of others that is unlikely to sit well with either the religious believers or the secular nonbelievers.

Thus the impasse that we seem to have reached. How then to move forward? The hope that animates this book is that our most productive move forward starts with a look back. By gaining clarity on the specific problem that the Enlightenment concept of other-directedness sought to solve, not only might we be led to a greater appreciation of its accomplishment, but we also can better appreciate what it leaves unsolved. Again, its specific accomplishment lies in demonstrating how egocentrism can be restrained without requiring recourse to the transcendent. But its limits are revealed in its incapacity to establish the sorts of intimate social bonds that today's critics of our atomistic and individualistic world seek to reanimate, and in its simple inability to gratify the deeper psychological yearning for intimacy and for exit from the confines of the self that the modern view of the autonomous individual seems to reify. What then beyond enlightened other-directedness do we need to satisfy these two needs? This is a staggeringly daunting question, but one to which the epilogue will return in an attempt to provide a prolegomena to a more fully sufficient answer. But even before that, there is much work to be done. And hence the two aims of this book: first, to demonstrate how the vision of other-directedness that emerged in the Enlightenment was developed as a means of mitigating egocentric self-preference independent of theological or philosophical concepts of transcendence; and second, to determine whether and how such a love can be preserved from degenerating into the self-love it was intended to remedy.

NOTES

1 See respectively Simon May, *Love: A History* (New Haven, CT: Yale University Press, 2011); Troy Jollimore, *Love's Vision* (Princeton, NJ: Princeton University Press, 2011); Pascal Bruckner, *The Paradox of Love* (Princeton, NJ: Princeton University Press, 2012), and Robert Spaemann, "The Paradoxes of Love," in *Love and the Dignity of Human Life: On Nature and Natural Law* (Grand Rapids, MI: Eerdmans, 2012); Barbara Frederickson, *Love 2.0: How Our Supreme Emotion Affects Everything We Feel, Think, Do, and Become* (London: Penguin, 2013). And at the intersection of love and psychology, see Berit Brogaard, *On Romantic Love: Simple Truths about a Complex Emotion* (Oxford: Oxford University Press, 2015); at the intersection of philosophy and history, see Ronald de Sousa, *Love: A Very Short Introduction* (Oxford: Oxford University Press, 2015).

2 Alain Badiou, *In Praise of Love* (New York: New Press, 2012), 16–17, 95. The last quoted phrase is delivered by Badiou's interlocutor Nicholas Truong with reference to Badiou's earlier claims; see Badiou, *The Meaning of Sarkozy*, tr. David Fernbach (London: Verso, 2008), 48–49.

3 Compare Luc Ferry, *On Love: A Philosophy for the Twenty-First Century* (London: Polity, 2013), 34, 52, 168, 170; to Badiou, *Praise of Love*, 57.

4 Ferry, *On Love*, 120; and Luc Ferry, *La révolution de l'amour: Pour une spiritualité laïque* (Paris: Plon, 2010), 88–89.

5 Jean-Claude Kaufmann, *The Curious History of Love* (Cambridge: Polity Press, 2011), 1, 5; see also esp. 12–13, 42, 45, 109–111, 116, 141–142, 147.

6 For these claims, see esp. Nicholas Wolterstorff, *Justice in Love* (Grand Rapids, MI: Eerdmans, 2011), esp. vii–viii, 1, 47–53; and Martha Nussbaum, *Political Emotions: Why Love Matters for Justice* (Cambridge, MA: Harvard University Press, 2013), esp. 2, 9–10. In the same vein see also Rebecca Kingston, *Public Passion: Rethinking the Grounds for Political Justice* (Montreal: McGill-Queen's University Press, 2011), esp. 12, 19, 61, 109, 143–148.

7 Nussbaum, *Political Emotions*, 17, 384; cf. 55, 70, 177, 315.

8 Nussbaum, *Political Emotions*, 3; cf. 166. For an earlier treatment of similar themes, see Romand Coles, *Rethinking Generosity: Critical Theory and the Politics of Caritas* (Ithaca, NY: Cornell University Press, 1997), vii.

9 In this vein see, e.g., Axel Honneth's recent characterization of "the morality of love" as a "specific kind of self-limitation" that enables us to realize our duties to others, in "Love, Society, and Agape: An Interview with Axel Honneth," *European Journal of Social Theory* 16 (2013): 251–252.

10 On the differences between altruism and love, see, e.g., Stephen G. Post, "The Tradition of Agape," in *Altruism and Altruistic Love: Science, Philosophy, & Religion in Dialogue*, ed. Post et. al. (Oxford: Oxford University Press, 2002), 53–59; and, in the same volume, Kristen Renwick Monroe, "Explicating Altruism," 106–107. Both essays also call attention to the particular limitations of "works that dichotomize altruism, focusing complex acts into only the bifurcated categories of egoism and altruism" (Monroe, "Explicating Altruism," 108; see also 114–115); for further critique of the limitations of the egoism–altruism dichotomy, see Neera Kapur Badhwar, "Altruism versus Self-Interest: Sometimes a False Dichotomy," in *Altruism*, ed. Ellen Frankel Paul, Fred D. Miller, Jr., and Jeffrey Paul (Cambridge: Cambridge University Press, 1993), 90–117.

11 See especially Nussbaum, *Political Emotions*, 137–160; and *Upheavals of Thought: The Intelligence of Emotions* (Cambridge: Cambridge University Press, 2001), esp. 401–454; and Michael Slote, *Moral Sentimentalism* (Oxford: Oxford University Press, 2010), 123–139. Other key recent studies of the political promise of these passions, and indeed affect more generally, that likewise call attention to their eighteenth-century origins include Kingston, *Public Passion*, esp. 182–210; Duncan Kelly, *The Propriety of Liberty: Persons, Passions, and Judgement in Modern Political Thought* (Princeton, NJ: Princeton University Press, 2011), esp. 1–12; Michael Frazer, *The Enlightenment of Sympathy: Justice and the Moral Sentiments in the Eighteenth Century and Today* (Oxford: Oxford University Press, 2010), esp. 168–182; and Sharon Krause, *Civil Passions: Moral Sentiment and Democratic Deliberation* (Princeton, NJ: Princeton University Press, 2008), esp. 1–26, 200–203.

12 Recent treatments of the relationship between dignity and the recognition of equality include George Kateb, *Human Dignity* (Cambridge, MA: Harvard University Press, 2011), esp. 6–9; and Michael Rosen, *Dignity: Its History and Meaning* (Cambridge, MA: Harvard University Press, 2012), esp. 38–54.

13 For very helpful introductions to the concepts of love in these traditions, see esp. the essays collected in Bruce Chilton and Jacob Neusner, eds., *Altruism in World Religions* (Washington, DC: Georgetown University Press, 2005); and several relevant entries in Yudit Kornberg Greenberg, ed., *Encyclopedia of Love in World Religions* (Santa Barbara, CA: ABC-CLIO, 2008).

14 The question of the degree to which romantic love predates Romanticism has long been a particular concern of Irving Singer's; see most recently his *Philosophy of Love: A Partial Summing-Up* (Cambridge, MA: MIT Press, 2009), 1–7; and at greater length, his earlier book *The Nature of Love, Vol. 2: Courtly and Romantic* (Chicago: University of Chicago Press, 1984), esp. 1–15 and 283–302.

15 Among the many influential studies of love that take these three types of love for their point of departure, see, e.g., Martin Luther King, Jr., *Strength to Love* (New York: Harper and Row, 1963), 36–37. Classic comparative studies of these concepts of love include Anders Nygren, *Agape and Eros*, trans. Philip S. Watson (New York: Harper and Row, 1969 [1932–1939]); and C. S. Lewis, *The Four Loves* (New York: Harcourt, 1960). Helpful more recent

surveys that structure their analyses around these three concepts include May, *Love: A History*, esp. 38–68, 81–118; and Carter Lindberg, *Love: A Brief History through Western Christianity* (Oxford: Blackwell, 2008), esp. 1–18.

16 Charles Taylor, *A Secular Age* (Cambridge, MA: Harvard University Press, 2007), 20, 374.

17 Spaemann, "The Paradoxes of Love," 1–2; in the same vein, see Singer, *Philosophy of Love*, 13–14. The Hume quotation is drawn from T 1.2.6.8.

18 Taylor, *A Secular Age*, 67; cf. esp. 16, 143, 245.

19 I am grateful to several colleagues, and especially Susan Collins, Patrick Deneen, and Michelle Schwarze, for encouraging me to develop this claim.

20 Plato, *Symposium*, trans. Seth Benardete (Chicago: University of Chicago Press, 2001), 210d–211d.

21 Plato, *Symposium*, 211c.

22 Plato, *Symposium*, 206a; cf. 207a. For commentary on the relationship of *eros* to transcendence, see, e.g., Glenn Most, "Six Remarks on Platonic Love," in *Erotikon: Essays on Eros, Ancient and Modern*, ed. Shadi Bartsch and Thomas Bartscherer (Chicago: University of Chicago Press, 2005), 42–43; and Aryeh Kosman, "Platonic Love," in *Virtues of Thought: Essays on Plato and Aristotle* (Cambridge, MA: Harvard University Press, 2014), esp. 32–36, 42.

23 On *eros* and possession, see esp. Nussbaum, *Upheavals of Thought*, 483–488. Nygren takes this aspect of *eros* – namely that it is, as Diotima says, "always dwelling with neediness" (203d) – as indicative of its fundamentally egocentric character; see *Agape and Eros*, esp. 174–179, 216. For the counterclaim, see, e.g., Kosman, "Platonic Love," 30ff; as well as Richard Kraut's claim that Diotima conceives of *eros* as "a complex combination of self-involving and other-regarding motives" ["Plato on Love," in *The Oxford Handbook of Plato*, ed. Gail Fine (Oxford: Oxford University Press, 2008), 286–310, quote at 293]; and Price's reading of the erotic desire to possess the beautiful as a manifestation of the desire for immortality [A. W. Price, *Love and Friendship in Plato and Aristotle* (Oxford: Oxford University Press, 1989), chapter 2].

24 The question of whether *eros* for the beautiful incorporates *eros* for a given individual has given rise to debates over whether Diotima's account is best read as "inclusive" or "exclusive." For overview see, e.g., Christopher Gill, "Platonic Love and Individuality," in *Polis and Politics: Essays in Greek Moral and Political Philosophy*, ed. Andros Loizou and Harry Lesser (Aldershot: Avebury, 1990), 69–71; Price, *Love and Friendship*, 45ff; and Ferrari's claim that the initiate described in Diotima's speech "subsumes in his ascent the inferior forms of love" [G.R.F. Ferrari, "Platonic Love," in *The Cambridge Companion to Plato*, ed. Richard Kraut (Cambridge: Cambridge University Press, 1992), 260].

25 Aristotle, *Nicomachean Ethics*, trans. Joe Sachs (Newbury, MA: Focus Press, 2002), 9.8, 1168b13–19.

26 Cf. Charles Kahn, "Aristotle and Altruism," *Mind* 90 (1981): 30ff; and Julia Annas, "Self-Love in Aristotle," *Southern Journal of Philosophy* 27 Supp.

(1988): 14–15. Especially helpful in this context is Price's observation that this passage describes "a higher possessiveness" (*Love and Friendship in Plato and Aristotle*, 113–114).

27 Aristotle, *Nicomachean Ethics* 9.8, 1168b30 and 1169b1; Plato, *Symposium*, 211b.

28 Aristotle, *Nicomachean Ethics* 9.8, 1169a3–15.

29 I examine the significance of this account at greater length in "Aristotle on the Greatness of Greatness of Soul," *History of Political Thought* 23 (2002): 1–20 (see esp. 18–19).

30 Aristotle, *Nicomachean Ethics* 8.3, 1156a5–1156b33; and *Nicomachean Ethics* 9.5, 1166b30–1167a5.

31 The degree to which this also holds true for Platonic *eros* has been a matter of recent scholarly debate. For a helpful account of the way in which the *eros* of the *Symposium* might incorporate a *philia*-like "other-directed service, which may well involve caring for others for their own sake," see the response given to Gregory Vlastos in Frisbee C.C. Sheffield, *Plato's Symposium: The Ethics of Desire* (Oxford: Oxford University Press, 2006), 154–182 (quote at 181).

32 On their incompatibility, see, most importantly, Nygren, *Agape and Eros*; for helpful commentary see Wolterstorff, *Justice in Love*, 26–27, 30, 39; and Lindberg, *Love: A Brief History*, 160. Against this view, see Pope Benedict XVI, *Deus caritas est*, 7–8 (the source of the "caricature" reference), and especially Josef Pieper, *Faith, Hope, Love* (San Francisco: Ignatius Press, 1997), 211–214.

33 Studies of Christian love, which treat these sources and from which I have learned much about *agape*, include Timothy P. Jackson, *The Priority of Love: Christian Charity and Social Justice* (Princeton, NJ: Princeton University Press, 2003), 1–27; Pieper, *Faith, Hope, Love*; and Edward C. Vacek, *Love, Human and Divine: The Heart of Christian Ethics* (Washington, DC: Georgetown University Press, 1994), esp. 116–156.

34 Matthew 22:36–40 (KJV).

35 Badiou, *Praise of Love*, 64.

36 In addition to the sources cited in n13, on the anticipation of the Gospel command in Judaism, see esp. Lenn E. Goodman, *Love Thy Neighbor as Thyself* (Oxford: Oxford University Press, 2008), 3–30; Chilton, "Altruism in Christianity," in *Altruism in World Religions*, 56–58; and Benedict XVI, *Deus caritas est*, 1.

37 Reeve captures something like what I have in mind here when he says of the *Symposium*: "Replace 'the beautiful itself' with the Christian 'God' and it is Augustine's story in the *Confessions*" [C. D. C. Reeve, *Love's Confusions* (Cambridge, MA: Harvard University Press, 2005), 114]. See also Vacek, *Love, Human and Divine*, esp. 50–51 and 98–102.

38 See, e.g., Harry Frankfurt, *The Reasons of Love* (Princeton, NJ: Princeton University Press, 2006), 71 and 77; Jackson, *Priority of Love*, 11; Wolterstorff, *Justice in Love*, 97; Vacek, *Love, Human and Divine*, 198ff and 243; and Pieper, *Faith, Hope, Love*, 221–222 and 237–238. Goodman advances similar claims in noting that self-regard is presumed in the Torah as the proper "gauge" for active caring for others, and that "the seedbed the Law seeks to

cultivate is an ethos in which ego is presumed but egoism rejected"; see *Love Thy Neighbor as Thyself*, 14–15.

39 Jean-Luc Nancy, without reference to theological categories, beautifully captures the difference between this self-love and simple egoism: "To love one's self is not the same as egoism. It is necessary to love oneself. Indeed, it's dangerous not to love oneself and worse still to hate oneself. But just as with the love of another, we have to distinguish between loving a favorite object, preferring oneself over all others, which is egoism and in which I relate to myself as to a prized possession or to what I 'have,' and loving oneself in the very fact that one exists, that one 'is' and in that sense, one is like any other, one has a unique 'price,' one counts in a unique way, for others as for oneself" [*God, Love, Justice, Beauty: Four Little Dialogues*, trans. Sarah Clift (New York: Fordham University Press, 2011), 127n2; cf. 80–81].

40 I'm grateful to Nicholas Wolterstorff for his emphasis on this point.

41 Kierkegaard, *Works of Love*, trans. Howard Song and Edna Song (New York: Harper, 1962), 70. For commentary, see Reeve, *Love's Confusions*, 3; Wolterstorff, *Justice in Love*, 28; cf. Nygren, *Agape and Eros*, 97.

42 King, *Strength to Love*, 69.

43 Ferry, *La révolution de l'amour*, 192, 297.

44 These moments all receive prominent attention in May, *Love: A History*; and Singer, *The Nature of Love*.

45 For a recent attempt to lay the blame at the Enlightenment's doorstep with regard to love in particular, see Kaufmann, *Curious History*, esp. 40–41.

46 Within recent political theory, foremost among these are the studies by Krause, Kelly, Kingston, and Frazer cited in n11. These studies are especially valuable for their collective illumination of the role of affect in judgment and especially in our deliberation about justice – a theme not unrelated to but ultimately distinct from my focus on relationship of love to our epistemic capacities.

47 Carl L. Becker, *The Heavenly City of the Eighteenth-Century Philosophers* (New Haven, CT: Yale University Press, 1932), 39; cf. Honneth, "Love, Society, and Agape," 250, 253–254, 257; and especially the helpful treatment of Grotius and Pufendorf by J.B. Schneewind, who observes that they were engaged in a project of "transforming the theological virtue of charity into a secular virtue," the import of which lies "not in its role in personal salvation, but in its ability to improve social life" [Schneewind, "The Misfortunes of Virtue," *Ethics* 101 (1990): 50]; for a similar claim regarding Hutcheson, see Terence Cuneo, "Reason and the Passions," in *The Oxford Handbook of British Philosophy in the Eighteenth Century*, ed. James A. Harris (Oxford: Oxford University Press, 2013), 244. More generally see Taylor, who calls explicit attention to the degree to which modern humanism recognized a necessity of providing "some substitute for *agape*," some "functional replacement either for Christian *agape*, or the disinterested benevolence of the neo-Stoics," one in which benevolence comes indeed to be recognized as an "*agape*-surrogate" (*A Secular Age*, 27, 245, 279–280; cf. 254, 261); and Kaufmann, who understands the Enlightenment's ambition as an attempt at "translating the Christian *agape* into a new and secular benevolence" (*Curious History*, 54). Helpful on

this front is Nygren's response: "the idea has often been put forward that it is possible to retain Christian ethics even while rejecting the religious content of Christianity. But the 'love for one's neighbor,' the 'general love of humanity,' which it is thus intended to retain turns out in the end to be something quite other than Christian love for one's neighbor. Nothing could be more disastrous for the Christian idea of love than that it should be identified with modern ideas of altruism, fellow-feeling, and so forth…Christian love has really nothing at all to do with such modern ideas" (*Agape and Eros*, 95–96). In recent political theory, a similar claim has been helpfully developed in Pierre Manent, *A World beyond Politics? A Defense of the Nation State*, trans. Marc LePain (Princeton, NJ: Princeton University Press, 2006), 187–188.

48 Happily several recent book-length studies have begun the examination of the eighteenth-century foundations and future prospects for true religion; see Gordon Graham, *Wittgenstein and Natural Religion* (Oxford: Oxford University Press, 2014), esp. 1–16; and Andre C. Willis, *Toward a Humean True Religion: Genuine Theism, Moderate Hope, and Practical Morality* (University Park: Penn State University Press, 2014).

49 I examine these concepts and the relevant literature at greater length in "Hume's Critique and Defense of Religion," in *Enlightenment and Secularism: Essays on the Mobilization of Reason*, ed. Christopher Nadon (Lanham, MD: Lexington, 2013), 89–101; and "Adam Smith on the 'Natural Principles of Religion'," *Journal of Scottish Philosophy* 13 (2015): 37–53.

50 On the implications of these eighteenth-century social developments for religion, see especially Taylor, *A Secular Age*, 194, 218.

51 An older but valuable comprehensive survey of the intellectual history of these concepts in the eighteenth century can be found in Norman Fiering, "Irresistible Compassion: An Aspect of Eighteenth-Century Sympathy and Humanitarianism," *Journal of the History of Ideas* 37 (1976): 195–218. Helpful more focused studies of these specific concepts include Patrick Frierson, "Learning to Love: From Egoism to Generosity in Descartes," *Journal of the History of Philosophy* 40 (2002): 313–338 and Sarah Marquardt, "The Long Road to Peace: Descartes' Modernization of Generosity in The Passions of the Soul (1649)," *History of Political Thought* 36 (2015): 53–83; Patrick Riley, "Introduction," in *Leibniz: Political Writings* (Cambridge: Cambridge University Press, 1998); David Lay Williams, "Spinoza and the General Will," *Journal of Politics* 72 (2010): 341–356; Michael Gill, "Shaftesbury on Love for Humanity" (unpublished ms.); Christian Maurer, "Hutcheson's Relation to Stoicism in the Light of His Moral Psychology," *Journal of Scottish Philosophy* 8 (2010): 33–49; and Sarah Moses, "'Keeping the Heart': Natural Affection in Joseph Butler's Approach to Virtue," *Journal of Religious Ethics* 37 (2009): 613–629.

52 See, e.g., in addition to those sources cited at n11, Michael Ure and Mervyn Frost, eds., *The Politics of Compassion* (London: Routledge, 2014), esp. 1–5.

53 Paul Tillich, *Love, Power, and Justice* (Oxford: Oxford University Press, 1954), 84, 117.

54 Benedict XIV, *Deus caritas est*, 18, 25, 30–31; see also King, *Strength to Love*, 21–22; and Pieper, *Faith, Hope, Love*, 148.

55 Kateb, *Human Dignity*, 127, 25.

56 Singer, *Philosophy of Love*, 16–20; see also Singer, *Nature of Love*, vol. 2: *Courtly and Romantic*, esp. 6–7.

57 Nussbaum, *Political Emotions*, 52; Sigmund Freud, *Civilization and Its Discontents*, trans. James Strachey (New York: W.W. Norton, 2010), 36, though cf. esp. 81–82, 91–95 and 145–146. For Taylor's response to Nussbaum (and Nietzsche) on this point, see *A Secular Age*, 625–634.

58 Ferry, *On Love*, 53.

59 Ferry, *La révolution de l'amour*, 24–25; and Ferry, *On Love*, 26, 37, 57. In this context cf. especially Taylor, *A Secular Age*, 374.

60 Luce Irigaray, *The Way of Love* (London: Continuum, 2002), 50, cf. 150.

2

Hume on Humanity

THE "POLITICS OF HUMANITY"

The sentiment of humanity has recently emerged as a prominent alternative to traditional conceptions of love. Martha Nussbaum, whose efforts to reawaken an appreciation of love within liberalism we have already had occasion to mention, in a separate recent book calls for an explicit shift "from a politics of disgust to a politics of humanity." Having witnessed the benefits of this "politics of humanity" in specific recent debates over sexual orientation and constitutional law, Nussbaum suggests that in our future debates over the family, employment, and the common good, the politics of humanity "must be enacted and reenacted in each of these areas, in each region of the country, each time a new issue comes along."[1] The rhetorical force of such a call is undeniable. Yet claiming that the politics of humanity is superior to the politics of disgust is far different from explaining the grounds of its superiority – or even what it is. What exactly then is this "politics of humanity" for which so much is being claimed?

For illumination, this chapter examines what is arguably the most complete exposition of the politics of humanity available to us: namely Hume's celebration of "humanity" as at once the proper foundation and the proper end of morality. Hume claims a great deal for the sentiment of humanity, indeed going so far as to say that "it can alone be the foundation of morals" (EPM 9.6). This is a remarkable and also an underappreciated claim, and what follows aims to present Hume's reasons for embracing it.[2] In so doing, it specifically aims to explain how Hume's championing of the sentiment of humanity emerged from his concern to

31

develop, contra the defenders of what he called the "selfish system of morals" (EPM App. 2.3), a defense of other-directed sentiment that is at once
capable of resisting or mitigating egoism, but also consistent with Hume's
epistemic commitments, and in particular his skepticism to transcendence. In addition, Hume presents humanity as an alternative not only
to love but also to such sentiments as benevolence and sympathy. What
follows thus also aspires to contribute to the debates among specialists
concerning humanity's relationship to these sentiments. Finally, I hope
that attending to Hume's arguments for humanity can also shed light
on the relationship between the components of the politics of humanity: secularism, other-directed values, and mutual recognition of shared
similarities. Yet for all this, the chief aim of what follows is to show how
Hume's understanding of the foundational import of the sentiment of
humanity emerged as a direct consequence of his conception of its capacity to manage self-love, and indeed to do so in a manner consistent with
his understanding of our cognitive capacities and limits.

LOVE, TRANSCENDENCE, AND HUMANITY

Before turning to Hume's conception of humanity, we need first to say
a few words about his views on love. Hume tends not to be regarded as
a central theorist of love, either by scholars of love or by Hume specialists. Hume in fact treats love in several places, most notably in Book 2,
Part 2 of the *Treatise*, explicitly dedicated to "Of Love and Hatred." But
his definitions of love and hatred here are in large part idiosyncratic to
Hume's own broader project, and on first glimpse seem to have little to
do with those traditional ways of conceptualizing love examined in the
previous chapter. Hume tends to define love as akin to esteem or admiration, insisting that "love and esteem are nearly the same passion, and
arise from similar causes" (EPM App 4.6n; cf. T 3.3.4.2), and locates
these causes in "accomplishments or services" possessed or done by others and which render them admirable to us (DP 2.2). In defining love
thus, Hume's aim is to demonstrate that love and hatred are merely the
manifestations of pain and pleasure that we experience upon beholding
certain qualities in others, and hence analogues of the pride and humility
we feel when we behold certain qualities in ourselves (see, e.g., T 2.2.1.9;
T 2.2.2; T 2.2.5.1; DP 2.3).[3]

Hume's most prominent treatment of love thus seems far removed
from any of the traditional concerns about transcendence. Yet some of
his other treatments of love face this concern squarely and indeed do

so in ways that have crucial consequences for his broader project as a moral philosopher. Two particular such treatments are especially important here: Hume's treatment of Platonic *eros*, and his treatment of what he calls "love of mankind" or "universal affection." The first of these he treats in a remarkable if relatively neglected passage at the end of his essay "Of Love and Marriage." The main theme of the essay as a whole is power relationships between the sexes, and the essay has been read as an attempt to describe an ideal of marriage founded on the conditions of perfect equality.[4] But for our purposes, its significance lies in its concluding discussion of Plato. Having traced the dissension that seems to plague modern marriages, Hume proposes to "deliver to them Plato's account of the origin of love and marriage" so as to restore harmony and equality (EMPL 560). What he ends up delivering is a truncated version of Aristophanes' speech in *Symposium* – a speech chiefly famous for its account of how the gods, fearing the power of men in their original state, divided each into two in order to curb man's power. The job of *eros*, as Aristophanes describes it, is to promote the efforts of these divided halves to reunite and thereby reestablish their lost wholeness and unity.[5]

But Hume proposes to go further and indeed "to carry on this fiction of Plato" by adding a new ending to the story – an ending that speaks directly to our concerns here. In Hume's addition the gods wish to repent for the misery they caused to men, who in their divided state had "become incapable of any repose or tranquility," and came to suffer from "such cravings, such anxieties, such necessities" that they were led to "curse their creation, and think existence itself a punishment." Taking pity on their suffering, Jupiter sends down two emissaries, Love and Hymen, "to collect the broken halves of human kind, and piece them together in the best manner possible" (EMPL 561). Initially they succeed – but success proves short-lived and dissension soon reappears. Hume traces this dissension to the helpers Love and Hymen called to aid them in their work. Hymen, we learn, allied himself with Care, "who was continually filling his patron's head with prospects of futurity; a settlement, family, children, servants; so that little else was regarded in all the matches they made." Love, for his part, allied with Pleasure – "who was as pernicious a counselor as the other, and would never allow Love to look beyond the present momentary gratification, or the satisfying of the prevailing inclination." The result was that Care worked to subvert what Love united, even as Pleasure worked to undo Hymen's pairings. This chaotic state required intervention by Jupiter, who ordered "an immediate reconcilement betwixt Love and Hymen," and also "laid his strict injunctions on

them never to join any halves without consulting their favourites Care
and Pleasure, and obtaining the consent of both to the conjunction"
(EMPL 562).

Hume's addition to Plato's *Symposium* speaks to several themes at
the heart of his own moral project and the present inquiry. The effect
of his revised account is to induce skepticism toward *eros*, and specifically skepticism toward its ability to promote anything like the sort of
self-transcendence Diotima had described. Where Diotima aims to free
the self from its bonds and to open it to a transcendent horizon, Hume's
account emphasizes the opposite: namely the simple inescapability of the
most basic concerns of the self, including especially fear, anxiety, pleasure, and pain. The liberating ascent to the transcendent in which the
Symposium's account of *eros* culminates has been rewritten by Hume
in such a way that liberation is replaced by a prenuptial contract that
mandates privileging the comfort and well-being of the self above all. Far
from promoting transcendence of the self, *eros* is circumscribed by the
self, and imprisoned within its limits.

Hume's rewriting of Plato thus seeks to induce skepticism toward the
notion that *eros* can promote self-transcendence. A similar sort of skepticism is to be found in Hume's comments on another type of love, namely
the "love of mankind." Hume's notorious denial that a universal love of
mankind is natural to human beings is well known to specialists.[6] In his
key passage on this front, Hume thus claims:

In general, it may be affirm'd, that there is no such passion in human minds,
as the love of mankind, merely as such, independent of personal qualities, of
services, or of relation to ourself. 'Tis true, there is no human, and indeed no
sensible, creature, whose happiness or misery does not, in some measure, affect
us, when brought near to us, and represented in lively colours: But this proceeds
merely from sympathy, and is no proof of such an universal affection to mankind,
since this concern extends itself beyond our own species. (T 3.2.1.12)

Hume's claim here is clear: the universal love of mankind – and by extension, agapic love in a more general sense – is a chimera for which we can
find no evidence in the human mind. In time we will need to examine
what Hume says here about the role that sympathy plays in this process. But for now what is especially interesting here is how Hume's argument against universal love compares to his discussion of *eros* in the
Symposium. Hume's claim here is not simply that all loves of others must
be chimerical, but, more precisely, that the universal and disinterested
love of others is a chimera – that is to say, love that is "independent of

personal qualities, of services, or of relation to ourself." Hume's clear emphasis is thus on the connection of love of others to concerns more conventionally associated with self-interest. Indeed just as Hume argued that we lack access to a transcendent *eros* free of self-interested concern for pleasure and tranquility, here he now suggests that we lack access to a universal love of others that transcends all concern for our individual selves. In this sense, in both *eros* and the "love of mankind," the self is the standard that properly serves at once as love's measure and its limit.

The key point here is that Hume's skepticism toward both erotic love and agapic love are grounded in a certain specific set of views about transcendence. In the previous chapter we already had occasion briefly to note Hume's views on self-transcendence in the context of Spaemann's insistence that Hume viewed all forms of self-transcendence as illusory. But Spaemann's claim perhaps requires additional nuance. For Hume himself does not seem to deny that human beings *aspire* to self-transcendence, and even believe themselves on occasion to achieve it. His claim is rather that this seeming self-transcendence is in fact an act of self-deception. Hume develops this point in an especially helpful way in the second section of the *Enquiry Concerning Human Understanding*. Emphasizing the degree to which thought seems "unbounded" and can in an instant transport us "into the most distant regions of the universe; or even beyond the universe, into the unbounded chaos," Hume explains that we often convince ourselves that "what never was seen, or heard of, may yet be conceived" (EHU 2.4; cf. EMPL 83). Yet Hume is skeptical of these seeming feats of self-transcendence; for all the "unbounded liberty" of our thought, closer examination reveals "that all this creative power of the mind amounts to no more than the faculty of compounding, transposing, augmenting, or diminishing the materials afforded us by the senses and experience" (EHU 2.5). Indeed, even the most transcendent categories – Hume specifically mentions "the idea of God" (EHU 2.6) – resolve into feelings and sensations. In Hume's language, all of our ideas are copied from impressions. For our inquiry, this means there can be no self-transcendence but only self-extension, as all contact with the seemingly transcendent – whether the beautiful, or the good, or God – is ultimately resolvable to an extrapolation from or extension of what is interior to or immediately present to the self.

From all of this several provisional conclusions can be drawn. First, Hume is skeptical of the legitimacy of traditional conceptions of love, especially erotic love and agapic or universal love. Second, his skepticism on this front emerges directly from his skepticism toward the notion that the self can be transcended or escaped in any genuine and legitimate sense. And third, Hume has epistemic arguments for his position: namely his argument concerning the nature of ideas and impressions. Taken together, these provisional conclusions point to a problem. That problem, put simply, concerns what substitute Hume might be able to propose for the older forms of love that his system militates against. And this problem turns out to be particularly acute for Hume in his capacities as a normative ethicist and political thinker. Hume, in short, is not Hobbes – that is, for all of his basic agreement with Hobbes's epistemic and ethical claims about the nature of the human mind and the primacy of self-concern, as a normative theorist Hume was deeply concerned to argue against the "selfish system" of morals that he himself associated with Hobbes – as we shall see in more detail subsequently. But in so doing, Hume sets up a challenge for himself. His normative commitments led him to argue for the superiority of other-directedness to self-centeredness. Yet his epistemic and ethical arguments against self-transcendence and transcendent love precluded his recurrence to traditional defenses of such concepts. Thus we wonder: what form of other-directedness is at once sufficiently robust to withstand Hobbesian egocentrism and yet commensurate with Hume's epistemic commitments? Hume's answer is the sentiment of humanity – a sentiment we need now to explore in detail.

HUMANITY: NORMATIVE DIMENSIONS

Hume's treatment of humanity has only relatively recently come to be a focus of specialists. Yet study of Hume's corpus as a whole reveals it to be a strikingly ubiquitous concept. And it is also a strikingly significant concept. For not only does Hume invoke humanity in a remarkable number of instances, he also attributes to it a remarkable significance and indeed primacy. Hume's key statement of humanity's primacy comes in the concluding section of his *Enquiry Concerning the Principles of Morals*, as we have already had occasion to note and which we will need to examine in more detail later. But this claim is itself consistent with his practical philosophy more generally, a philosophy consistently animated by his concern to encourage the growth and spread of humanity. This is especially evident in Hume's virtue theory. The centrality of humanity to this theory is clear from Hume's portraits of both the best and the worst characters. These portraits tend to suggest that it is the presence or absence of humanity that in fact determines the virtuousness or viciousness of a character. Hume introduces this claim in the *Treatise*, arguing that "no character can be more amiable and virtuous" than that of the "greatest humanity" (T 3.2.1.6). He develops it further in his later writings; thus in the second *Enquiry*, the model character is introduced as a man "of honour and humanity" (EPM 9.2), the portraits of ideal statesmen in Hume's *Essays* often emphasize their prominent humanity (e.g., EMPL 549), and his portraits in the *History of England* of Bacon – for Hume, the peak of human wisdom and virtue (EMPL 83) – likewise celebrate humanity (H 4.327, 4.359, 5.86).[7] Hume's critiques of viciousness similarly focus on humanity and its absence; thus his claims that the worst heart is one "destitute of humanity or benevolence," and the viciousness of a Nero is explained as a deficiency in "sentiments of duty and humanity" (EMPL 269; EPM App. 1.12). Even the notorious "sensible knave" – the classic free rider who discovers his advantage in pursuing self-interest and disregarding justice – is faulted for having "no relish for virtue and humanity, no sympathy with his fellow-creatures, no desire of esteem and applause" (EPM 9.22–23; EMPL 169).

Hume's celebration of humanity extends to his political theory; a remarkable number of his observations on peoples and cultures ancient and modern are efforts to demonstrate that humanity is in fact "the chief characteristic which distinguishes a civilized age from times of barbarity and ignorance" (EMPL 274).[8] In this vein Hume's *History* begins with the assumption that ancient nations were devoid of justice and humanity (H 1.15), and his portraits of ancient Anglo-Saxons (H 1.185) and ancient Gauls (EMPL 206) alike distinguish these rude originals from their successors explicitly on humanity's grounds. Moreover, Hume discovers a "want of humanity and of decency" not merely in barbarism's rudeness but also in the very peaks of ancient civilization (EMPL 246). This theme is especially pronounced in the second *Enquiry*; among its favorite tropes is the ancient obsession with courage and bravery (e.g., EPM n31, 7.13, 7.15, 7.25), which necessarily must "sound a little oddly in other nations and other ages" and especially ours, for today we recognize that "martial bravery" often "destroyed the sentiments of humanity; a virtue surely much more useful and engaging" (EPM 7.13–14). And Hume even goes a step further, reminding us that when the ancients mentioned sentimentalized humanity at all, they did so not to sing its praises but to warn against its seductions (EPM App. 4.14). Humanity is thus the line of demarcation that separates ancients from moderns. "Among the ancients, the heroes in philosophy, as well as those in war and patriotism, have a grandeur and force of sentiment, which astonishes our narrow souls." Yet moderns enjoy a greater gift, even if the ancients themselves would consider it "romantic and incredible": namely "the degree of humanity, clemency, order, tranquillity, and other social virtues, to which, in the administration of government, we have attained in modern times" (EPM 7.18; cf. EMPL 94).

This explicit recognition of the connection between humanity and modernity on the one hand and humanity and morality on the other in part explains Hume's campaign on behalf of modernity itself. And not just "modernity" in some abstract sense; his discussions of specific modern institutions are, to a remarkable degree, structured around explicit arguments that these institutions are preferable to their forebears on the grounds of their superior capacity to promote humanity. A glimpse of this is offered in a comparison of ancient and modern educational institutions, the latter of which "instil more humanity and moderation" (EMPL 94). Hume's key claims on this front, however, are to be found in the context of his development of certain of his foundational political ideas, including his advocacy of commercial society, his strategies to minimize faction, and his advocacy of post-Christian secularization. Hume's argument on the first front begins with his belief that science and humanity have "so close a connexion" (H 2.519), and is further developed in his claim that "a serious attention to the sciences and liberal arts softens and humanizes the temper, and cherishes those fine emotions, in which true virtue and honour consists" (EMPL 170). It reaches a peak in his claim that "*industry, knowledge,* and *humanity*, are linked together by an indissoluble chain, and are found, from experience as well as reason, to be peculiar to the more polished, and, what are commonly denominated, the more luxurious ages" (EMPL 271). Commerce – both material and interpersonal – is thus to be welcomed for its contributions to spreading humanity.[9]

The spread of humanity is to be further welcomed for its capacity to mitigate the threats that factionalism and civil war pose to stability. In the same passage in which Hume distinguishes civilization from barbarism on the grounds of humanity, he also observes that among the advantages of rule by "humane maxims" rather than "rigour and severity" is that such maxims are less likely to promote rebellion: "factions are then less inveterate, revolutions less tragical, authority less severe, and seditions less frequent" (EMPL 273–274). And humanity not only mitigates the threat of disorder from factions but also mitigates the destabilizing potential of religion. The critique of religion that Hume develops across his corpus is notoriously complex and well beyond our scope; here we note only that several of Hume's key distinctions of true from false religion rest on consequentialist considerations of whether a given religion promotes or inhibits humanity. Thus where polytheism allows "knavery to impose on credulity, till morals and humanity be expelled from the religious systems of mankind," theism "justly prosecuted" serves to "banish every thing frivolous, unreasonable, or inhuman from religious worship" and thereby promote justice and benevolence (NHR 9.1; cf. DCNR 86). However critical Hume may have been of the destructive potential of superstition and enthusiasm, he consistently argues that the "proper office of religion" is in fact the regulation of men's hearts so as to "humanize their conduct" (DCNR 82).

Humanity thus plays a crucial role in Hume's practical writings and forms a prominent element of his normative prescriptions on a wide range of fronts. Yet it is in his moral philosophy that humanity plays its most important role. Nowhere is this import more evident than in the conclusion to the second *Enquiry*. Here Hume forthrightly tells us that it is humanity – and indeed humanity alone – that makes morality itself possible:

The notion of morals implies some sentiment common to all mankind, which recommends the same object to general approbation, and makes every man, or most men, agree in the same opinion or decision concerning it. It also implies some sentiment, so universal and comprehensive as to extend to all mankind, and render the actions and conduct, even of the persons the most remote, an object of applause or censure, according as they agree or disagree with that rule of right which is established. These two requisite circumstances belong alone to the senti-ment of humanity here insisted on. (EPM 9.5)[10]

Hume reiterates this point in the paragraph that follows. While humanity may not be as strong as the passions derived from self-love, "it can alone be the foundation of morals, or of any general system of blame or praise" (EPM 9.6). This is an arresting statement; Hume's pronouncement that humanity "alone" can be the foundation of morals attests to a primacy of humanity in his moral philosophy that parallels if not exceeds its primacy in his political philosophy. But all of this necessarily leads us to wonder what exactly Hume found in humanity to make it worthy of this primacy. Put differently: why exactly does Hume credit "humanity" as at once the proper foundation and the proper end of morality? And what exactly might his decision to privilege humanity in this way and to this degree have to do with the critiques of love and transcendence examined in the first part of this chapter?

HUMANITY: EPISTEMIC DIMENSIONS

Hume offers two reasons for the primacy of humanity. The first concerns his understanding of the purpose of moral philosophy itself, and specifically its role, as Hume conceived it, in encouraging other-directedness. The second reason concerns the fundamental commitments of his epistemology, and particularly his conception of the limits and the capacities of human understanding – limits that preclude self-transcendence, and capacities that involve the principles of association that help us get along in the world.

Hume's understanding of the purpose of moral philosophy, it is generally agreed, underwent a transformation over time – a transformation coeval, perhaps not coincidentally, with his reconsideration of the primacy of humanity itself. As many have noted, in the *Treatise* Hume understood himself to be an "anatomist" rather than a "painter" (T 3.3.6.6), and his well-known letter to Francis Hutcheson from the same time would seem to reaffirm that the author of the *Treatise* was concerned mostly to provide a phenomenological rather than a normative account of morality. Yet by the time he began the second *Enquiry*, Hume's aims had shifted in a decidedly more normative direction.[11] These ambitions are especially evident in his efforts in the second *Enquiry* to respond to what he regarded as an especially worrisome phenomenon, one that we have already had occasion to note – namely the ascendency of the "selfish system of morals" that Hobbes and Mandeville had championed (EPM App. 2.3). The specter of this selfish system indeed looms large throughout the second *Enquiry* – thus Hume's striking warnings regarding men of "the most depraved disposition" who further "encourage that depravity," claiming that "all *benevolence* is mere hypocrisy, friendship a cheat, public spirit a farce, fidelity a snare to procure trust and confidence" (EPM App. 2.1). Clearly Hume worries that their arguments have been widely influential, noting that even decent men, "without any bad intention," frequently "discover a sullen incredulity" toward expressions of benevolence and public spirit, and sometimes "deny their existence and reality" (EPM 6.21; cf. 5.3). Hume's own response is to attempt to rescue "more generous motives and regards" from those detractors who insist on the "deduction of morals from self-love" (EPM 5.4–6) – an aim that requires us to "renounce the theory, which accounts for every moral sentiment by the principle of self-love" and instead "adopt a more public affection, and allow, that the interests of society are not, even on their own account, entirely indifferent to us" (EPM 5.17).

The normative overtones of such injunctions are impossible to miss, and mark an important departure from the *Treatise*. Yet this shift presents important challenges of its own. Chief among these is the question of how Hume might provide a defense of the superiority of other-directedness and "public affection" to egoism – and indeed a defense consistent with his epistemic commitments and his skepticism toward transcendence in particular. The precise nature of Hume's skepticism has of course long been a subject of controversy among specialists, and the delineation of different strands (dogmatic, mitigated, realist, Pyrrhonian) remains a perennial exercise. Yet all conceptions of Hume's skepticism, however else they might differ, recognize that a principal aim of his skeptical arguments demonstrating the limits of understanding is to check a propensity to make practical inferences from a priori or theological propositions.[12] That is, in demonstrating that the human understanding is "by no means fitted for such remote and abstruse subjects" (EHU 1.12), Hume famously insists that we would do well to turn away from the transcendent and to focus our attention instead only on empirical phenomena known by experience, all else being "entirely arbitrary" (EHU 4.9; cf. 11.23; EPM 2.5). But this move, familiar to students of Hume's epistemology, has implications for his normative project and the place of humanity in it. Specifically, Hume's skepticism necessarily rendered unavailable to him in his struggle against the selfish system the resources afforded by traditional theories of love insofar as it precluded recourse to the theological or teleological commitments characteristic of the transcendent theories of love.[13] It is here, at the intersection of his skeptical epistemology and his normative morality, that we find an initial reason for Hume's insistence on humanity's primacy.[14] For in the first instance, humanity is a response to the selfish system commensurate with Hume's skeptical epistemological commitments. Many scholars have noted that a key aim of Hume's account of sympathy is to provide a sentimentalist alternative to theological or teleological accounts of the origin of moral distinctions.[15] Humanity is likewise clearly intended as a contribution to this same "humanistic" project.[16]

Yet this immediately raises two questions. First, if indeed humanity does the same work as sympathy, what exactly did Hume think he was gaining in shifting from his emphasis on sympathy in the *Treatise* to his emphasis on humanity in the second *Enquiry*? Second, what relationship does humanity bear to his epistemology in its totality, which of course involves much more than skepticism? The answer to the first of these questions ultimately depends on the answer to the second; what

immediately follows thus focuses on this latter question, leaving the former for the next section. The latter question is especially urgent given
recent reconsiderations of Hume's epistemology that have done much to
show that skepticism captures only part of his intent; a significant effect
of the debate over what has come to be called the "new Hume" has been
to compel us to reconsider Hume's epistemology as only partly critical or
negative by recalling us to the import of its more constructive or positive
side.[17] Studies of this side – his naturalism as opposed to his skepticism –
focus especially on its accounts of those aspects of our minds that enable
us to remedy gaps in our understanding that would otherwise render
impossible our practical navigation of the world. Particularly important
on this front has been the debate over Hume's account of "natural belief"
– that is, our necessary belief in causation, the persistence of personal
identity, and continued existence of a mind-independent external world
– beliefs that Hume regards as incapable of epistemic validation but yet
indispensable to our practical existence.[18] But for students of his practical
philosophy and his theory of humanity in particular, the most important
mechanism of our minds is that which provides us with another set of
"natural instincts," without which there would be "an end at once of all
action" (EHU 5.5–8, cf. 5.22): the association of ideas.

   That Hume's doctrine of association is central to his project is clear;
in his own Abstract of the *Treatise* he famously identifies it as his key
innovation (Abstract 35). Its significance lies chiefly in the supplement
that it provides to his well-known "copy principle": the claim that ideas
are merely copies of our impressions derived from our senses (T 1.1.1.7).
Hume understood that such an account alone could hardly explain
the existence of our many ideas that are not traceable in any direct or
obvious way to experience. These ideas, he explains, are not copies of
impressions but rather products of a recombination of simple ideas in
the imagination – acts of "compounding, transposing, augmenting, [and]
diminishing" of the sort that we have already had occasion to note above
(EHU 2.5). In this sense, associationism replaces transcendence as the
mechanism that explains our capacity to generate ideas that might seem
on their face to go beyond ordinary and direct sense experience.

   Hume specifically identified three sorts of relations that make certain
ideas particularly susceptible to association: resemblance, contiguity, and
causation (T 1.1.4; EHU 3.2; Abstract 35). These relations apply to either
the relation between an idea and its object or between two ideas; thus
whenever either an idea and an object or two ideas are related by similarity (resemblance), close proximity (contiguity), or seeming necessary

connection (causation), Hume posits that one will call forth the other. The significance of this discovery lies in its capacity to rescue us from the morass in which skepticism might otherwise seem to land us; Hume himself credits associationism as the source of "the only links that bind the parts of the universe together, or connect us with any person or object exterior to ourselves" (Abstract 35). This is a striking claim, and its practical significance has not gone unnoticed. Many have particularly noted its implications for Hume's theory of sympathy in the *Treatise*, explicitly presented in terms of associationism. Yet for all the agreement on the centrality of association in sympathy, there is considerable disagreement on the fate of association in Hume's mature ethics. Some have argued that in his later works Hume simply drops association altogether.[19] Others have responded that his later works in fact retain a "continued general commitment to associationism," even if for various prudential reasons Hume chose not to highlight it to the same degree as he had in the *Treatise*.[20] On the grounds of evidence to be examined subsequently, the latter camp seems to have the stronger case in this debate. Yet there is also reason to believe that the question on which debate to now has turned – does Hume keep or drop associationism? – fails to speak to the most important question raised by his late ethics. The crucial question isn't *whether* Hume retains associationism but rather *which* associationism he retains.

The key fact here is that in the *Treatise*, sympathy involves both contiguity and resemblance, whereas in the second *Enquiry* Hume splits this association up, identifying sympathy with contiguity, and humanity with resemblance.[21] In the *Treatise*, Hume presents his case in his account of how sympathy enables us to experience the affective states of others – the indispensable element in the larger process of generating moral norms in the absence of access to those foundations that Hume considered epistemically unavailable. Here he particularly insists that we are necessarily more affected by what is close to us than by what lies at a distance: "the sentiments of others have little influence, when far remov'd from us, and require the relation of contiguity, to make them communicate themselves entirely" (T 2.1.11.6). He reiterates the same point elsewhere: "We sympathize more with persons contiguous to us, than with persons remote from us: With our acquaintance, than with strangers: With our countrymen, than with foreigners" (T 3.3.1.14). This leads him ultimately to observe:

Now as every thing, that is contiguous to us, either in space or time, strikes upon us with such an idea, it has a proportional effect on the will and passions, and commonly operates with more force than any object, that lies in a more distant and obscure light. Tho' we may be fully convinc'd, that the latter object excels the former, we are not able to regulate our actions by this judgment; but yield to the sollicitations of our passions, which always plead in favour of whatever is near and contiguous. (T 3.2.7.2; cf. 3.3.1.15, 2.3.7.3)

Clearly contiguity plays a role in sympathy – indeed a role that we can already see to be hardly unproblematic insofar as contiguity relations weaken as they widen. But in the *Treatise* sympathy is generated by resemblance as well as contiguity. Thus at one place Hume accounts for the influence of pity and compassion in terms of resemblance, arguing that "we have a lively idea of every thing related to us" as "all human creatures are related to us by resemblance" (T 2.2.7.2). Elsewhere he applies this to sympathy, suggesting that it is in fact precisely our awareness of our "very remarkable resemblance" to others that "must very much contribute to make us enter into the sentiments of others" (T 2.1.11.5), a point further developed in Hume's emphasis on the "*immediate* sympathy, which men have with characters similar to their own" (T 3.3.3.4). Thus resemblance and contiguity each play a key role in the process of enabling us to enter into the sentiments of others in the *Treatise* – a point underscored in Hume's claim that "we must be assisted by the relations of resemblance and contiguity, in order to feel the sympathy in its full perfection" (T 2.1.11.8). But what happens to this claim in the second *Enquiry*?

FROM SYMPATHY TO HUMANITY

In the second *Enquiry*, contiguity comes to be associated with sympathy and in fact comes to be identified as sympathy's chief disadvantage, while resemblance comes to be associated with humanity and indeed comes to be seen as humanity's chief advantage. Hume's appreciation of this distinction and its implications for his normative project to combat the selfish system explains his shift from sympathy to humanity, and provides an answer to the question of what exactly the later account of humanity adds to his earlier account of sympathy. In brief, a humanity associated with resemblance offers two distinct advantages over a sympathy associated with contiguity: first, it provides a means of establishing a universal or comprehensive morality that transcends the partiality endemic to both the selfish system and to systems of sympathy dependent on contiguity relations; and second, it provides a mechanism that self-corrects for such partialities by establishing a common point of view intrinsic to humanity itself. In this way, humanity reveals itself as a response to the challenge of egocentrism that avoids the pitfalls of both sympathy and love.

Hume's first important discussion of humanity in the second *Enquiry* comes in Section 5, Part 2. Hume introduces this account with an account of sympathy – and specifically of sympathy's shortcomings. In this vein he claims that sympathy "is much fainter than our concern for ourselves, and sympathy with persons remote from us, much fainter than that with persons near and contiguous" (EPM 5.42). Two points here bear emphasizing. First, Hume here explicitly identifies sympathy not with associationism in general but specifically with contiguity; and second, he uses this point to illustrate not an advantage of sympathy but its weakness. Indeed the aim of this passage is to demonstrate precisely the incapacity of a sympathy tied to contiguity to forge affective bonds that transcend gaps in contiguity – both in terms of space (here represented by the difficulty of sympathizing with those far removed from us geographically) and in terms of time (here represented by the difficulty of sympathizing with those far removed from us historically). But this presents a real problem – a problem that indeed goes straight to the heart of Hume's concern to respond to the selfish system. We have already seen that Hume regards universal love as a chimera, and hence unavailable as a response to the selfish system. But now it seems that sympathy too has its shortcomings. Yet if not to sympathy then, to what exactly can we turn to "render our sentiments more public and social"?

Hume's answer is that humanity succeeds where sympathy falls short. Thus in what follows we learn that humanity promotes "acquaintance or connexion," for "in proportion as the humanity of the person is supposed to encrease, his connexion with those who are injured or benefited, and his lively conception of their misery or happiness; his consequent censure or approbation acquires proportionable vigour" (EPM 5.43). Humanity's capacity to promote such connections – and particularly connections between those far removed or noncontiguous to us – is an especially prominent element of Hume's second key discussion of humanity in the EPM. Thus in its concluding section Hume argues that when regarded from the perspective of humanity, "no character can be so remote as to be, in this light, wholly indifferent to me" (EPM 9.7), and that "there is no circumstance of conduct in any man, provided it have a beneficial tendency, that is not agreeable to my humanity, however remote the person" (EPM 9.8). In contrast to sympathy then, humanity is not at all limited by contiguity relations. Indeed this is one of the two reasons why Hume insists that humanity "alone" can be the foundation of morals: because it alone is "so universal and comprehensive as to extend to all mankind, and render the actions and conduct, even of the persons the most remote, an object of applause or censure" (EPM 9.5). Humanity is "comprehensive" – the sentiments that arise from it are universal in their scope as they "comprehend all human creatures," even and especially the most remote (EPM 9.5, 9.7).

Humanity thus clearly succeeds where both universal love and sympathy fall short. Universal love is admirable, but beyond the capacities of our self-interested natures to sustain; humanity, in contrast, is capable of forging bonds with even the most distant others. And indeed it forges these bonds in a way that sympathy cannot: where sympathy is always limited by contiguity, humanity transcends gaps in contiguity and "extends to all mankind." But what explains humanity's capacity to extend beyond the boundaries that seem to be imposed on sympathy, and thereby to create the connections to others that an otherwise unavailable universal love would have us strive to realize? The answer would seem to lie in humanity's relationship to the epistemic principles of resemblance. In the *Treatise* and elsewhere Hume insists that the three principles of association are the "only" links that "connect us with any person or object exterior to ourselves" (Abstract 35; T 1.4.6.16; EHU 3.2). We have every reason to believe that Hume retains this view in the second *Enquiry*; certainly he never suggests that he has discovered any other principle of connection. This fact, in conjunction with Hume's silence on causality and his explicit critique of the limits of contiguity relations, leaves only resemblance. Hume himself had earlier attested to the role of resemblance in our relations with others. In the *Treatise* he had repeatedly noted that our perception of the world begins with "the relation of objects to ourself," since "ourself is always intimately present to us" (T 2.1.11.8; cf. 2.3.7.1, 2.1.11.4; DP 3.4). Having studied ourselves we turn next to compare others to us. What we immediately recognize is our resemblance, a process Hume explains a passage cited in the previous section:

We have a lively idea of every thing related to us. All human creatures are related to us by resemblance. Their persons, therefore, their interests, their passions, their pains and pleasures must strike upon us in a lively manner, and produce an emotion similar to the original one; since a lively idea is easily converted into an impression. (T 2.2.7.2)

Hume repeats and extends the claim in a second passage previously cited:

Now 'tis obvious, that nature has preserv'd a great resemblance among all human creatures, and that we never remark any passion or principle in others, of which, in some degree or other, we may not find a parallel in ourselves. The case is the same with the fabric of the mind, as with that of the body. However the parts may differ in shape or size, their structure and composition are in general the same. There is a very remarkable resemblance, which preserves itself amidst all their variety; and this resemblance must very much contribute to make us enter into the sentiments of others, and embrace them with facility and pleasure. (T 2.1.11.5)

This process explicitly described in the *Treatise* is, I think – with one crucial caveat to be explained later – the process implicitly at work in the account of humanity in the second *Enquiry*. Indeed taken together, (i) Hume's failure to revise his claim that association relations are our "only" links to others; (ii) his explicit insistence on the limits of contiguity-based sympathy in the second *Enquiry*; (iii) his detailed accounts of resemblance relations in the *Treatise*; (iv) and his specific employment of the term "humanity" to describe this process, collectively suggest that Hume has precisely this process of reflection on the resemblance of others to ourselves implicitly in mind in arguing for humanity's primacy in the second *Enquiry*. Yet the import of this association of humanity with resemblance is that it enables humanity to be truly comprehensive in a way that sympathy cannot. Sympathy, it is generally agreed, is a spectatorial process.[22] Hume's central account of sympathy makes this clear: "when any affection is infus'd by sympathy, it is at first known only by its effects, and by those external signs in the countenance and conversation" (T 2.1.11.3). Sympathy thus clearly begins with what can be seen by the spectator or "the observation of external signs" (T 2.1.11.4). But seeing of course requires proximity, and hence the dependence of sympathy on contiguity: to "please the spectator," spectators need to be sufficiently close to actors to observe them (T 3.3.1.8). It is in this vein that the *Treatise* emphasizes that pity too "depends, in a great measure, on the contiguity, and even sight of the object" (T 2.2.7.4). But where sympathy and pity require the close proximity that spectatorship demands, humanity is free from dependence on contiguity because resemblance relations take place entirely in the imagination and independently of the external senses limited by the demands of contiguity. It is thus that Hume, whenever he offers examples of association by resemblance, specifically emphasizes the capacity of resembling images to make the distant or "absent" seem immediate (e.g., EHU 5.15).[23]

Humanity's first advantage over sympathy is its comprehensiveness – that is, that it is capable of extending universally in precisely the way envisioned by both an unavailable universal love and an inefficacious contiguity-limited sympathy. This is, however, only one of two

advantages. Humanity's primacy, Hume also argues, owes to the fact
that it not only *extends* universally, but is also *felt* universally – humanity, that is, not only *embraces all*, but is also *experienced by all*. Hume
makes this point repeatedly in his analysis of humanity, and indeed does
so in a language clearly indebted to his theory of resemblance. In this
vein he strikingly insists that humanity is a sentiment "common to all
mankind," that it in turn generates sentiments that are "the same in all
human creatures," and that it is "diffused, in a greater or less degree,
over all men, and is the same in all" (EPM 9.5, 9.7, 9.9). This explicit
reliance on the language of resemblance emerges most clearly in his
claim that "the humanity of one man is the humanity of every one"
(EPM 9.6). But Hume's emphasis on our sameness with regard to our
possession of humanity comes to be amplified only when he describes
the operations of humanity. For not only is humanity possessed by all
and not only does it operate similarly in all, but it also recommends the
same objects as valuable to all: humanity "recommends the same object
to general approbation, and makes every man, or most men, agree in the
same opinion or decision concerning it" (EPM 9.5). And herein lies not
only humanity's clearest debt to resemblance but also its most distinctive
feature: namely its capacity to guarantee that "the same object touches
this passion in all human creatures" and thereby produce in all men "the
same approbation or censure" (EPM 9.6–7).

Hume clearly recognizes the momentous import of his claim. Humanity,
insofar as it is uniformly experienced and its substantive determinations
of value are universally similar, is precisely what enables us to establish universal norms in a pluralistic world without requiring recourse to
the transcendent categories that he has already judged unavailable. But
humanity has a further advantage – and indeed one that again suggests
its superiority to sympathy. Hume consistently argues that sympathy
requires correction by judgment, as is well known; not only is sympathy
limited in scope and unable to extend beyond boundaries of contiguity, but within its boundaries it is also prone to distort the phenomena
it treats. Thus even as sympathy functions to extend us outside of ourselves and correct partialities to which self-love renders us susceptible, its
dependence on contiguity can also distort our judgments of objects closest
to us. Thus it is that the sympathy that was originally proposed as a remedy for the partiality endemic to self-love itself needs a remedy capable of
ameliorating the "partiality" or "unequal affection" to which sympathy
itself, when unregulated, gives rise (e.g., T 3.2.2.8, 3.2.5.8). Clearly this
worries Hume: "there is no quality in human nature, which causes more

fatal errors in our conduct, than that which leads us to prefer whatever is present to the distant and remote" (T 3.2.7.8). It is for this reason that the *Treatise* invokes the need for recourse to a "common point of view" that affords the impartiality necessary to correct the distortions to which sympathy is prone; thus by "judgment" or "reflection" we "correct the momentary appearances of things" (see T 3.3.1.11, 3.3.1.15–18, 3.3.1.21, 3.3.1.30).[24]

All of this is present in the second *Enquiry* as well. Here too we are reminded that in all instances in which we are affected by a "less lively sympathy" – Hume has here in mind another case involving "distant ages" and "remote nations" – we need to take recourse to that "judgment" that "corrects the inequalities of our internal emotions and perceptions" (EPM 5.41; cf. T 3.3.3.2). But what is new here is that "reflection" is now no longer the only mechanism we have at our disposal to help us "correct these inequalities" (EPM n25).[25] Humanity itself plays a key role in this corrective process, and in fact provides its own specifically noncognitive route to a common point of view. Thus Hume explains that he who would make normative judgments with which he expects others to concur must transcend his "peculiar" sentiments and "particular" circumstances; he must

choose a point of view, common to him with others: He must move some universal principle of the human frame, and touch a string, to which all mankind have an accord and symphony. If he mean, therefore, to express, that this man possesses qualities, whose tendency is pernicious to society, he has chosen this common point of view, and has touched the principle of humanity, in which every man, in some degree, concurs. While the human heart is compounded of the same elements as at present, it will never be wholly indifferent to public good, nor entirely unaffected with the tendency of characters and manners. And though this affection of humanity may not generally be esteemed so strong as vanity or ambition, yet, being common to all men, it can alone be the foundation of morals, or of any general system of blame or praise. One man's ambition is not another's ambition; nor will the same event or object satisfy both: But the humanity of one man is the humanity of every one; and the same object touches this passion in all human creatures. (EPM 9.6)

Here again the central problem concerns the mechanism of the necessary shift from a private or individual perspective to the more public or common point of view. But now the route is different. In the *Treatise*, the "common point of view" could be achieved only via cognition, and specifically cognition that corrects distorted sentiments. The challenges involved in squaring this position with this Hume's sentimentalism have long been appreciated.[26] But in the passage from the second *Enquiry*

quoted here, Hume provides a quite different route to the common point
of view – indeed one commensurate with his sentimentalism – in insisting
that the common point of view is established when one's judgments and
sentiments are in accord with the "affection of humanity" that is itself a
"universal principle of the human frame." In addition, this account of the
common point of view is independent of all reference to spectators – a
crucial difference from the *Treatise* account. There the common point of
view without which "'tis impossible men cou'd ever agree in their sentiments and judgments" is achieved by spectators who transcend their partialities by taking on the only perspective "which might cause it to appear
the same to all of them" – the perspective of the agent, "the only interest
or pleasure, which appears the same to every spectator" (T 3.3.1.30).
The second *Enquiry*'s account, on the other hand, is developed wholly
without reference to spectatorship; in this account the sameness that collective ethical deliberation requires is established neither by reciprocal
and reiterated intersubjective exchanges nor by the efforts of spectators
sympathetically entering into the affective states of agents, but by the
sameness that is the result of a sentiment which is the same in all, which
extends to all, and which recommends the same object to the approbation of all. Humanity, that is, itself provides us with a "common point of
view" precisely because it is "common to all men" and generates the same
judgment in all men. What this common judgment is – and indeed what
humanity itself is – is the next subject to which we must turn.

HUMANITY AND "COOL PREFERENCE"

The foregoing has sought to illuminate two of the most important aspects
of Hume's conception of humanity: first, its relationship to his epistemology and to his theory of associationism in particular; and second, Hume's
views on the advantages of shifting from the sympathy of the *Treatise* to
the humanity of the second *Enquiry*. But we have yet to address the most
important question regarding humanity: what exactly is it? The answer is
hardly obvious. In one sense, as we have seen, humanity is clearly aligned
with sympathy. Hume himself often links humanity with sympathy via
the coordinating conjunction (e.g., EPM 5.45, 6.3, 9.12, n60), and many
scholars have regarded humanity and sympathy as simply equivalent.[27]
Hume, however, also couples humanity with benevolence (e.g., EPM 2.5,
5.18, 6.21, 9.20) – a fact that has led other scholars to equate humanity
with benevolence.[28] Yet in the end it seems clear that Hume uses the single term humanity in *both* senses; at times humanity is clearly meant to

denote an ethical virtue (as we saw previously in our treatment of its normative dimensions); at other times it clearly denotes the mechanism that gives rise to our moral distinctions (as we saw earlier in our treatment of its epistemic dimensions and its relationship to sympathy). In light of this, the crucial task for interpreters is less to justify why humanity is better understood as either sympathy or benevolence than to identify what exactly Hume thinks humanity is, and explain what about it renders humanity capable of contributing, as Hume thinks it does, to both the phenomenological or descriptive project associated with sympathy, as well as the normative or prescriptive project associated with benevolence.[29]

What then is humanity? Hume's definition is simple but subtle: humanity is our preference for the well-being of others. Hume presents this definition several times in the second *Enquiry*, and it is particularly evident in the concluding section. Here humanity is introduced as the most important of those "generous sentiments" that "direct the determinations of our mind, and where every thing else is equal, produce a cool preference of what is useful and serviceable to mankind, above what is pernicious and dangerous" (EPM 9.4). Humanity, that is, generates "that applause, which is paid to objects, whether inanimate, animate, or rational, if they have a tendency to promote the welfare and advantage of mankind" (EPM 9.12, cf. 9.8). In this sense, humanity is the answer to the rhetorical question implied in the title to Section 5 of the second *Enquiry* ("Why Utility Pleases"), and is distinguished as the aspect of our minds that determines us to regard the well-being of others as an end, and to bestow approbation on whatever is capable of promoting that end (T 3.3.1.9):

How, indeed, can we suppose it possible in any one, who wears a human heart, that, if there be subjected to his censure, one character or system of conduct, which is beneficial, and another, which is pernicious, to his species or community, he will not so much as give a cool preference to the former, or ascribe to it the smallest merit or regard? Let us suppose such a person ever so selfish; let private interest have ingrossed ever so much his attention; yet in instances, where that is not concerned, he must unavoidably feel *some* propensity to the good of mankind, and make it an object of choice, if every thing else be equal…We surely take into consideration the happiness and misery of others, in weighing the several motives of action, and incline to the former, where no private regards draw us to seek our own promotion or advantage by the injury of our fellow-creatures. And if the principles of humanity are capable, in many instances, of influencing our actions, they must, at all times, have *some* authority over our sentiments, and give us a general approbation of what is useful to society, and blame of what is dangerous or pernicious. (EPM 5.39)

Hume's definition of humanity is important both as a statement of what humanity is as well as what it is not. Humanity is neither an affective state that leads us to feel deeply for others, nor is it valuable principally as a motive to action. In this sense, humanity is something very different from either pity or benevolence as they tend to be understood today. Humanity of course clearly resembles pity and benevolence in some key respects. In the *Treatise* Hume himself had described pity as "a concern for, and *malice* a joy in the misery of others, without any friendship or enmity to occasion this concern or joy," and benevolence "a desire of the happiness of the person belov'd, and an aversion to his misery" (T 2.2.7.1, 2.2.9.3; cf. 2.2.9.15, 2.2.6.3–4). The core of each of these – a concern for the well-being of another – is retained in humanity. But humanity conspicuously lacks the deeply affective aspects of pity and benevolence.[30] Humanity is rather a "natural affection," part of "the original constitution of the mind," a simple given that establishes our "cool preference" for what is beneficial over what might be harmful to others (EPM 5.3–4, cf. 5.17, 5.39, 5.42–44, 9.4, App. 1.3).

This "cool preference" cannot be emphasized strongly enough. For not only does it distinguish humanity from pity or benevolence, it also distinguishes it from love. Love too has often been understood as sharing the concern for the well-being of others that Hume places at the core of humanity; to take just one example of the contemporary discussions examined in our introductory chapter, love is often seen as an account of "our experiences of wanting the best for the beloved." But wanting the best in the sense that love does goes well beyond simple cool preference for well-being; as the same author also insists, love is "an emotional, affirming participation in the dynamic tendency of an object to realize its fullness."[31] But humanity, insofar as its concern for others is both established by and also limited to this simple cool preference, functions very differently from love. And this is key for Hume and the consistency of his project. As we saw earlier, Hume was steadfast in the *Treatise* in insisting that there is "no such passion in human minds, as the love of mankind, merely as such" (T 3.2.1.12). But his concept of humanity as a mere cool preference for the well-being of others is consistent with this denial of universal love as well as with Hume's claim that "'tis seldom men heartily love what lies at a distance from them" (T 3.3.1.18). For while humanity leads us to be concerned with others, this concern is consistently expressed as a matter of "cool preference," far different from the warmth that animates traditional conceptions of love.[32] All told then, humanity occupies a unique place among the other-directed or social virtues. It shares with other social virtues concern with the well-being of others. Yet it can't be assimilated to the sentimentalized social virtues associated with feeling appropriately (such as pity, compassion, or benevolence), nor to those active social virtues associated with acting well (such as generosity, liberality, or beneficence). Humanity occupies a different place altogether; rather than either prompting affect or action, it serves as a determining ground that establishes social actions and dispositions as preferable to selfish ones.

Humanity is thus at once distinct from pity and benevolence and love. But it is also distinct from sympathy. Sympathy, as we have seen, is first and foremost a mechanism of "communication" (T 2.2.7.5, 2.2.9.13, 2.3.6.8, 3.3.1.7).[33] Specifically it is that mechanism of communication that enables us, in our relations with others, to "receive by communication their inclinations and sentiments" and thereby "enter into" their affective states (T 2.1.11.2, 2.2.5.14–15). Humanity, however, is defined wholly without reference to those forms of communication that establish the sort of intimate identification that produces deep affective bonds. Thus in sharp contrast to the sympathy of the *Treatise* that enables us to "enter so deep" into the feelings of others (T 2.1.11.7), the humanity of the second *Enquiry* is championed not because it enables us to enter into the perspectives of others and feel their pain and partake in their suffering, but because it does nothing more (and indeed nothing less) than produce in us that decidedly "cool" preference for the well-being of others. This preference, moreover, is established without any intimate knowledge of the particular situation of another; we are rather led by humanity to prefer that other human beings be benefited rather than harmed, no matter how distant they are from us and no matter how little we know of their conditions.[34]

Those partial either to the traditional conceptions of love or to contemporary defenses of affective imaginative identification with others are likely to find Hume's turn from sympathy to humanity disappointing. But Hume himself regards this turn as a significant move forward, and it is important to see why. We know already that Hume thinks that universal love asks too much of individuals like ourselves who for both moral reasons (the ubiquity of self-interest) and epistemic reasons (the limits of our reason) are incapable of self-transcendence. But sympathy itself seems to ask almost as much of human beings as love. First, the sympathy of the *Treatise* relies on a complex and perhaps too-clever-by-half account of infusion via the spectator's conversion of original impressions into ideas into secondary impressions to form the foundation of moral distinctions

(T 2.1.11.3). But more importantly, it requires ordinary moral agents to develop a very high degree of sensibility. The account of humanity in the second *Enquiry* asks for much less by comparison. First, it traces our concern for others not to intersubjective processes but rather to an "original" or "antecedent" principle of "our nature" (EPM n19, 5.46; T 3.2.1.6). In this sense, far from requiring such intersubjective processes for a generation of moral distinctions, these distinctions are antecedently established by the ordinary operations of our nature. Thus where the turn to sympathy had been before justified as necessary given the unavailability of certain foundations, in locating this "cool preference" in "our nature," Hume points to a very different origin for moral distinctions – one that indeed is consummately immanent, requiring neither a capacity of the self to access the transcendent (as does love), or a capacity of the self to engage in intersubjective exchange that would also bring it outside itself (as does sympathy).[35]

Humanity conceived as a "cool preference" also has a second advantage over both love and sympathy. As Hume conceives it, humanity demands from us only that level of affective concern for others that is accessible to most human beings. Hume repeatedly insists in this vein that humanity is a minimal disposition that asks its possessor merely to prefer that others be benefited rather than harmed, in only those instances in which all else is equal and in which self-interest is not at stake. And herein lies perhaps the most striking feature of his account. His argument for humanity as the only sentiment on which a moral system can be founded is itself founded on the important claim that humanity extends to all and is felt by all, as we have seen. But what may be most remarkable about humanity is how little it in fact demands of us, for while its strength is manifested in its aggregate operations, unto itself it is "somewhat small and delicate" – indeed "weak" and "faint" (EPM 9.9, 9.4). And this weakness of humanity is, somewhat paradoxically, the key to its strength.[36] For humanity succeeds at its aim of restraining self-love not because it is capable of overpowering the instinctive sentiments of self-love within the moral psychology of the individual. Instead, humanity succeeds at the task of mitigating self-love within society precisely on the grounds that in asking so little from each individual it leads large collections of individuals to generate certain prosocial norms. And it is this belief that animates the concluding statement on humanity in the second *Enquiry* – a statement that not only reveals humanity's place in Hume's project but also binds it to our inquiry on love: namely that it is not by the sympathy or imagination of the individual but by those "universal principles" that "arise from humanity" that "the particular sentiments of self-love [are] frequently controuled and limited" (EPM 9.8).[37]

CONCLUSION

Humanity, understood as a cool preference for the well-being of others, is ultimately an independent category, substantively independent of benevolence and sympathy and love yet capable of contributing to the projects with which sympathy and benevolence and love are often associated. In determining our preference that others be benefited, it lays a foundation for our approval and ultimately our practice of the social virtues that work to promote the well-being of others. In generating a universal preference for the well-being of others, humanity provides a foundation for our collective construction of norms. Humanity thus plays a crucial role in the project of mitigating egocentrism and encouraging other-directedness that is our primary focus. But attending to Hume's theory of humanity has three additional benefits besides: first, it can clarify how we ought to characterize Hume's ethics as a whole; second, it can clarify what exactly is at stake in the call of Nussbaum and other contemporary defenders of sentimental other-directedness for a renewed "politics of humanity"; and third, it helps us to understand better the advantages as well as potential challenges inherent to the shift from traditional love to sentimental other-directedness.

With regard to Hume, attending to his theory of humanity can help us clarify how we might characterize his ethics on two fronts. The first concerns the tension between his reputation as a human nature theorist and his reputation as a theorist of intersubjectivity. Many have taken Hume to have founded his political theory on his vision of "the constant and universal principles of human nature" that form the foundation of his "science of man" (EHU 8.7, T Intro 6–10).[38] Others, however, have understood his project quite differently, emphasizing less his claims on behalf of a universal human nature than his claim that it is the "intercourse of sentiments" in intersubjective social interaction that produces that "general unalterable standard" by which we judge what is properly praised or blamed (EPM 5.42).[39] But how are these two readings – each of which captures some crucial side of Hume's project – to be reconciled? It is precisely here that we see an important benefit of attending to his theory of humanity. Reestablishing humanity as central to his project not only does justice to Hume's own intentions, but it also provides an alternative to both the thoroughgoing naturalistic and the thoroughgoing constructivist readings of his project. For it is clear that while Hume, in his mature ethics, hardly denies the role of intersubjective and reciprocal exchanges of approbation and disapprobation in shaping norms, by privileging the "original principle" of humanity as the foundation of morality Hume establishes a standard by which the moral effects of these various intersubjective processes can themselves be judged.

Attending to the place of humanity in Hume's thought can also help resolve a second dichotomy. Hume is still frequently celebrated today as the architect of a positivistic social science; on the basis of both his famous distinction between "is" and "ought" and his debate with Hutcheson, Hume has been regarded as principally dedicated to articulating a descriptive or phenomenological social science free of all normative injunction.[40] Yet this is difficult to square with the second *Enquiry*, which argues that "the end of all moral speculations is to teach us our duty," and concludes with Hume's explicit hope that his work will "contribute to the amendment of men's lives, and their improvement in morality and social virtue" (EPM 1.7, 9.14). In light of such, other interpreters have emphasized that his aims are at once normative as well as descriptive.[41] Attending to the role of humanity in Hume's thought, I have sought to show, provides further support for the latter view. Grounding his system in a sentiment that accounts for the origins of judgment (that is, which promotes the phenomenological aims of sympathy) and at once also establishes a "rule of right" in the form of an attachment to "public good" (that is, which promotes the prosocial or other-directed normative aims associated with benevolence), Hume suggests that these two projects are neither discrete nor incompatible.

Attending to Hume's theory of humanity thus has great potential payoffs for our understanding of Hume himself. Yet it can also do much to illuminate what is at stake in the contemporary call for a renewed "politics of humanity," and indeed just what the "politics of humanity" is. Several possibilities present themselves on this latter front. It may be that the politics of humanity is simply a *humanistic* politics – a secular alternative to any one of several available political theologies. Or it may be that the politics of humanity is a politics dedicated to the preeminence of *humane values* – pity or compassion or benevolence. Or perhaps the politics of humanity is simply one dedicated to recognition of our *shared humanness* – a politics grounded in shared commonalities that make it possible to speak of our common "humanity" with others. Nussbaum herself nods in each of these directions at different times; sometimes the politics of humanity is an alternative to a politics of disgust practiced by "large segments of the Christian Right," sometimes it is a politics founded on such other-directed values as "respect" or "love," and sometimes (indeed most often) it is a politics founded on sympathy, or the "capacity for imaginative and emotional participation in the lives of others."[42] But by attending to Hume's vision of a politics of humanity we can better understand the relationship of these three elements of such a politics: humanism, humane values, and "humanness." In Hume's theory, as we have seen, the case for the primacy of humanity is first established in the context of the unavailability of certainty in matters extending beyond experience; humanity, that is, first emerges as a "humanist" response to the epistemic unavailability of the transcendent categories foundational to a political theology or a teleological politics. Further, the specific form of humanity to which Hume turns – humanity defined as a preference for the well-being of others – establishes the grounds of our preference for the socially beneficial or "humane" over the socially destructive or selfish. And insofar as this humanity is shared by all and extends to all human beings connected to us by resemblance, it serves to connect human beings universally and define our "shared humanness."

Hume's theory of humanity is thus a core element of his own larger project, and an important point of reference for understanding the contemporary politics of humanity. Yet the principal import of Hume's theory of humanity lies in the way in which it serves as a substitute for the traditional conception of other-directed love. As we have seen, Hume shares with the defenders of agapic or universal other-love a concern to manage self-love, yet parts with the defenders of universal love in finding such a love, however admirable its normative ambitions may be, simply beyond our limited capacities. Humanity, however, seeks to reach a similar goal – but does so in a way that asks considerably less of us. To be humane in Hume's sense we need not love our neighbor in any of the more transformative or affective senses that both the traditional conception of love as well as our own instinctive understandings of love tend to regard as central to the experience of genuine love. To be humane in Hume's sense it is rather sufficient that we merely have a cool preference for his well-being – a desire that he not be harmed, and above all that he not be harmed by us. That he could be an object of any greater degree of care is not part of humanity's concern, as Hume envisions it. And this last point is particularly crucial, for herein lies the key difference between Hume's theory of humanity and both the traditional concept of love and the politics of humanity described by Nussbaum. Nussbaum's politics of humanity calls for a level of emotional intimacy with strangers she

explicitly labels "love," as well as for a "transformation at the level of
the human heart" capable of promoting "deep social transformations."⁴³
But it is here that Hume's concept of humanity and the contemporary
politics of humanity part ways. Hume's theory is dedicated less to effecting the social change that a politics of love envisions than to achieving a
decidedly more realist (and in Hume's mind more pressing) aim: namely
to articulate a response to the selfish system that is at once consistent
with his epistemological commitments yet sufficiently robust to preserve
what is best in modernity from degenerating into egocentrism. In this
sense Hume's concept of humanity establishes the ground for a minimal
ethics appropriate to a secular age – indeed a minimalism in the realm of
social values that complements and parallels a more familiar minimalism
associated with liberal theories of procedural justice. In so doing Hume
at once illuminates both the advantages and the limits of the politics
of humanity – advantages and limits well captured by Deleuze in his
account of Hume's "true morality": "It does not involve the change of
human nature but the invention of artificial and objective conditions in
order for the bad aspects of this nature not to triumph."⁴⁴

NOTES

1   Nussbaum, *From Disgust to Humanity: Sexual Orientation and Constitutional
    Law* (New York: Oxford University Press, 2010), xix–xx.
2   The role of humanity in Hume, and especially its normative role, has been
    largely underemphasized by commentators; important exceptions include
    Robert Shaver, "Hume on the Duties of Humanity," *Journal of the History
    of Philosophy* 30 (1992): 545–556; Andrew Sabl, "Noble Infirmity: Love
    of Fame in Hume," *Political Theory* 34 (2006): 548; Scott Yenor, "Revealed
    Religion and the Politics of Humanity in Hume's Philosophy of Common
    Life," *Polity* 38 (2006): esp. 405–412; Remy Debes, "Humanity, Sympathy
    and the Puzzle of Hume's Second Enquiry," *British Journal for the History
    of Philosophy* 15 (2007): 27–57; Jacqueline Taylor, "Humean Humanity
    Versus Hate," in *The Practice of Virtue*, ed. Jennifer Welchman (Indianapolis,
    IN: Hackett, 2006), 182–203, and Taylor, "Hume on the Importance of
    Humanity," *Revue Internationale de Philosophie* 67 (2013): 81–97. Taylor
    ("Humean Humanity vs. Hate," 182, 196–199) and Shaver ("Hume on the
    Duties," 545–546, 552–555) are especially helpful in presenting humanity
    as a supplement to justice that sensitizes us to cruelty and promotes social
    stability in a way that procedural liberalism alone cannot.
3   Helpful specialist studies of this aspect of Hume's theory of love include
    Christine Korsgaard, "The General Point of View: Love and Moral
    Approval in Hume's Ethics," *Hume Studies* 25 (1999): esp. 5–6; Elizabeth
    S. Radcliffe, "Love and Benevolence in Hutcheson's and Hume's Theories of

the Passions," *British Journal for the History of Philosophy* 12 (2004): esp. 639–641; and Nancy Schauber, "Complexities of Character: Hume on Love and Responsibility," *Hume Studies* 35 (2009): esp. 41–44.

4   See Sarah M. S. Pearsall, "Hume – and Others – on Marriage," in *Impressions of Hume*, ed. Marina Frasca-Spada and P. J. E. Kail (Oxford: Oxford University Press, 2005), 276–279.

5   Plato, *Symposium*, 189d–193d.

6   Hume's claims on this front have also been engaged by nonspecialists; see, e.g., Peter Singer, "Ethics and Intuitions," *Journal of Ethics* 9 (2005): 333–337.

7   See also Shaver, "Hume on the Duties," 546–547, which also helpfully notes that humanity provides a "check" on exploitation of the weak. Eric Schliesser provides an illuminating account of the evolution of Hume's views on Bacon in "The Science of Man and the Invention of Usable Traditions," in *Conflicting Values of Inquiry: Ideologies of Epistemology in Early Modern Europe*, ed. Tamás Demeter, Kathryn Murphy, and Claus Zittel (Leiden: Brill, 2014), 306–336.

8   For this claim, see Neil McArthur, *David Hume's Political Theory: Law, Commerce, and the Constitution of Government* (Toronto: University of Toronto Press, 2007), 8, 18; Sharon R. Krause, "Hume and the (False) Luster of Justice," *Political Theory* 32 (2004): 636–637; Taylor, "Hume's Later Moral Philosophy," in *The Cambridge Companion to Hume*, ed. David Fate Norton and Jacqueline Taylor, 2nd ed. (Cambridge: Cambridge University Press, 2009), 338–339, and "Hume on the Importance of Humanity," 89–91, 94, 96; and Yenor, "Revealed Religion," 410.

9   See Yenor's excellent account of how "the ethic of humanity, among its other meanings, implies sufficiency and comfort in an entirely human world" ("Revealed Religion," 408–411; quote at 409). On how commerce promotes these ideals, see Christopher J. Berry, "Hume and the Customary Causes of Industry, Knowledge, and Humanity," *History of Political Economy* 38 (2006): 291–317.

10 Hume's description of humanity as a "sentiment" is striking. While consistent with his accounts of humanity elsewhere (e.g., T 3.2.5.6; EPM 7.14) and with his tendency to regard virtue as a sentiment or quality of mind (T 3.1.1.26, 3.1.2.3), it departs from traditional understandings of humanity and stands in particular tension with Cicero's understanding of humanity as the cultivation or perfection of our natures; in this vein see the discussion of *humanitas* as embracing both *philanthropia* and *paideia* in M. L. Clarke, *The Roman Mind* (London: Cohen and West, 1956), 135–145. As a consequence of this shift Hume occupies a key transitional point between the classical focus on the individual character virtues and the modern focus on social sentiments or values.

11 On this shift, see esp. James Fieser, "Is Hume a Moral Skeptic?" *Philosophy and Phenomenological Research* 50 (1989): 95–96; Kate Abramson, "Sympathy and the Project of Hume's Second Enquiry," *Archiv für Geschichte der Philosophie* 83 (2000): esp. 49, 64–66, 71; James Moore, "Utility and Humanity: The Quest for the *Honestum* in Cicero, Hutcheson, and Hume," *Utilitas* 14 (2002): 379–380; and Annette C. Baier, "*Enquiry Concerning the*

Principles of Morals: Incomparably the Best?" in *A Companion to Hume*, ed. Elizabeth S. Radcliffe (Oxford: Blackwell, 2008), 293–320.

12 Several studies examine Hume's aims to combat religion via a skepticism culminating in secularism; see, e.g., Jennifer A. Herdt, *Religion and Faction in Hume's Moral Philosophy* (Cambridge: Cambridge University Press, 1997); Michael B. Gill, *The British Moralists on Human Nature and the Birth of Secular Ethics* (Cambridge: Cambridge University Press, 2006), esp. 205–208; and John Rawls, *Lectures on the History of Moral Philosophy* (Cambridge: Harvard University Press, 2000), 12–14. This is particularly well expressed in Yenor's claim that Hume "endorses the revolutionary aspiration of making God obsolete" ("Revealed Religion," 405; cf. 398, 407–408, 413); and Aryeh Botwinick's account of Hume's "'separate peace'" with religion [*Ethics, Politics and Epistemology: A Study in the Unity of Hume's Thought* (Lanham, MD: University Press of America, 1980), 170–171]. These studies have emerged in tandem with a renewed emphasis on Hume's Hobbesianism; see Stephen Buckle, "Hume in the Enlightenment Tradition," in *Companion to Hume*, 33–34; Russell Hardin, *David Hume: Moral and Political Theorist* (Oxford: Oxford University Press, 2007), esp. 2, 6–7, 23, 212–224; and Paul Russell, *The Riddle of Hume's Treatise: Skepticism, Naturalism, and Irreligion* (Oxford: Oxford University Press, 2008), esp. 61–69. Russell offers a particularly useful formulation in his recent claim that among Hume's aims is "discrediting religious morality and putting in its place a secular morality based on the secure and credible foundations of a proper understanding of human nature and the human condition" ["Hume's Anatomy of Virtue," in *The Cambridge Companion to Virtue Ethics*, ed. Daniel C. Russell (Cambridge: Cambridge University Press, 2013), 114–115].

13 The distance of Hume's ethics from Christian ethics is well established; see, e.g., Baier's description of EPM as "anti-Christian manifesto" ("Incomparably the Best," 298, 309, 311, 314–315; quote at 315). Hume's relationship to ancient systems is more complex. They are often sympathetically compared; see, e.g., Moore, "Utility and Humanity," 365–386 (which identifies Hume's humanity with Cicero's *honestum* at 385–386); Peter Jones, *Hume's Sentiments: Their Ciceronian and French Context* (Edinburgh: University of Edinburgh Press, 1982); and John W. Danford, *David Hume and the Problem of Reason: Recovering the Human Sciences* (New Haven, CT: Yale University Press, 1990), 161. But others offer reasons to question this association; see esp. Krause, who notes that Hume frequently employs the language of the noble and praiseworthy as if they are unproblematic (e.g., EPM 1.7, 5.3, 8.7), yet his ambition to incorporate the noble "within the confines of his empiricist method" faces a challenge as it "uses the language of nobility and elevation while rejecting the framework of independent value that had once given it meaning" – leading Krause rightly to wonder "what could Hume mean by the perfection of the man, given the empiricist, antiteleological character of his moral science?" ("Hume and Justice," 629, 635, 645–646).

14 In this sense, attending to the role of humanity provides further reasons to think Hume's practical philosophy is inseparable from his epistemology – a

view helpfully developed by Botwinick (*Ethics, Politics and Epistemology*, esp. 85), though recently challenged by McArthur (*Hume's Political Theory*, esp. 5).

15 An excellent discussion of sympathy's role as a nonfoundational alternative to theologically grounded systems is offered in Herdt, *Religion and Faction*, esp. 2, 58–60, 80–81. In a similar vein, see the discussion of sympathy as a substitute for the civic relations of neo-Aristotelian civic humanism in Christopher J. Finlay, *Hume's Social Philosophy: Human Nature and Commercial Sociability in* A Treatise of Human Nature (London: Continuum, 2007), 105ff; and the discussion of justice as a mediator between relativism and teleology in Krause, "Hume and Justice," 647.

16 See, e.g., Becker, who regards Hume as "representative of his century" in sharing its characteristic attachment to secularized humanity (Carl L. Becker, *The Heavenly City of the Eighteenth-Century Philosophers* (New Haven, CT: Yale University Press, 1932), 39; cf. 40–41, 130); see also Clifford Orwin, "Montesquieu's *Humanité* and Rousseau's *Pitié*," in *Montesquieu and His Legacy*, ed. Rebecca E. Kingston (Albany: SUNY Press, 2009), 141, 146.

17 For an introduction, see esp. Rupert Read and Kenneth A. Richman, eds., *The New Hume Debate* (London: Routledge, 2007).

18 Kemp Smith is commonly credited with reawakening interest in the role of natural belief in Hume; see *The Philosophy of David Hume* (London: Macmillan, 1941), 443–458.

19 Thus Taylor argues that Hume "sets the hypothesis regarding association to one side" having come to see it as "problematic" ("Hume's Later Moral Philosophy," 315, 319–322; see also "Hume on the Importance of Humanity," 84), and Terence Penelhum has suggested that the technical details of association simply "ceased to interest him" ["Hume's Moral Psychology," in *The Cambridge Companion to Hume*, ed. David Fate Norton and Taylor, 2nd ed. (Cambridge: Cambridge University Press, 2009, 242]; see also Nicholas Capaldi, *David Hume: The Newtonian Philosopher* (Boston: Twayne, 1975), 179].

20 See esp. Remy Debes, "Has Anything Changed? Hume's Theory of Association and Sympathy after the *Treatise*," *British Journal for the History of Philosophy* 15 (2007): esp. 314–315, 325, 330; and Abramson, "Sympathy and the Project," 71, 78–80.

21 It should be said that Hume is not indifferent to the role of causality (e.g., T 2.1.11.6), but this is not emphasized in the second *Enquiry*.

22 See, e.g., Abramson, "Sympathy and Hume's Spectator-centered Theory of Virtue," in *Companion to Hume*, esp. 240.

23 Botwinick rightly notes that Hume fails to recognize in an explicit way the limits of spectatorial ethics (*Ethics, Politics and Epistemology*, 165–166), yet his substitution of humanity for sympathy may well testify precisely to such an awareness.

24 See esp. Rachel Cohon, "The Common Point of View in Hume's Ethics," *Philosophy and Phenomenological Research* 57 (1997): 829–833; and Charlotte R. Brown, "Hume on Moral Rationalism, Sentimentalism, and Sympathy," in *Companion to Hume*, 234–238.

25 The parallels between the *Treatise* account and the EPM account are very nicely traced in Debes, "Has Anything Changed?" 318–322; see also Abramson's helpful account of how Hume sought to create "safeguards for the intersubjectivity of our moral sentiments" ("Sympathy and the Project," 54–55; and Debes, "Humanity, Sympathy and the Puzzle of Hume's Second Enquiry," 39–40). I differ from Abramson in thinking that Hume's retention of the language of the moral point of view can testify only to his continued engagement with the problem of partiality, and cannot establish that Hume regarded sympathy as the only – or even the best – solution to it.

26 For an important effort at such, see Cohon, "Common Point of View," esp. 828, 833; though cf. EPM n24.

27 Among political theorists the most prominent defender of this view is Rawls (see *Lectures*, 101–102); cf. Abramson's claim that the second *Enquiry*'s "'principle of humanity'" is "shorthand for the imaginative process described explicitly in the *Treatise*, and there named 'extensive sympathy'," ("Sympathy and the Project," 55; cf. 78); Rico Vitz, "Sympathy and Benevolence in Hume's Moral Psychology," *Journal of the History of Philosophy* 42 (2004): 262–263, 271–272; Baier, "Incomparably the Best," 307, 309–310.

28 See, e.g., David Wiggins, *Ethics: Twelve Lectures on the Philosophy of Morality* (Cambridge, MA: Harvard University Press, 2006), 107; and McArthur, *Hume's Political Theory*, 8, 17; cf. Herdt, *Religion and Faction*, 75–77; Shaver, "Hume on the Duties," 546; Capaldi, *Hume*, 182–184; cf. 180. Taylor seems closest to the mark in noting that Hume uses the terms humanity, general benevolence, and sympathy at various times "to refer to the capacity that explains why we tend to be pleased by others' happiness or pained by their misery" ("Hume's Later Moral Philosophy," 319). Among the most important treatments in this vein is that of Debes, which begins with the observation in the second *Enquiry* that there is an "equivalence" between benevolence and humanity ("Humanity, Sympathy and the Puzzle," 29), but goes on to demonstrate the significance of the distinction between the principle of humanity and the sentiment of humanity, and also provides an insightful analysis of both benevolence and humanity as species of "cool preference" (31–32).

29 Doing so may also help to mitigate the common complaint that Hume's use of terms is imprecise or even "sloppy" (Baier, "Incomparably the Best," 309; Taylor, "Hume's Later Moral Philosophy," 323; Debes, "Humanity, Sympathy and the Puzzle," 29; Vitz, "Sympathy and Benevolence," 261, 272). It may also shift debate away from distinguishing the "principle of humanity" from the "sentiment of humanity"; see, e.g., Debes, "Humanity, Sympathy and the Puzzle," 32. Hume is, I think, quite conscious of what is at stake in applying a single category to both normative and descriptive phenomena, and his decision to do so requires us to account for his intention in doing so (cf. Debes, "Humanity, Sympathy and the Puzzle," 41).

30 In this sense, humanity seems less a principle "by which a person desires to give aid to others" (Vitz, "Sympathy and Benevolence," 271), than one with

"little coercive force," which "need not lead to any intentions or action" (Baier, "Incomparably the Best," 309–310). Insofar as he emphasizes human- ity's coolness, Hume also seems to draw back from the view that humanity is best regarded as a sense of commonality "which makes us respond emotion- ally at least, if not with action, to the situations and emotional experiences of others" (Taylor, "Humean Humanity versus Hate," 192), or as "an ethical attitude and virtue that reflects the capacity to overcome prejudice and pro- mote the decent treatment of others" (Taylor, "Hume on the Importance of Humanity," 82). Wiggins raises a related point in his perceptive study of the concept of solidarity, in which he calls attention to Hume's conspicuous fail- ure to account for "something which is coeval with weak benevolence or fel- low-feeling but utterly special, namely our primitively prohibitive aversions, the visceral horror we feel at the slaughter of the innocent or the repaying of good with gratuitous evil, the indignation that seizes us against the ill- usage of defenceless persons, the way our blood runs cold at the sight of an unprovoked wounding or injury" ("Solidarity and the Root of the Ethical," *Tijdschrift voor Filosofie* 71 (2009): 247). Hume's defense of humanity as cool preference indeed seems unable to account for this – a fact that will importantly distinguish it from Rousseau's concept of pity and Smith's con- cept of sympathy alike, as we shall see subsequently.

31 Edward C. Vacek, *Love, Human and Divine: The Heart of Christian Ethics* (Washington, DC: Georgetown University Press, 1994), 34 and 44.

32 Vitz rightly calls attention to humanity as an original principle ("Sympathy and Benevolence," 263, 271; cf. Taylor, "Hume's Later Moral Philosophy," 321; Debes, "Humanity, Sympathy and the Puzzle," 52), yet humanity needs to be explicitly distanced from love insofar as love requires more than the recognition of resemblance (cf. Vitz, "Hume and the Limits of Benevolence," *Hume Studies* 28 (2002): 279). This "minimal" conception of humanity may also serve to defend Hume from the charge that his shift from sym- pathy is a "retreat" to an "uncharacteristic idealism" (Krause, "Hume and Justice," 642).

33 On sympathy as communication, see David Owen, "Hume and the Mechanics of Mind: Impressions, Ideas, and Association," in *Cambridge Companion*, 89–92; and James Farr, "Hume, Hermeneutics, and History: A 'Sympathetic' Account," *History and Theory* 17 (1978): 289–299, 306–307; see also Capaldi's claim that "to reject sympathy is to reject the importance of the communication of vivacity as the connecting link of the three books of the *Treatise*" (*Hume*, 185).

34 Hume's caveats that we prefer that others be benefited rather than harmed only when "everything else is equal" and we are free of all "private regards" and "particular biass" (EPM 9.4; 5.39; 5.43) must be kept in mind here so as to ensure that his theory of humanity not be thought inconsistent with his conceptions of the relationship of self-interest to concern for others expressed elsewhere (e.g., T 2.3.3.6).

35 On these grounds I question the "no-change" hypothesis emphasizing con- tinuity between sympathy in T and humanity in EPM; see Debes, "Has

Anything Changed?" 314–315; Abramson "Sympathy and the Project," 48, 53, 55; Vitz, "Sympathy and Benevolence," 268, 274; Vitz, "Hume and the Limits of Benevolence," 286–287. So too I would question the suggestion that humanity in the EPM is a retreat from or attenuation of the theory of sympathy in T [see, e.g., Rawls, *Lectures,* 101–102; Selby-Bigge's introduction to his edition of the *Enquiries,* xxv–xxvii; and cf. John B. Stewart, *The Moral and Political Philosophy of David Hume* (New York: Columbia University Press, 1963), 331].

36   For a structurally similar formulation with regard to Rousseau (and indeed one to which we will need to return in the next chapter), see Jonathan Marks, "Rousseau's Discriminating Defense of Compassion," *American Political Science Review* 101 (2007): 727–739.

37   Here lies my difference with Debes, who argues that humanity is "fundamentally dependent on sympathy" and indeed requires sympathy to "activate" it ("Humanity, Sympathy and the Puzzle," 28, 35, 40–41, 46, 52–54, 56), and that "no notion of humanity as a concern for others merely as such *could* exist in the *Enquiry,*" for "any actual concern for another's well-being is instead necessarily mediated by sympathetic representation" (47). I agree that adding sympathy to humanity enlivens it, just as it would any other form of association (see, e.g., T 1.3.9.6; Vitz, "Hume and Limits of Benevolence," 271). At the same time, the process by which humanity is *expressed* – a process in which intersubjectivity and enlivening by sympathy are indeed instrumental – is, I think, practically and conceptually distinct from the grounds on which humanity's authority is *established.* Yet on this front, others have wondered whether Hume's effort "to ground the moral in the natural" in his account of humanity isn't "fundamentally question-begging." In one sense this seems right; the absence of a metaphysical defense of humanity's naturalness indeed raises the question of the extent to which Hume's account is "a genuine advance in a theoretical account of the origin of moral distinctions *qua* moral" (Herdt, *Religion and Faction,* 77–78). At the same time, Hume's defense of humanity's superiority ultimately seems to be conceived on practical rather than metaphysical grounds – that is, on the grounds of the accessibility and reliability that is the consequence of its substantive minimalism, and which, together with its comprehensiveness and universality, distinguish it as a chief ally in the political project of mitigating egotism.

38   Representative and particularly useful is Berry, "Hume's Universalism: The Science of Man and the Anthropological Point of View," *British Journal for the History of Philosophy* 15 (2007): 535–550, esp. 538ff; see also Beauchamp's claim that "morality, for Hume, is contingent on human nature, which alone is the source of moral universality" ("The Sources of Normativity in Hume's Moral Theory," in *Companion to Hume,* 493).

39   See, e.g., Abramson, "Sympathy and the Project," 52–53.

40   Most recently, Hardin has argued that Hume is a "proto-social scientist" with no substantive moral theory whatsoever (*Hume: Moral and Political Theorist,* 3, 6, 23–28, 53, 125, 171, 209, 230).

41 See, e.g., Finlay, *Hume's Social Philosophy*, 5; Krause, "Hume and Justice," 629–631, 634; Penelhum, "Hume's Moral Psychology," 267–268.

42 Nussbaum, *From Disgust to Humanity*, xiv–xxiii, 47–51, 204–209.

43 Nussbaum, *From Disgust to Humanity*, xx.

44 Gilles Deleuze, *Empiricism and Subjectivity: An Essay on Hume's Theory of Human Nature*, trans. Constantin V. Boundas (New York: Columbia University Press, 1991), 50.

3

Rousseau on Pity

Recent calls for the resuscitation of love within contemporary politics and in contemporary liberalism in particular have also taken the form of calls for a "politics of compassion." In this vein a recent volume explicitly dedicated to the "politics of compassion" develops several of the claims that we have seen made on behalf of the "politics of humanity."[1] But here again we need to pause and ask: what exactly does a "politics of compassion" entail? And more specifically: how does this compassion compare to traditional conceptions of love, and are there in fact reasons to prefer a "politics of compassion" to the liberal vision of a society driven by self-love?

For guidance we can again turn to the Enlightenment. Just as Hume's study of the sentiment of humanity offered an entry point into the politics of humanity, so too Rousseau's treatment of compassion can provide a helpful point of entry into the "politics of compassion." Rousseau has often been credited as one of the founders of the politics of compassion, and the preeminent role that compassion or *pitié* plays in his system has been often noted by specialists.[2] But Rousseau's conception of pity is particularly important for our purposes because of what it shares with several of the other eighteenth-century concepts of sentimentalized other-directedness that are our focus here. First, like his fellow eighteenth-century theorists, Rousseau defends compassion on the grounds of its capacity to mitigate the worst effects of self-love – effects Rousseau treated in great detail and arguably with greater acuity than any other eighteenth-century thinker. Second, and especially important for our larger argument in this book, Rousseau defends compassion on the grounds that it gratifies longings for self-transcendence in ways commensurate with the Enlightenment's broader skepticism toward the human capacity to realize transcendence.

On the first front, that of mitigating self-love, pity plays a key normative role in Rousseau's system – albeit a negative role. Many scholars have noted this crucial normative role but have developed it in a different mode. Several scholars present pity as a character virtue, valuable for its capacity to promote the realization of the good life.[3] Others present pity as a civic virtue, valuable for how it can promote the realization of the good society.[4] Yet while there is textual warrant for each view, a third possibility exists: namely that Rousseau valued pity not because it promotes the realization of an individual or political *summum bonum*, but because it can make possible avoidance of a specific *summum malum*: namely the degeneration of society into an unjust state of war in which the weak are dominated by the strong as a result of the liberation of self-love encouraged by modernity. It is on this side of pity that what follows concentrates, specifically arguing that the aim of pity is not to promote the realization of a warmer or more intimate society built on love. Instead pity's project is specifically negative and not positive: to neutralize self-love rather than to realize transformative affective bonds with others.[5]

On the second front, concerning pity's relationship to transcendence, pity is also valuable for how it serves to resolve the potential tension between our longings for transcendence and our incapacities to access the transcendent as traditionally understood. The tension here lies primarily in the fact that Rousseau believes us to be caught between a desire to escape the confines of the self on the one hand and an incapacity to liberate ourselves from the gravitational pull of self-love on the other. And this tension is further exacerbated by Rousseau's conviction that our efforts at self-transcendence are thwarted not only by the power of our self-love, but also by our limited cognitive capacities; born in sensation and refined via a long course of cognitive development, human understanding, even when fully developed, cannot provide us direct access to God's will or to full knowledge of the beautiful. Yet all is not lost. Rousseau himself sees that another possibility exists. For even if an escape from the self that a vertical ascent to the transcendent would make possible is in fact precluded, a sort of self-transcendence on the horizontal plane may yet be possible if some way of extending ourselves beyond ourselves to others can be shown to be within our capacity. Herein lies pity's promise. Rousseauan pity is a remarkable phenomenon insofar as it utilizes

resources inherent to the self, and specifically self-love guided by cognition, to help the self extend beyond itself – in Rousseau's idiom, "to
develop his heart and extend it to his fellows" (E 13:378; OC 4:510) – in
ways that are both morally and politically healthy.

Rousseau's theory of pity – and in particular his theory of "developed" pity that will be our focus – thus contributes to his broader practical political project of mitigating self-preference and ensuring equality,
and itself emerges from a less well-appreciated but central side of his
project: his epistemology. Rousseau's accounts of our cognitive capacities and development are less well appreciated than his politics and his
accounts of the passions. Yet his epistemology is a central component of
his moral psychology and his political theory, and attending to his treatment of pity can be of particular assistance in making these connections
evident.[6] But to appreciate the full significance of Rousseau's theory of
pity and its cognitive aspects in particular we need to begin with his specific treatments of love.

EROS, PATRIOTISM, AGAPE

Rousseau's legacy as a theorist of love is nearly the direct opposite of
Hume's. Where Hume's thoughts on love have largely been disregarded,
Rousseau's thoughts on love have long been valued as preeminent contributions to the history of Western thinking on love, as well as core elements of his own broader project. On the former front, Rousseau has long
been – and indeed continues to be – credited as a father of Romanticism.[7]
On the latter front, specialists have often testified to the prominence
and indeed preeminence of love in his moral and political thought.[8] And
rightly so: reading across Rousseau's corpus we find love credited as "the
supreme happiness of life" (E 13:497; OC 4:653), as one of the "sweetest
sentiments known to men" (SD 3:46; OC 3:168), and indeed "the greatest, the strongest, the most inextinguishable" of Rousseau's own needs
(C 5:348; OC 1:414) – and all this without saying anything of the ubiquity of love as the driving force of Rousseau's renowned *Julie*, often said
to be the most popular novel of the eighteenth century.[9]

Yet setting aside Rousseau's most hyperbolic claims about love, what
is more significant for our purposes is his unique substantive definition
of love and its limits. Rousseau regards love as the preeminent expression of our longing to transcend our individual selves. In this of course
he harkens back to the older tradition with which we have been engaged.
But Rousseau ultimately stands apart from this tradition, for while he

agrees with the tradition on the nobility of love's longing for transcendence he breaks with the tradition in insisting that its form of transcendence is beyond our capacities to attain. On Rousseau's view, the same self that love so ardently wishes to go beyond itself inevitably tethers the self and places insurmountable limits on its aspirations. And it is this paradox – that love seeks a self-transcendence that the self is constitutionally incapable of realizing – that serves as a red thread connecting at once Rousseau's views on three different types of love, and also establishes the link between Rousseau's conception of pity and his conceptions of these three types of love: romantic love, patriotic love, and Christian love, all of which demand attention.

We begin with Rousseau's view of romantic love. Rousseau's conceptions of *eros* and romantic love have been the subject of many studies.[10] Rather than try to replicate these, what follows focuses on one particular aspect of his conception of *eros* and romantic love, namely (and in keeping with the main themes of our study), the way in which Rousseau understands the relationship of *eros* and romantic love to transcendence. What is notable in Rousseau's understanding of this relationship is his consistent emphasis on the fact that romantic love seeks a self-transcendence that the self itself necessarily resists and ultimately thwarts. In describing the way in which love longs for transcendence Rousseau uses language and imagery familiar from Diotima, confessing in *Emile* that "in love everything is only illusion. I admit it. But what is real are the sentiments for the truly beautiful (*le vrai beau*) with which love animates us and which it makes us love" (E 13:570; OC 4:743). Love animates in us a longing for "the truly beautiful" and specifically aims to liberate us from the confines of the self – as Rousseau says, to detach us "from the baseness of the human *I*" (E 13:570–571; OC 4:743). But this is a strikingly hard task, as Rousseau's accounts of his romantic encounters in his autobiographical writings attest. In each of these episodes, Rousseau seeks to lose himself in union with his partner, but finds himself unable fully to participate in this union because of an acute and often painful self-consciousness that always returns him to himself; thus his affair with Madame de Warens is haunted by a guilt and "invincible sadness" that "poisoned its charm" (C 5:165; OC 1:196), his affection for Sophie d'Houdetot is plagued by a sensitivity to "the shame of seeing myself humiliated" (C 5:377; OC 1:448), and his raptures for "Sara" are colored by "humiliation" stemming from his incapacity to prevent himself from seeing himself as he is, in all his pathos (LS 12:264; OC 2:1290). In each of these episodes, union is ultimately thwarted by the more powerful gravity of a self-concern that necessarily

and irresistibly recalls Rousseau back to himself (see also C 5:183; OC
1:219 and C 5:212; OC 1:253–254). And this side of Rousseau's conceptions of *eros* and romantic love is on particular display in his account
of the needs that led him to pursue his relationship with his companion
Thérèse Levasseur:

The first of my needs, the greatest, the strongest, the most inextinguishable, was
entirely in my heart: it was the need for an intimate society as intimate as it
could be; it was above all for this that I needed a woman rather than a man, a
lover rather than a friend. This peculiar need was such that the closest union
of bodies could not even be enough for it: I would have needed two souls in
the same body; since I did not have that, I always felt some void. (C 5:348; OC
1:414–415)

Herein lies the key problem. *Eros* generates the need for a union with
another that takes us beyond ourselves. Yet the fact of our physical cor-
poreality renders this an impossible dream. Romantic love is thus born
from a desire of the self to transcend itself, and thwarted by the fact that
the embodied self cannot be transcended.[11]

A similar problem lies at the heart of Rousseau's conception of patriotic love. To be sure, there are clear differences between Rousseau's treatments of patriotism and romantic love. Yet, patriotic love of fatherland
and fellow-citizen, like romantic love, is ultimately governed by concerns
for the self, and by self-love in particular. As Rousseau indeed makes
clear, and many have rightly seen, the sort of patriotism he recommends
is not to be confused with disinterestedness or self-abnegation. In sharp
contrast, so far from calling for an overcoming or denial of the self,
Rousseau's key treatments of patriotism often insist that extension rather
than transcendence of self-concern is patriotism's proper aim.[12] Thus
even as Rousseau marvels at the seemingly selfless dedication of the true
citoyen and *citoyenne* (E 13:164; OC 4:249), he presents another side of
the story in his discussions of patriotism elsewhere, and especially in the
Political Economy. Here, in the course of his defending his claim that "it
is certain that the greatest miracles of virtue have been produced by love
of fatherland," Rousseau goes on to explain that the patriotism he champions here is not one founded on renunciation of the self but rather a
"feeling of humanity" that has been "concentrated among fellow citizens"
and reinforced by awareness of the "common interest that unites them,"
and indeed one that combines "the force of self-love (*amour-propre*) with
all the beauty of virtue" (DPE 3:151; OC 3:254–255). In this sense, the
love of one's community that Rousseau so frequently and so prominently

celebrates is not a repudiation of self-love but rather the extension of self-love such that it embraces the community as a whole; patriotic love, like romantic love, thus necessarily begins and ends with the self.

And with this we come to Christian love. Rousseau is not often regarded as a theorist of Christian charity, and for good reason: his comments on charity are few in number and much less prominent than his treatments of *eros* and of patriotism.[13] But they deserve attention nevertheless, particularly in light of the insight they can offer into Rousseau's views on love more generally. Certainly the most prominent of Rousseau's discussions of Christian love is his brief reference to charity in the *Social Contract*. In the course of his defense of civil religion in the penultimate chapter of the *Social Contract*, Rousseau presents a critique of Christianity which argues in part that insofar as "Christian charity makes it hard to think ill of one's neighbor," it can only be suited to a state in which "all citizens without exception would have to be equally good Christians," as a single knave could take advantage of a meek citizenry (SC 4:221; OC 3:466).[14] But this functionalist critique of charity was only one side of Rousseau's more extended engagement with Christian love – engagements that span both his personal and his philosophical writings.

Rousseau's early writings contain a set of prayers thought to be composed in the period between 1738 and 1739 while he was in residence with Mme. de Warens at Les Charmettes.[15] These prayers are striking for many reasons, not least of which is their emphasis on love; indeed central to the second of these prayers in particular is Rousseau's explicit proclamation of his wholehearted love for God ("Oh my God, I adore you with all the extent of my force ...") and the way in which Rousseau's love animates his love for neighbors: "stir up in our hearts the love that we owe to your paternal tenderness, and to all your benefits; the respect and the veneration that we owe to your immense Majesty, and your formidable power; and the charity that we owe to our neighbor" (FG 12:158–159; OC 4:1035–1036). And this was hardly only the faith of his youth; as late as 1762, Rousseau would still insist to religious authorities, "I am a Christian, and sincerely Christian, according to the doctrine of the Gospel," by which he specifically understood "that whoever loves God above all things and his neighbor as himself is a true Christian" of the sort that he sought to "strive to be" (LB 9:47; OC 4:960). It is to this same doctrine that the Vicar professes himself to subscribe, exhorting remembrance that "the true duties of Religion are independent of the institutions of men; that a just heart is the true temple of the divinity; that in every country and in every sect the sum of the law is to love God

above everything and one's neighbor as oneself" (E 13:479; OC 4:631–
632). And so too in *Julie* St. Preux insists "that there is no way to love the
master sincerely without loving all those who are dependent upon him:
a truth which serves as foundation to Christian charity" (J 6:380; OC
2:462; cf. J 6:294: OC 2:356–357).

Yet these more conventional restatements of the great commandment
need to be set next to a very different presentation of the great commandment in *Emile*. In a key footnote Rousseau presents a conception
of Christian love that brings this love within the ambit of the key themes
of *Emile*. But in so doing Rousseau presents the foundations of Christian
love very differently:

> Even the precept of doing unto others as we would have them do unto us has no
> true foundation other than conscience and sentiment; for where is the precise rea-
> son for me, being myself, to act as if I were another, especially when I am morally
> certain of never finding myself in the same situation? And who will guarantee me
> that in very faithfully following this maxim I will get others to follow it similarly
> with me? The wicked man gets advantage from the just man's probity and his
> own injustice. He is delighted that everyone, with the exception of himself, be
> just. This agreement, whatever may be said about it, is not very advantageous for
> good men. But when the strength of an expansive soul makes me identify myself
> with my fellow, and I feel that I am, so to speak, in him, it is in order not to suffer
> that I do not want him to suffer. I am interested in him for love of myself, and the
> reason for the precept is in Nature itself, which inspires in me the desire of my
> well-being in whatever place I feel my existence. From this I conclude that it is
> not true that the precepts of natural law are founded on reason alone. They have
> a base more solid and sure. Love of men derived from love of self (*l'amour des
> hommes dérivé de l'amour de soi*) is the principle of human justice. The summa-
> tion of all morality is given by the Gospel in its summation of the law. (E 13:389n;
> OC 4:523n)

Rousseau's footnote raises a host of fundamental issues to which we will
need to return later, including especially the way in which it describes the
process of how we experience the sufferings of others. But for now, the
most fundamental issue it raises concerns its conception of the Gospel's
"summation of the law." Jesus's own account of the summation of the
law, as Rousseau himself elsewhere suggests, rests of course on two principles: first, love of God; and second, love of neighbor as self. Rousseau's
restatement here is of course wholly silent on the first commandment. Yet
with divine love off the table, love of others has to be reconceived, and
on these grounds Rousseau identifies "love of men derived from love of
self" as the principle of justice. Now, the ways in which this conception

of neighbor love differs from the traditional conception are obvious. But what bears emphasizing here is the way in which this new formulation of neighbor love connects to Rousseau's conceptions of romantic love and patriotic love. What is striking is that neighbor love as presented here, just like romantic love and patriotic love, is circumscribed by self-love; so far from representing a transcendence of self-love and self-concern, *agape* comes to be reconceived as an extension of self-love to others.

From all of this, we can conclude that Rousseau thinks that love, in at least three of its most important forms, is incapable of realizing full self-transcendence. But at this point we might wonder why exactly he thinks this, and why exactly this matters. To the first question, Rousseau seems to think that love must necessarily succumb to self-love for two reasons. The first is the sheer power of self-love itself. One of the foundational principles of the moral psychology that Rousseau develops in *Emile* is that all of our passions owe their origin to self-love and that self-love is necessarily inescapable: "the source of our passions, the origin and the principle of all the others, the only one born with man and which never leaves him so long as he lives is self-love (*l'amour de soi*) – a primitive, innate passion, which is anterior to every other, and of which all others are in a sense only modifications" (E 13:363; OC 4:491). As we have seen, his views on romantic love, patriotic love, and Christian love all attest to this foundational conviction about the power and ubiquity of self-love. But to this is joined a second conviction that reinforces his conception of love's limited powers of self-transcendence. This concerns Rousseau's understanding of the foundations and limits of our capacities. While Rousseau often invokes a longing for transcendence, his discussions of our moral and epistemic capacities largely tend to emphasize the impossibility of transcendence as traditionally understood.

Rousseau attests to these longings in several places. In this vein, the first *Discourse* opens praising the powers of the man who can "dissipate, by the light of his reason, the darkness in which nature had enveloped him; rise above himself (*s'élever au-dessus de soi-même*); soar intellectually into celestial regions; traverse with giant steps, like the sun, the vastness of the universe" (FD 2:4; OC 3:6). So too the *Moral Letters* celebrate "great geniuses, the astonishment and honor of their species," who "in some manner break through the barrier of the senses, soar into the celestial and intellectual regions, and raise themselves as far above the ordinary man as nature raises this latter above the animals" (ML 12:188; OC 4:1098). Indeed in the *Moral Letters* Rousseau's longings

for philosophical transcendence of the sort that Diotima's speech rendered familiar are especially clear, as evident in his celebration of "those
involuntary raptures (*ces transports involontaires*) that sometimes seize
a sensitive soul in the contemplation of the morally beautiful and the
intellectual order of things, that devouring ardor that suddenly comes
to enflame the heart with love of the celestial virtues, that sublime going
astray that raises us above our being, and carries us into the empyrean
next to God himself" (ML 12:190; OC 4:1101).[16] But even here, enraptured by such transcendence, Rousseau goes on to emphasize the fleetingness and ephemerality of these experiences – "ah, if this sacred fire could
last ..." (ML 12:190; OC 4:1101; cf. J 6:570; OC 2:694–695 and RSW
8:45–46; OC 1:1046). As this suggests, and as we will continue to see,
Rousseau's epistemological discussions tend rather to insist that insofar
as the origins of ideas lie in sensation, our capacity to transcend our
sensory faculties is impossible in a lasting way; the notion that we could,
through our own efforts, raise ourselves "next to God himself" is absent
from Emile's education in particular.

As to the second question – why all of this emphasis on the relationship of love to self-transcendence matters – the answer is that it matters for reasons that have to do with pity itself. Rousseau's account of
pity proceeds along on the same lines as his treatments of love: pity –
and specifically the developed pity that will be our primary focus in
what follows – is at its heart an attempt to transcend the self and join
with others. In this sense, pity is not only a sentiment that regulates or
restrains self-love (though it most certainly is that), but it is also the sentiment that gratifies longings for self-transcendence given the inaccessibility of transcendence as traditionally understood. In this sense, pity
aspires to the same end as love. Yet pity's advantage lies in the fact that
where love demands an engagement with and a dependence on entities
beyond the self – whether God, or the beautiful, or merely other beings
capable of reciprocating our love (e.g. E 13:365; OC 4:494) – pity is
self-contained and depends on nothing beyond resources immediately
available to the self in order to extend us beyond ourselves to others;
thus pity, as Manent explains, "does not demand any moral transformation or transcendence of the self" and "its wellspring is the selfishness of
each person."[17] Pity, we might say, draws on certain elements internal to
us – and specifically certain elements of our moral psychology and our
cognition – to extend ourselves out of ourselves in ways that are beneficial rather than pernicious to the social order and to our individual
well-being.

Rousseau's first and likely best-known account of pity comes in the *Second Discourse*. Here he offers his account of the "natural pity" (*pitié naturelle*) (SD 3:48; OC 3:170–171) experienced by the savage in the state of nature. While our primary interest here is developed pity, a brief examination of the main features of natural pity can help to bring into relief the distinguishing features of developed pity, and especially its cognitive elements.

Rousseau twice defines natural pity in the first half of the *Second Discourse*, each time in similar terms. His first definition is offered in the Preface, in which he claims to perceive in the original state of the human soul "two principles anterior to reason": on the one hand the principle that interests us in our own self-preservation, and on the other that which "inspires in us a natural repugnance to see any sensitive being perish or suffer, principally those like ourselves" (SD 3:14–15; OC 3:125–126). His second definition is given in his critique of Hobbes; here he insists that Hobbes failed to notice that principle which "tempers the ardor he has for his own well-being by an innate repugnance to see his fellow suffer" (SD 3:36; OC 3:154). Both definitions, with their similar terms and language, introduce three central questions touching pity: first, the question of *what* the proper aim or end or purpose of pity is; second, the question of *how* pity proposes to achieve this aim or end; and third, the question of *for whom* pity is properly felt. These three questions form the focus of Rousseau's treatment of natural pity in the *Second Discourse* as well as his account of developed pity elsewhere, and thus demand our attention.

What then is the point of pity? Here there can be little doubt: the purpose of pity is to restrain our pursuit of self-interest in the service of our preservation. Pity, we are thus repeatedly reminded, prompts repugnance at the suffering of others to such a degree that its possessor will be reticent to inflict suffering on others; even in pursuing self-preservation he will thus be "restrained by natural pity from harming anyone himself" (SD 3:48; OC 3:170). Hence Rousseau's claims that pity was "given to man in order to soften, under certain circumstances, the ferocity of his *amour-propre* or the desire for self-preservation before the birth of this love" (SD 3:36; OC 3:154), and also that "pity is a natural feeling which, moderating in each individual the activity of love of oneself, contributes to the mutual preservation of the entire species" (SD 3:37; OC 3:156). Rousseau seems to find a beauty in this arrangement insofar as it suggests something like an internally well-regulated machine; pity, we are thus told, in nature "takes the place of laws, morals, and virtue" and provides an internal self-regulation that harmonizes the interests of the individual with those of the species without requiring externally imposed positive laws or moral norms (SD 3:37; OC 3:156). This self-regulation is moreover within the reach of all, however underdeveloped. In this vein, natural pity is sufficient to communicate to all their duties to others, absolving them of having to rely for their knowledge of these duties on either reason and "belated lessons of wisdom" (SD 3:15; OC 3:126; cf. SD 3:37–38; OC 3:156–157), or on revelation and "supernatural gifts" (SD 3:20; OC 3:134). Reason and revelation claim to be able to teach "that sublime maxim of reasoned justice" represented by the golden rule, but "natural feeling" alone is sufficient to inspire the less perfect but more useful "maxim of natural goodness" (SD 3:37–38; OC 3:156).

All of this is clear enough from Rousseau's account. What is less obvious but perhaps more important is how pity achieves this admirable harmony of potentially competing interests. Explaining how natural pity works, Rousseau in the definitions quoted previously twice says that it is the experience of *seeing* that prompts repugnance. The empirical evidence that Rousseau marshals in defense of his position shows just what he has in mind; thus the sad lows of the soon-to-be-slaughtered cattle are said to be prompted by the "horrible sight that strikes them," the anguish of the prisoner who "sees outside" the beast destroying the baby is said to be the necessary result of what any would "suffer at this sight," and the tragedies on stage are what give rise to the tears of spectators at the theater (SD 3:36; OC 3:154–155).[18] Rousseau even goes so far as to speak of "the suffering animal" (*l'animal souffrant*) and "the observing animal" (*l'animal Spectateur*) (SD 3:37; OC 3:155). But why is he so concerned to emphasize this aspect of pity? He seems to do so for two reasons, each of which helps to set the stage for his account of developed pity. First, the fact that pity is activated by sight is crucial. Sensation, Rousseau frequently argues, is the only cognitive mechanism active in the human being's undeveloped state; thus in both his account of the natural savage in the *Second Discourse* as well as that of the child in the first three books of *Emile* Rousseau insists that in our undeveloped state, sensation is the whole of cognition. As a result, natural pity's efficacy depends entirely on its capacity to exploit the only resources available to undeveloped minds.

Natural pity's special relationship to sight also suggests a second aspect of its cognitive significance, one that specifically concerns what an underdeveloped mind lacks. Rousseau calls attention to certain of these deficiencies in accounting for the savage's incapacity for love. Love itself depends on "certain notions of merit or beauty that a savage is not capable of having, and on comparisons he is not capable of making," suggesting a necessary connection of the capacity to generate "abstract ideas of regularity and proportion" to the heart's susceptibility "to the feelings of admiration and love" (SD 3:39; OC 3:158; see also E 13:364; OC 4:493). And like love, pity too is constituted by epistemic capacities. The savage mind, in particular, lacks a capacity for reflection; natural pity, we are thus told, is "a virtue all the more universal and useful to man because it precedes in him the use of all reflection" (SD 3:36; OC 3:154), that it is "the pure movement of nature prior to all reflection" (SD 3:36; OC 3:155), and that it is what "carries us without reflection to the aid of those whom we see suffer" (SD 3:37; OC 3:156). But what exactly does Rousseau mean when he says that pity is anterior to "reflection"? In some sense he clearly means that pity is pre-cognitive (or to use Derrida's formulation, "prereflexive"): that natural pity is a sentiment that is felt rather than an idea or compound sentiment that can be thought.[19] Rousseau himself suggests as much when he calls pity one of the "two principles anterior to reason" (SD 3:14–15; OC 3:125–126). Yet we should take care not to reduce 'prior to reflection' to 'prior to cognition.' Rousseau's use (indeed his repeated use) of the language of "reflection" suggests a particular kind of cognition – indeed a type of cognition that stands in a particular relationship to sight. Reflection, that is, is not merely meditation or reverie but a specific type of cognition which proceeds in two stages: first the spectator's act of looking outward, and second the spectator's subsequent receipt of the image upon its return; in this sense reflection suggests both the *going-out* that sight makes possible as well as a *bringing-back* to the self that depends on epistemic abilities beyond sight. Yet this second stage is impossible for natural man given his epistemic limits; reflection's work comes only after *amour-propre*: "Reason engenders *amour-propre* and reflection fortifies it; reason turns man back upon himself, it separates him from all that bothers and afflicts him" (SD 3:37; OC 3:156).[20] This is the key fact that developed pity will in time draw upon. For now though, the claim is that where developed pity will draw upon cognition, natural pity operates independently of all cognition save sensation; hence Rousseau's comparison of the philosopher, reasoning himself out of pity, to the savage who "for want of wisdom and reason" is always "heedlessly yielding to the first feeling of humanity" (SD 3:37; OC 3:156; see also ML 12:189; OC 4:1099; and LdA 10:273–274; OC 5:28–29).

Before turning to developed pity, two last sides of natural pity demand brief mention. One concerns the proper objects of natural pity – that is to say, those for whom natural pity is to be felt. Here too Rousseau gives a seemingly clear answer that perhaps conceals some deeper challenges. Throughout the account of natural pity in Part One of the *Second Discourse*, Rousseau repeatedly suggests that natural pity is to be felt for our fellows: "*nos semblables*." But who exactly are our fellows? This is a more difficult question that it might first seem.[21] Natural man is famously bestial, more sensing than thinking, and Rousseau suggests he has more in common with animals than with man as we know him today (SD 3:27; OC 3:143). Incapable of reason, his fellows cannot be those who reason; incapable of speech, his fellows cannot be those who speak. Rather they are any and all that feel – a category that explicitly includes animals: "if I am obliged to do no harm to someone like me, it is less because he is a reasonable being than because he is a sensitive being," itself a quality "common to beast and man" and which establishes certain duties of one to the other (SD 3:15; OC 3:126).[22] More implicitly, this category would also seem to include those who are similar, but distant. Our fellows (*nos semblables*) need not necessarily be our neighbors (*nos prochains*) – a point that will be important later when we come to examine the specific differences between pity and charity.

Finally, we should note that the question of whether Rousseau in fact offers one or two theories of pity has long exercised scholars and has generated a large literature; as will become clear, what follows sides with the view that the accounts of pity in the *Essay on the Origin of Languages* and in *Emile* are consistent with that found in the *Second Discourse*.[23] But my own reasons for finding these consistent are somewhat different than those often given. The consistency of these various articulations of pity lies in the fact that they are dedicated to the same end: namely restraint of self-love. Yet they are distinct on two grounds. First, they each address themselves to managing very different types of self-love; where the natural pity of the *Second Discourse* is charged with managing *amour de soi*, the developed pity of *Emile* is charged with managing *amour-propre*: tasks that, for all their similarities, present quite different challenges. Second, the specific challenge posed by *amour-propre* consists in its propensity to extend ourselves beyond ourselves; in this sense those developed beings who experience *amour-propre* will be uniquely subject to a longing for self-transcendence unknown to natural savages and other undeveloped beings. Managing the unique challenges posed by the developed human being's will to extend himself beyond himself is thus a key aim of developed pity. Succeeding at this task will require developed pity to regulate extension beyond itself by drawing on epistemic capacities of comparison, imagination, judgment, reason, and reflection for its mitigation. Developed pity is thus a cognitive sentiment.[24]

DEVELOPING PITY: EPISTEMIC ELEMENTS
IN THE *ESSAY*

Rousseau's account of natural pity in the *Second Discourse* lays an important foundation insofar as it clearly defines *what* pity does (manages self-love), *how* pity does it (via appeals to the cognitive category of sensation), and *for whom* pity is felt (our fellows). Yet putting matters this way reveals that a great deal of work remains to be done. Specifically, the inevitable process of human development raises specific challenges on all three fronts insofar as it introduces a new sort of self-love (*amour-propre*), stimulates the cultivation of epistemic capacities beyond simple sensation (including reason, imagination, judgment, and reflection), and indeed so alters the human being that in his developed state he has a wholly new notion of his fellows or *semblables*. These three transitions help explain why Rousseau shifts his attention from the natural pity examined to this point to what he calls "developed pity," which is the subject of the accounts of pity found in chapter 9 of the *Essay on the Origin of Languages* and Book 4 of *Emile*, each of which clearly go well beyond the account in the *Second Discourse*. At the same time certain key differences distinguish these two later accounts from each other. The most significant is that in *Emile*, *amour-propre* becomes a central category of analysis, whereas the *Essay* account proceeds entirely without reference to *amour-propre*. Instead, the *Essay* focuses almost exclusively on a different side of developed pity, namely its epistemic elements – and herein lies its chief significance. In presenting developed pity, Rousseau might be said to divide the labor between his two texts, allowing the *Essay* to present its cognitive elements without reference to moral development, where *Emile* 4 seems to presume precisely such a cognitive development to have already taken place, allowing its account to focus on the way in which epistemic development impacts moral development. It is on this distinction that the present analysis is offered, beginning with the account in the *Essay* insofar as it enables us to isolate with precision the cognitive elements of pity absent from the *Second Discourse* but which will play a decisive role in *Emile*.

The key texts here are the second and third paragraphs of chapter 9 of the *Essay*. The richness of the former demands quotation in full:

Social affections develop in us only with our enlightenment. Pity, although natural to the heart of man, would remain eternally inactive without the imagination that puts it into play. How do we let ourselves be moved to pity? By transporting ourselves outside of ourselves (*en nous transportant hors de nous-mêmes*); by identifying ourselves with the suffering being. We suffer only as much as we judge he suffers; it is not in ourselves, it is in him that we suffer. Consider how much this transport presupposes acquired knowledge! How could I imagine evils of which I have no idea? How would I suffer in seeing someone else suffer if I do not even know that he is suffering, if I do not know what he and I have in common? He who has never reflected cannot be clement, or just, or pitying – no more than he can be wicked and vindictive. He who imagines nothing feels only himself; he is alone in the midst of mankind (*il est seul au milieu du genre humain*). (EL 7:306; OC 5:395–396)

A tremendous amount of work is being done here and requires some disaggregation. First and most significantly, Rousseau here introduces a key feature of pity: namely its capacity to "transport ourselves outside of ourselves." In this sense, and in light of the terms of our larger inquiry, pity enables us not only to form bonds with others but also, in some sense that will demand further investigation, to engage in the sort of self-transcendence that we have seen to be of great interest to Rousseau.[25] But second, and nearly as significantly, Rousseau here describes a new type of pity, one not given by natural sentiment but one developed in us via "our enlightenment" (*nos lumières*). Rousseau's decision to use this fact as his line of demarcation is unto itself significant; here it is not our moral development or the awakening of *amour-propre* that matters, but the cultivation of our minds. A sensitivity to this can help to open up the richness of his account. For what exactly does our enlightenment here consist in? As several have noted, the developed capacity for imagination is of clear and crucial significance for the exercise of developed pity. Rousseau elsewhere is clear that "it is only imagination which makes us feel the ills of others" (E 13:384; OC 4:517), and recognition of this has helped account for the consistency of this account with that of the *Second Discourse*, as well as the import of the cognitive in developed pity.[26] Yet – and this is the point to be emphasized – to suggest that a cultivation of imagination constitutes the whole or even the most notable side of the epistemology of developed pity would do pity a disservice. Far from exhausting the epistemic elements of developed pity, imagination is one element among many, and indeed itself depends on other prior epistemic developments.

To some degree this has been recognized; a number of commentators have explicitly noted that the exercise of pity involves reason as much as imagination.[27] But even "reason" fails to capture the full range of epistemic faculties necessary for developed pity. The evidence for this lies in the paragraph itself. Here we learn not only that pity requires imagination for its activation, but that imagination requires for its activation several other capacities. The first of these is the capacity to form ideas. In this vein Rousseau suggests that the very "transport" of the self outside the self that imagination makes possible itself "presupposes acquired knowledge" – and indeed knowledge of several types; thus we are told that we can imagine no evils of which we have no prior "idea," we cannot feel another's suffering unless we "know" she suffers, and we cannot feel her suffering if we do not "know" what that other has in common with us. Not far below the surface of the seemingly simple invocation of imagination there thus lie three remarkably complex forms of knowledge: first, a knowledge of the phenomenon that causes the sufferer to suffer; second, knowledge that the sufferer is herself suffering; and third, a knowledge of the way in which the sufferer and the spectator are similar. Each of these, of course, presumes a great deal of cognitive sophistication that goes well beyond anything of which natural savages were capable. But even this is not enough; Rousseau also insists that the experience of pity requires further cognitive capacities. Two are explicitly mentioned. The first is judgment.[28] Clearly the feelings we feel for others, however spontaneous they may seem to us in experiencing them, are themselves conditioned by the judgments we make about their suffering; hence Rousseau's claim that "we suffer only as much as we judge he suffers." Given the attention he gives elsewhere to the development of the capacity for judgment, this is significant. As we shall see, judgment of several types – that of the spectator judging the degree to which the sufferer feels his pain, that of the spectator judging the degree to which the sufferer ought to feel his pain, that of the spectator judging the degree to which he himself would or ought to feel such pain in a similar situation – will be central to the three "maxims" of pity that Rousseau will present in Book 4 of *Emile*. Second, Rousseau also insists that beyond judgment, imagination, and knowledge, we also require a capacity for reflection; as he insists, "he who has never reflected cannot be clement, or just, or pitying." It is an observation that, more than any other, suggests the distance of developed pity from the natural pity of the *Second Discourse*.

Rousseau's key paragraph in the *Essay* thus lays out a host of preconditions for the experience of pity – preconditions that not only suggest its complexity and sophistication compared to natural pity, but which also intersect with the central epistemic categories that he elsewhere treats in great detail. At the same time, this account presents a challenge. Given the remarkable gap that separates the natural man and his natural pity from the developed man who experiences developed pity one might not unreasonably wonder how exactly Rousseau envisions this transition. Put differently, what does Rousseau think needs to be done to enable the individual to experience developed pity? It is a complex question that requires a great deal of elaboration; indeed it is to this question that the first three books of *Emile* seem to be dedicated. Yet Rousseau provides the core elements of his answer in the third paragraph of chapter 9 of the *Essay*:

> Reflection is born of compared ideas, and it is the multiplicity of ideas that leads to their comparison. He who sees only a single object has no comparison to make. He who sees from his childhood only a small number and always the same ones still does not compare them, because the habit of seeing them deprives him of the attention needed to examine them; but as a new object strikes us we want to know it, we look for relations between it and those we do know; it is in this way that we learn to consider what is before our eyes, and how what is foreign to us leads us to examine what touches us. (EL 7:306; OC 5:396)

Here again several important claims are being set forth. The first concerns a specific epistemic transition central to the transition from natural to developed pity, namely the transition from sensation to comparison. As we saw in the account in the *Second Discourse*, natural pity was elicited by sight. But now Rousseau suggests that sight is in some sense not enough. What is needed is not sight but comparison – that is, not simply the apprehension of one object but the capacity to simultaneously apprehend and understand the relationships between two objects. But why is this so important for pity? Elsewhere Rousseau explains that development of the capacity to compare multiple objects is a crucial prerequisite for moral judgment; thus in the trajectory several times sketched in *Emile*, children should begin by sensing and learning how to sense well and accurately, only afterward moving to compare the objects of their sensations in manners enabling them to cultivate the capacity to discriminate and judge between them, as well as a capacity to judge the relationship of these objects to themselves. The development of pity follows the same trajectory, we can now see. Thus while a capacity for pity may be natural, its full actualization requires not only sensation but also the capacity for reflection built on comparison – which itself requires additional epistemic virtues, including attention, curiosity, and willingness to experience that which is new and foreign. In the absence of such cognitive talents pity is likely to remain potential rather than actual.[29] And this fact, in turn, may well explain Rousseau's insistence that for all his natural pity, natural man is the natural enemy of all he does not know: "so much naturalness and so much inhumanity" and "so much love for their family and aversion for their species" (EL 7:306; OC 5:396).

This final formulation suggests the magnitude of the challenge that pity faces, particularly under the conditions of modernity. Natural pity, at its best, may lead to love among intimates yet is powerless to restrain (indeed perhaps even encourages) animosity to strangers. Even if it were the case that some vestige of natural pity still persists today – a possibility that Rousseau seems very much to doubt, insisting that modern society's inequality and agitated passions "stifl[e] natural pity" (SD 3:52; OC 3:176) – it could do little to restrain self-love in the great society. For this task, that of restraining *amour-propre*, only developed pity is sufficient, and it is the burden of the account given in *Emile* to explain how the developed cognition of developed pity serves to restrain developed self-love and simultaneously lead us out of ourselves to others in a salutary way.

DEVELOPED PITY: FROM EPISTEMOLOGY TO ETHICS IN *EMILE*

The account of developed pity in the *Essay* marks a significant shift from the account of natural pity in the *Second Discourse*. This shift, as we have seen, largely involves the way in which developed pity draws on certain cognitive developments not present to natural man. Yet the account of developed pity in the *Essay* remains incomplete insofar as it fails to broach the central task: namely to demonstrate how developed pity can promote the specifically moral goals of mitigating those dangers posed by developed self-love and enabling us to achieve self-transcendence on the horizontal if not the vertical plane. It is to this moral task that Rousseau dedicates his account of developed pity in Book 4 of *Emile*. That this account comes only in Book 4 is itself significant; Book 4 is itself largely the story of Emile's awakening to the possibility of self-extension and thereby self-transcendence in all of its different modalities, from *eros* to *amour-propre* to *pitié* to religion. Each of these phenomena, and *amour-propre* perhaps most explicitly and obviously, is defined by the effort to extend one's being out of or beyond one's self, and on these grounds pity's intimate relationship to *amour-propre* in particular has often been emphasized.[30] Yet for all it shares with *amour-propre* and with these other phenomena, pity is unique insofar as it provides a means of extending the self beyond itself that is at once both morally and politically healthy (unlike many expressions of *amour-propre*), and furthermore is self-sufficient insofar as its expression (unlike many expressions of *eros* and faith) is independent of recourse to transcendent categories. Put differently, pity at once establishes minimal relations with others and also gratifies our longings for some minimal degree of self-transcendence without depending on any resources beyond those already immanent to the developed self.

Demonstrating this claim is the burden of this section. Yet to do this, it will be necessary to say a further word about the larger trajectory of *Emile* and the place of the account of developed pity in its broader narrative. Briefly, the developed pity of Book 4 deserves to be seen in the context of two of the central projects of *Emile*: first, the project to render Emile both good for self and good for others; and second, the project of cultivating not only Emile's character but also his mind. Rousseau of course devotes much of his Preface and the early part of Book 1 to clarifying the first project. In his idiom, the challenge before him is to demonstrate whether it is in fact possible to transcend the division between one who lives solely for others and one concerned to live only for himself (see, e.g., E 13:163–165; OC 4:248–251). Seen in the light of this project, developed pity takes on a special significance, insofar as it is precisely that passion which brings pleasure and sweetness to the self at the same time that it reveals itself as the quintessential expression of being for others. Developed pity, that is, may well be the only passion that, in the metaphor with which we began, gratifies both poles of the flattened line.

Developed pity is also significant for the way in which it serves to contribute to what is perhaps the main goal of the first three books of *Emile*, namely the proper formation of the mind via cultivation of specific epistemic faculties and virtues. In this way, pity presumes several epistemic developments central to the account of Emile's cognitive development given in Books 1–3; indeed, so far from emerging out of nowhere, the account of pity that we are given in Book 4 is itself the culmination of a long prior developmental process. This is an intricate process that demands careful reconstruction; here we note only those features that bear specifically on pity. The first and foundational stage is sensibility; "at the beginning of life when memory and imagination are still inactive, the child is attentive only to what affects his senses at the moment," and thus the child's entire epistemic training is strictly limited to learning how to sense well and accurately at the outset (E 13:193; OC 4:284). The aim of this stage is to teach the child to experience pain and pleasure in such a way that he becomes maximally effective at pursuing the gratification of his most natural passion, the desire for self-preservation; early education is thus "a sort of experimental physics relative to his own preservation" (E 13:263–264; OC 4:369–370). But even here crucial lessons are taught that will in time serve to prepare him for developed pity. Many of Emile's early lessons famously involve learning how to live with 'skinned knees' of some sort or another. Rousseau thinks this important because such experiences not only help to develop courage and self-command and resilience (E 13:207; OC 4:299–300), but also because the experience of one's own pain makes possible a capacity to experience and understand the pain experienced by others: "the man who did not know pain would know neither the tenderness of humanity nor the sweetness of commiseration" (E 13:219; OC 4:313–314; cf. LP 2:131; OC 3:236).[31]

Thus even in the stage of nascent sensibility important cognitive lessons are clearly being taught. Even so, in this premoral and pre-cognitive period the subject is almost exclusively concerned with satisfying the self-interests needed to preserve its being (E 13:231; OC 4:329), and hence "the only lesson of morality appropriate to childhood" is "never to harm anyone" (E 13:239; OC 4:340) – the negative morality of natural pity. Yet this stage is not destined to last. True morality of course begins only at the moment when reason enables us to know the difference between good and evil, and conscience leads us to love the former and despise the latter (E 13:196; OC 4:288 and E 13:371; OC 4:501), and hence the full development of morality requires judgment as well as conscience. Indeed, these developments are ultimately more important than even imagination. To the degree that developed pity has been regarded as an intellectual sentiment rather than simply one that is passively felt, imagination is often given pride of place as the most significant cognitive faculty for pity. But Rousseau himself often downplays and almost disparages imagination when comparing it to other higher-order cognitive capacities. This is particularly evident in his association of imagination with sensation:

Before the age of reason the child receives not ideas but images; and the difference between the two is that images are only absolute depictions of sensible objects, while ideas are notions of objects determined by relations. An image can stand all alone in the mind which represents it, but every idea supposes other ideas. When one imagines, one does nothing but see; when one conceives, one is comparing. Our sensations are purely passive, while all our perceptions or ideas are born out of an active principle which judges. (E 13:243; OC 4:344)

This is a striking statement for several reasons, not least of which is the fact that for Rousseau the imagination is more closely assimilated to the senses than to intellect proper. Imagination is indeed only one faculty among many, and perhaps not the highest at that – and certainly not alone sufficient for the experience of developed pity, insofar as the latter (as we have already been told and will soon again be told) requires the capacity for comparison and judgment that imagination alone cannot provide.

In any case, Emile's cognitive development is largely complete by the time we reach the account of pity at the start of Book 4. Two crucial paragraphs near the end of Book 3 show just how far Emile has come, and serve to remind the reader of the chief stages of the cognitive development:

At first our pupil had only sensations. Now he has ideas. He only felt; now he judges; for from the comparison of several successive or simultaneous sensations and the judgment made of them is born a sort of mixed or complex sensation which I call an idea.

And further:

Simple ideas are only compared sensations. There are judgments in simple sensations as well as in the complex sensations which I call simple ideas. In sensation, judgment is purely passive. It affirms that one feels what one feels. In perception or idea, judgment is active. It brings together, compares, and determines relations which the senses do not determine. (E 13:353–354; OC 4:481)

A tremendous amount of work is being done in these paragraphs.[32] But for now what matters is how the cognitive attainments here described bear on Rousseau's theory of pity. To this end what matters are three capacities in particular: Emile's ability to form ideas, his ability to compare, and his ability to judge. Each of these epistemic attainments will soon prove itself necessary for the experience of developed pity, as Emile shifts from his early limited experiences of "only natural and purely physical knowledge," to the knowledge needed by a fully developed being – that is, not only "the essential relations of man to things" but also "the moral relations of man to man" (E 13:358–359; OC 4:487; cf. E 13:364; OC 4:493).

It is then the burden of Book 4 to take this next step and to show exactly how Emile's appreciation of these "moral relations" is an extension of his appreciation of the "essential relations" in which the tutor has been schooling him to this point. The key virtue for the appreciation and proper negotiation of these moral relations is, of course, developed pity, and what remains for us to show is how Rousseau's account of such in the beginning of Book 4 stands within the context of the larger projects of *Emile* that we have sketched previously. In brief, Rousseau's account of developed pity in *Emile* aims to fulfill two goals: first, it shows how exactly one can be both for one's self and also for others; and second, it shows how exactly the cognitive elements of developed pity can mitigate the most potentially destabilizing elements of self-love and enable us to achieve some degree of self-transcendence. The opening of Book 4 particularly signals its commitment to the first of these. Here Rousseau claims that the self-love that directs each man to "his own preservation" is itself "always good and always in conformity with order" and is also the source of the initial expressions of our love of others; thus the child's first instinct is to love himself and then "to love those who come near him" for the possible contributions these others might be able to make toward assisting his efforts at self-preservation (E 13:363; OC 4:491–492). This is a remarkable claim for several reasons, not least of which is the challenge it offers to Christian love – a point to which we will need to return later. But for now, our focus needs to be not on the self-love of *amour de soi* but the self-love of *amour-propre*, which is the main focus of Book 4.

Amour-propre is famously of central interest to Rousseau. This interest owes largely to the fact that *amour-propre* is at once the source of what is best and what is worst in the developed human being. On the one hand, *amour-propre* enables us to escape the limits of ourselves. On the other hand, this very move beyond ourselves to others not only marks the end to our self-sufficiency but also the beginnings of a possible dependence on others – a dependence that brings with it a host of familiar worries about duplicity, anxiety, and egocentrism. But what determines whether *amour-propre* promotes our well-being or our corruption, whether it stays healthy or becomes "inflamed"?[33] Book 4 of *Emile* offers a clue. "Let us extend *amour-propre* to other beings," Rousseau explains: "We shall transform it into a virtue." Rousseau's reasoning is that *amour-propre* is rendered safe by being dispersed: "the less the object of our care is immediately involved with us, the less the illusion of particular interest is to be feared," and for this reason Emile must be always kept "at a distance from himself" (E 13:409; OC 4:547–548; cf. E 13:312; OC 4:430). And this is a lesson Emile is portrayed as having learned well; thus his profession in the sequel to his story that he has been taught to "open my soul only to the most noble, to attach it only to the worthiest objects that are my fellows, to extend, so to speak, the human I over all of humanity, and in this manner to preserve myself from the vile passions that concentrate it" (ES 13:686; OC 4:883).

Several remarkable moves are being made in these passages. First, Rousseau here suggests that the remedy for self-love lies in self-love itself; self-love properly directed toward others, that is, helps to mitigate the more dangerous threats posed by a self-love that is concentrated within itself. Second, self-love reveals itself to be capable of serving as a vehicle for self-transcendence; Rousseau's innovation on this front lies in his inversion of the traditional assumption that transcendence requires a rejection or overcoming of self-love. Self-love, properly directed, can bring us out of ourselves in ways that again promote transcendence on a horizontal if not on the vertical plane. But for our purposes what is especially significant here is that pity is also dedicated to realizing these same ends. Pity, that is, restrains the most pernicious elements of self-love and also makes possible a self-transcendence. Moreover, it does so by requiring nothing beyond those resources that are already available to the developed self, and specifically the cognitive resources that enable developed pity both to replicate what is best and most healthy in *amour-propre* as well as mitigate the most pernicious tendencies of *amour-propre*.

The story of pity in Book 4 begins with the observation of Emile's incapacity to experience pity prior to the awakening of his imagination in adolescence. Hence the child Emile "knows what it is to suffer, for he has himself suffered," yet for now he "hardly knows that other beings suffer too." The use of the senses is not enough for developed pity: merely "to see it without feeling it is not to know it." Yet once his imagination has been awakened, "he begins to feel himself in his fellows" (E 13:373–374; OC 4:504–505). Progress is being made. Emile no longer exhibits "insensibility" or indifference characteristic of one who has "reflected little on sensitive beings." At the same time, while he may no longer be "stupid" he is not yet "learned." And it is only at this point at which he has "already compared too many ideas to feel nothing and not enough to have a conception of what he feels" that he begins to feel pity:

Thus is born pity, the first relative sentiment which touches the human heart according to the order of nature. To become sensitive and pitying, the child must know that there are beings like him (*êtres semblables à lui*) who suffer what he has suffered, who feel the pains he has felt, and that there are others whom he ought to conceive of as able to feel them too. In fact, how do we let ourselves be moved by pity if not by transporting ourselves outside of ourselves and identifying with the suffering animal, by leaving, as it were, our own being to take on its being? We suffer only so much as we judge that it suffers. It is not in ourselves, it is in him that we suffer. Thus, no one becomes sensitive until his imagination is animated and begins to transport him out of himself (*le transporter hors de lui*). (E 13:374; OC 4:505–506)

Here, of course, Rousseau offers his reprise of the passage from the *Essay* that we have already examined; here too, pity requires knowledge of the idea of suffering, transportation of ourselves out of ourselves through imagination, and judgment of the suffering that others experience. Yet these sides of pity come to take on a new meaning in the *Emile* account, and in two ways. First, we now know where these cognitive elements come from, as the first three books of *Emile* provide a detailed account of the developmental process that is merely sketched in the *Essay*. Even more importantly, the context of the *Emile* narrative makes clear why the cognitive elements are so important. On this front, the key fact is the focus on *amour-propre* that dominates Book 4 and provides the immediate context of the discussion of pity even though it was almost entirely absent from the *Essay*.

Rousseau presents the dangers of *amour-propre* in his account of "the point at which *amour de soi* turns into *amour-propre*." For Emile this moment is precisely that at which "the first glance he casts on his fellows leads him to compare himself with them," and here "the first sentiment aroused in him by this comparison is the desire to be in the first position." This is a precarious moment, as it will determine "whether among these passions the dominant ones in his character will be humane and gentle or cruel and malignant…of beneficence and commiseration or of envy and covetousness" (E 13:389; OC 4:523–524; cf. E 13:365; OC 4:494). What inclines Emile one way rather than another, and prevents him, as a developed being who compares himself to others, from harming others in pursuit of his goals? The answer is pity, for it is pity that enables him to know the conditions of those below him, and that leads him to be reticent to exert his power over them.[34] Pity thus utilizes the mechanism of *amour-propre* – the desire to live outside of or beyond one's self – to counteract the inclinations of a developed being to egocentrism, thereby minimizing self-centeredness even while encouraging other-directedness:

> To excite and nourish this nascent sensibility, to guide it or follow it in its natural inclination, what is there to do other than to offer the young man objects on which the expansive force of his heart can act – objects which swell the heart, which extend it to other beings, which make it find itself everywhere outside of itself (*qui le fassent par tout retrouver hors de lui*) – and carefully to keep away those which contract and concentrate the heart and tighten the spring of the human *I*? (E 13:374–375; OC 4:506)

The exercise of pity – and specifically developed pity governed by cognition – makes possible at once the mitigation of the destructive

self-love that would "contract and concentrate the heart" and the gratification of the desire for self-transcendence that is embodied by the
"expansive force" of the heart and its longing to extend to others.

Rousseau elaborates on how developed pity will serve both to contain
self-love and promote self-transcendence in the three illustrative "maxims" of pity that he uses to "summarize all the preceding reflections"
(E 13:375; OC 4:506). All three maxims suggest that developed pity
depends upon our cognitive capacities in order to both restrain self-love
and promote self-transcendence; in so doing they reaffirm the general
insistence that the "truth of sentiments depends in large measure on cor-
rectness of ideas" (E 13:380; OC 4:512). Rousseau's first maxim is thus
that "it is not in the human heart to put ourselves in the place of people
who are happier than we, but only in that of those who are more pitiable" (E 13:375; OC 4:506). Implicit in this are a host of intellectual acts,
not least of which is the judgment of relative position – a judgment that
requires not only the capacity to determine the degree of happiness felt
by other individuals, but also the capacity to compare this degree of happiness to the degree we experience in our own right. And this capacity is
crucial for quite practical reasons. To know that others are unhappy and
indeed more unhappy than one's self will lead the possessor of developed
pity to see one's self in their place – an absolutely crucial sentiment for
the mitigation of the potentially destructive desire to be superior to others, given all the cruelty it threatens.

This is extended in the second maxim: "one pities in others only those
ills from which one does not feel oneself exempt" (E 13:375; OC 4:507).
Here a second important step is taken, at once cognitive and practical.
The cognitive element concerns reflection; where in the first maxim, what
matters was judgment of the feelings of others, what matters in the second
maxim is the capacity to bring this judgment back to the self – in its terms,
to realize that the unhappiness felt by others now may well be felt by us
in the future. Indeed Rousseau himself explicitly says that the "reflection"
that "each may be tomorrow what the one whom he helps is today" is
precisely what lays the ground for "making him humane" (E 13:376–377;
OC 4:507).[35] The cognitive aspects at work here thus include not only the
capacity to recognize one's essential equality with others insofar as we are
equally vulnerable to suffering, but also a capacity to reflect on the essential precariousness of our well-being. In so doing the pitier manifests precisely the disposition that Rousseau hopes the auditor of the Vicar's creed
to cultivate, namely that of one who has been taught "to regret the errors
of my fellows, to be touched by their miseries, and to pity them more than

to envy them" and be "moved with compassion for human weaknesses by the profound sentiment of his own" (E 13:424; OC 4:564) – affirming that indeed "it is only the sentiment of our own failings that impels us to forgive those of others" (J 6:381; OC 2:463–464).

Finally the third maxim reveals the import of exhibiting judgment and reflection together: "the pity one has for another's misfortune is measured not by the quantity of that misfortune but by the sentiment which one attributes to those who suffer it" (E 13:377; OC 4:508).[36] In developing this claim, Rousseau goes on to reprise many of his epistemological concerns – including the place of "imagination," and "memory" and "physical sentiment": thus "one pities an unhappy man only to the extent one believes he is pitiable. The physical sentiment of our ills is more limited than it seems. But it is by means of memory, which makes us feel their continuity, and of imagination, which extends them into the future, that they make us truly pitiable" (E 13:377; OC 4:508). This particular form of reflective judgment also promotes a practical egalitarianism. "To the man who thinks, all the civil distinctions disappear," as a capacity for developed pity enables its possessor to see through the inequalities of society and see "the same sentiments in the hod-carrier and the illustrious man" (E 13:377; OC 4:509) – a capacity whose practical and political significance is immediately obvious. Indeed it is in this sense that developed pity points to Rousseau's politics. However absent pity may be from the explicit story of the *Social Contract*, pity is a key element of the moral psychology that its citizens are expected to have if they are to overcome their propensity to self-preference and to value others as genuine equals.

The maxims thus show how Emile can use his cognitive capacities both to mitigate his destructive self-love and also gratify his desires to extend his being to others. But it is only later in the text that Rousseau shows us the end product of this process in all its glory. In what is perhaps the central passage on pity in Book 4 of *Emile*, Rousseau aims to demonstrate nothing less than that "the love of mankind is nothing other than the love of justice," and that the root of this greatest of loves is precisely love of self "extended" to "other beings":

To prevent pity from degenerating into weakness, it must, therefore, be generalized and extended to the whole of mankind. Then one yields to it only insofar as it accords with justice, because of all the virtues justice is the one that contributes most to the common good of men. For the sake of reason, for the sake of love of ourselves, we must have pity for our species still more than for our neighbor (*nôtre prochain*), and pity for the wicked is a very great cruelty to men. (E 13:409–410; OC 4:547–548)

Rousseau's formal claim here is that pity gains strength in becoming dispersed, and indeed reaches its fruition in being dispersed universally across "the whole of mankind." Rousseau at times calls this virtue not pity but "humanity."[37] In this vein the *Second Discourse* thus asks, "what are generosity, clemency, humanity, if not pity applied to the weak, to the guilty, or to the human species in general?" (SD 3:37; OC 3:155). So too in a crucial passage in Book 4 of *Emile*, Rousseau explains that while a pitying individual's "sensibility will in the first place be limited to his fellows, and for him his fellows will not be unknowns," in time, and "only after having cultivated his nature in countless ways" – ways that explicitly include "many reflections" on his own sentiments and those of others – will he "get to the point of generalizing his individual notions under the abstract idea of humanity" (E 13:387; OC 4:520).

The imaginative extension of ourselves to others that pity makes possible at once serves the dual purposes of mitigating our destructive self-love and gratifying our desires to transcend ourselves on the horizontal plane. This may be nowhere more evident than in the striking locution that Rousseau twice uses to describe the experience of self-love's extension to others. Pity, as described here, aims not only to enable us to feel what others feel. The true aim of pity is to extend ourselves in such a way that we find ourselves in others – hence the claims that "when the first development of his senses lights the fire of imagination, he begins to feel himself in his fellows (*à se sentir dans ses semblables*)" (E 13:373; OC 4:504), and that "when the strength of an expansive soul makes me identify myself with my fellow, and I feel that I am, so to speak, in him (*je me sens pour ainsi dire en lui*), it is in order not to suffer that I do not want him to suffer" (E 13:389n; OC 4:523n). As a result of this transport of ourselves into others, their suffering becomes a matter of our own self-interest insofar as we ourselves will feel what they feel. This is remarkable on two fronts. First, the self-transcendence that Rousseau here describes is one demanding nothing more than self-love guided by imagination. Second, the self-transcendence that leads us to feel ourselves in others not only gratifies longing for transcendence but also mitigates the more dangerous sides of *amour-propre* that might lead us to become agents of harm to those others in whom we in some sense reside.

PITY: BENEFITS AND CHALLENGES

Developed pity is thus a remarkable phenomenon. First, it dedicates itself to mitigating the dangers of self-love. Second, it mitigates self-love without recourse to transcendence. Third, it establishes our connection to others not on an unavailable transcendence but on capacities to feel and to imagine and to judge readily available to all developed human beings; in this way it provides on the horizontal plane a sort of simulacrum of the self-transcendence that is unavailable on the vertical plane. In each of these ways, pity is a useful substitute for traditional forms of love requiring appeals to transcendent categories, one especially to be welcomed by all concerned to fashion a counterweight sufficiently robust to balance self-love in the absence of a foundational appeal to divine love. Yet pity also has its limits, and two are especially noteworthy. First, pity is often too weak to prompt beneficent action. Second, pity, even at its best, often threatens to reify the very egocentrism it aims to mitigate.

On the first front, Rousseau often warns that Emile be preserved from "that sterile and cruel pity" that "is satisfied with pitying ills it can cure" and never results in "active beneficence" (E 13:407; OC 4:545); across his works he has little good to say about the "cruel pity that turns one's eyes away from other people's ills in order to dispense oneself from relieving them" (ML 12:203; OC 4:1118) or "that heartless pity that is content to turn away its eyes from ills it could relieve" (J 6:436; OC 2:532) and the sterile pity of the theater that attracts the eyes of all yet never leads to "the slightest act of humanity" (LdA 10:268; OC 5:23; cf. E 13:406; OC 4:544).[38] Rousseau is thus conspicuously worried by the prospect of inefficacious pity, yet there is relatively little in his account of his account of pity itself that might serve to alleviate this concern and transform pity into an active disposition. Jean-Jacques' pupil is briefly said to be "loving" (E 13:383; OC 4:516), yet the far more pronounced thrust is on the tutor's emphatic insistences that he not be brought up to become "a male nurse or a brother of charity" (E 13:384; OC 4:517), or even worse, "a knight errant, a redresser of wrongs, a Paladin" (E 13:406; OC 4:544).

On the second front, Rousseau repeatedly attests to his concern that pity may exacerbate rather than mitigate egocentrism. This concern manifests itself in three ways. First, pity can encourage pride insofar as a feeling of compassion can prompt feelings of superiority to the recipients of compassion.[39] Rousseau himself calls this "the error most to be feared," in part "because it is the most difficult to destroy," but in part because of the threat pity poses to equality: "In pitying them, he will despise them; in congratulating himself, he will esteem himself more, and in feeling himself to be happier than them, he will believe himself worthier to be so" (E 13:400; OC 4:536–537). Second, Rousseau not only worries that pity promotes pride, but he also worries that insofar as pity brings pleasure it leads those who experience it to value their subjective feelings over the actual welfare of others. Emile is explicitly taught pity for the "inner enjoyment" it provides (E 13:410; OC 4:548), and insofar as pity is pleasant or "sweet" it allows its possessor in a worrisome way to "share" others' suffering without having to "feel" it (E 13:382; OC 4:514 and E 13:373; OC 4:504). Third, pity not only threatens to degenerate into passive quietism, but it also can, in certain circumstances, lead us to become the agents of suffering to certain types of others. In discussing patriotism, Rousseau suggests that other-directed sentiments such as pity need to be "compressed" in order to be rendered active (e.g., DPE 3:151; OC 3:254). This process, however, has its dark side; as has been noted, not only does compression intensify the feeling of other-identification to such a degree that it can become indistinguishable from civic enthusiasm, but it is also capable of coexisting with – and even contributing to – the most destructive sorts of behavior toward all others who lie outside the intimate circle in which compressed pity is experienced.[40] In the *Essay* in particular it is clear that an energetic pity that is concentrated among our immediate fellows can prompt not only love for those we identify as our fellows but also hate and inhumanity toward those outside our circle (EL 7:306; OC 5:396).

These aspects of pity help clarify how far distant pity is from both Christian and contemporary conceptions of compassion, and also how much it shares with the Enlightenment conceptions of sentimentalized other-directedness that are the focus of this study. Today we often conceive of compassion as a warm, affective response to the suffering of others, one indeed capable of creating intimate bonds of care and concern for the well-being of others beyond ourselves. But Rousseau's pity is quite different on several fronts, as we have seen. First, where contemporary compassion is warm, Rousseauan pity is cold; so far from promoting active beneficence, pity is dedicated to the negative end of restraining self-love and minimizing harm. Second, where contemporary compassion justifies concern for others on the value inherent to others – whether this value is understood to emanate from their inherent dignity and rights or simply the ways in which we resemble others – the motivating force behind Rousseauan pity is not other-directed concern but self-love. In this sense, pity is a precarious foundation on which to build a warmer and more caring society, and indeed seems less to emanate from a lofty idealism than from a hard-headed "moral realism."[41] Ultimately, insofar as pity seems dedicated more to mitigating self-love's abuses rather than to promoting love's benefits, it seems not subversive of but precisely in keeping with the minimal morality of liberalism.[42]

On these same fronts pity reveals its distance from traditional Christian love. Rousseau's concept of pity has been described as "his version of charity."[43] Yet pity stands in fundamental opposition to *agape* in several respects. First, pity for others is grounded not in the love of the divine, but in love of ourselves. While Rousseauan pity shares with Christian love an insistence on the intimate connection of self-love to love of others, Rousseau understands this connection to be founded on our basic neediness – a neediness that he has explicitly proclaimed to be natural and "good" in itself. This, however, is far removed – to say the very least – from the claim that we must first love God with the whole of our being and only then love our neighbor as we love ourselves. The unavailability of the transcendent thus compels Rousseau's move to establish love of others on the alternative foundation of the love of self, and it is here that we most clearly see the degree to which he was concerned to flatten the triangle into a line.[44] Second, the others that are specifically designated as the objects of our proper pity are not in fact our neighbors or those real people closest to us with whom we live, but the species in its collectivity, an abstraction that can never be seen but only imagined.[45] Humanity, the perfection or *telos* of developed pity, is indeed specifically conceived as the opposite of neighbor-love: not love of those near to us, but pity for those distant. Rousseau, in one of his most normative moments in *Emile*, insists: "Men, be humane. This is your first duty. Be humane with every station, every age, everything which is not alien to man. What wisdom is there for you save humanity?" (E 13:209; OC 4:302 and J 6:127; OC 2:156). The pity that when fully developed manifests itself as humanity is thus not merely an ethical duty but wisdom itself, albeit a wisdom very different from that which begins with the fear of the Lord or that which aspires to the possession of the good and true and beautiful (see esp. ML 12:198; OC 4:1112–1113).

The same factors that distinguish Rousseau's pity from contemporary compassion and Christian love also suggest its affinities with the other eighteenth-century theories of other-directedness that are our focus here. First, insofar as its primary aim is the negative restraint of harms emanating from aggressive self-love rather than the positive promotion of acts of beneficence, it shares the central aim of Hume's concept of humanity, dedicated as we have seen to establishing a minimally sufficient "cool preference" for the well-being of others rather than encouraging love or positive benevolence. Second, Rousseau's pity is precisely both wide and weak in the same ways that we saw Hume's concept of humanity to be. Third, insofar as pity forges its minimal bonds with others on the foundations afforded by those resources immanent to the developed self, and its epistemic resources in particular, it shares Hume's aim of creating bonds via immanent resources – in Hume's case, the capacity for associative resemblance – rather than access to the transcendent.

Rousseau's pity thus shares much with Hume's humanity including especially the concern to further commitments to decency and non-malfeasance characteristic of liberal societies that lack access to more robust forms of love.[46] Yet it also leaves several questions unanswered, and in so doing anticipates two eighteenth-century theories of other-directedness it remains for us to examine. First, neither humanity nor pity provide motives or incentives to act for others; indeed however effective pity and humanity may be at restraining self-love so that we not become agents of harm to others, they offer us little incentive to exert ourselves to become the agents of the promotion of the well-being of others. Second, even as humanity and pity draw on cognitive processes that reveal each to be considerably more complex than mere subrational affects, neither pity nor humanity are fully justifiable by reason. In his key footnote on Christian love in *Emile*, Rousseau, as we have seen, insists that neighbor love must be based on the sentiment of self-love precisely because we lack compelling "reason" beyond self-love for justifying love of others. Smith's theory of sympathy and Kant's theory of love, however, will aim to provide, in their respective ways, both positive incentives and legitimizing reasons for other-directed behavior that at once build on and seek to go beyond the essential foundations laid by Hume's humanity and Rousseau's pity.

NOTES

1 Michael Ure and Mervyn Frost, eds., *The Politics of Compassion* (London: Routledge, 2014). Several essays in this volume assess the benefits and limits of compassion in the contemporary political context; especially useful is Iain Wilkinson's effort "to develop a new sociology of humanitarian sentiment and moral sensibility" in part out of eighteenth-century materials in his essay on "The New Social Politics of Pity" (121–135; quote at 123). For further studies, see Martha Nussbaum, "Compassion: The Basic Social Emotion," *Social Philosophy and Policy* 13 (1996): 27–58; Maureen Whitebrook, "Compassion as a Political Virtue," *Political Studies* 50 (2002): 529–544; as well as those pieces cited in Jonathan Marks, "Rousseau's Discriminating Defense of Compassion," *American Political Science Review* 101 (2007): 727.

2 Clifford Orwin in this vein describes Rousseau as "that thinker whose contribution was greatest" to the rise in compassion, and indeed the thinker

who "presided over the dawn of political compassion"; see his "Rousseau and the Discovery of Political Compassion," in *The Legacy of Rousseau*, ed. Clifford Orwin and Nathan Tarcov (Chicago: University of Chicago Press, 1997), 296. Also, in keeping with accepted practice among specialists (see, e.g., Marks, "Rousseau's Discriminating Defense," 727n4), I follow Rousseau in using pity and compassion interchangeably to refer to the same sentiment.

3   On pity, together with *amour-propre*, as instrumental to provision of such goods as the mutual recognition essential to realization of the good life for a human being, see N. J. H. Dent, *Rousseau* (Oxford: Basil Blackwell, 1998), esp. 113ff. For a recent development of this perspective, see esp. Frederick Neuhouser, *Rousseau's Theodicy of Self-Love: Evil, Rationality, and the Drive for Recognition* (Oxford: Oxford University Press, 2008). On the specific question of the degree to which pity can be understood as a virtue, see Paul Audi, "La pitié est-elle une vertu?" *Dix-huitième Siècle* 38 (2006): 463–480.

4   For the view that pity's chief value lies in its civic function, and particularly its capacity to promote "social cohesion," see esp. Mira Morgenstern, *Rousseau and the Politics of Ambiguity* (University Park: Penn State University Press, 2000), 55–119 (on "social cohesion" specifically see 56 and 62–63). For a valuable recent development of this theme beyond Rousseau, see esp. Rebecca Kingston, *Public Passion: Rethinking the Grounds for Political Justice* (Montreal: McGill-Queen's University Press, 2011).

5   An especially helpful account of pity's "negative" aspects with which what follows largely concurs is offered in Richard Boyd, "Pity's Pathologies Portrayed: Rousseau and the Limits of Democratic Compassion," *Political Theory* 32 (2004): 519–546 (see esp. 522 and 537).

6   What follows thus aims to trace the implications of Rousseau's account of cognitive development for one side of our moral development. I examine Rousseau's account of cognitive development and its foundations in sensory epistemology in "Rousseau's Virtue Epistemology," *Journal of the History of Philosophy* 50 (2012): 239–263; for further recent studies, see, e.g., Annette Pierdziwol, "Extending Nature: Rousseau on the Cultivation of Moral Sensibility," in *Contemporary Perspectives on Early Modern Philosophy: Nature and Norms in Thought*, ed. Martin Lenz and Anik Waldow (Dordecht: Springer, 2013), 135–158; and Denise Schaeffer, *Rousseau on Education, Freedom, and Judgment* (University Park: Penn State University Press, 2014), esp. 36–62.

7   See, e.g., Irving Singer, *The Nature of Love*, vol. 2: *Courtly and Romantic* (Chicago: University of Chicago Press, 1984), 303–343; and Simon May, *Love: A History* (New Haven, CT: Yale University Press, 2011), 152–164. For a more skeptical view, see Isaiah Berlin, *The Roots of Romanticism*, ed. Henry Hardy (Princeton, NJ: Princeton University Press, 1999), 7, 52–53.

8   Key studies of Rousseau's political thought that emphasize love, and especially *eros*, include Joel Schwartz, *The Sexual Politics of Jean-Jacques Rousseau* (Chicago: University of Chicago Press, 1984); Allan Bloom, *Love and Friendship* (New York: Simon and Schuster, 1993), 39–156; and

Elizabeth Rose Wingrove, *Rousseau's Republican Romance* (Princeton, NJ: Princeton University Press, 2000).

9   For our purposes, it is worth noting that Rousseau himself frames *Julie* not simply as a study of romantic love but of pity and humanitarianism as well. The important second preface to *Julie* thus defends its presentation of the novel's love story on the specific grounds that in reading it "one learns to love mankind" (J 6:9; OC 2:14), and Julie's lover professes at the outset that it is specifically to her pity that he is most attracted (J 6:26; OC 2:32). In light of the present chapter's themes, see also David Gauthier's reading of how Julie's love can be understood as an aspiration toward unity that can be fulfilled only via transcendence of this world; see his *Rousseau: The Sentiment of Existence* (Cambridge: Cambridge University Press, 2006), 99–106.

10 In addition to those studies cited in n8, see esp. the reading of Rousseau's concept of extension of being as a modification of Platonic *eros* given in Laurence Cooper, *Eros in Plato, Rousseau, and Nietzsche: The Politics of Infinity* (University Park: Penn State University Press, 2008), 135–173. Cooper's sensitivity to the significance of Rousseau's account of the desire to extend and enlarge one's being (see esp. 135–136, 141–149) has been especially helpful for my understanding of pity.

11 May captures something like what I want to argue when he says that the lover "becomes authentic through love" insofar as "he becomes not selfless, but a self. He doesn't lose himself, but finds himself. Even when he strives to transcend nature he seeks to be guided by, and in a sense to actualize, his own nature" (*Love: A History*, 164).

12 On ancient patriotism in Rousseau, see, e.g., Shklar, *Men and Citizens: A Study of Rousseau's Social Theory* (Cambridge: Cambridge University Press, 1969), esp. 156–157. For contemporary application, see Nussbaum, *Political Emotions: Why Love Matters for Justice* (Cambridge, MA: Harvard University Press, 2013), 30, 44–45. Next to these should be set Anna Stilz's recent effort to draw from Rousseau "a more liberal and rationalist theory of civic solidarity" as an alternative to more familiar culturally grounded arguments for patriotism in her *Liberal Loyalty: Freedom, Obligation, and the State* (Princeton, NJ: Princeton University Press, 2009), 113–136 (quote at 115).

13 A key exception is Mark Cladis, "Redeeming Love: Rousseau and Eighteenth-Century Moral Philosophy," *Journal of Religious Ethics* 28 (2000): 221–251. My view is closer to those who have emphasized the differences between Rousseauan pity and Christian love (see n43 in this chapter).

14 A helpful recent reading of Rousseau's civil religion is provided in Charles L. Griswold, Jr., "Liberty and Compulsory Civil Religion in Rousseau's *Social Contract*," *Journal of the History of Philosophy* 53 (2015): 271–300.

15 See the editor's note at OC 4:1763–1764; for commentary on the prayers, see Charles A. Spirn, *Prayer in the Writings of Jean-Jacques Rousseau* (New York: Peter Lang, 2008), 25–41.

16 On the aspiration to transcendence in Rousseau, see also Cooper, *Eros in Plato, Rousseau, and Nietzsche*, 134–135, 156, 160. David Lay Williams has laid out perhaps the most developed case for the substantive role

played by transcendent ideas in Rousseau's moral and political philosophy; see *Rousseau's Platonic Enlightenment* (University Park: Penn State University Press, 2007), esp. xxvii–xxix, 76–88, 98–106.

17 Pierre Manent, *A World beyond Politics? A Defense of the Nation State*, trans. Marc LePain (Princeton, NJ: Princeton University Press, 2006), 190.

18 Relevant to Rousseau's account of what the spectator feeling pity sees – but pointing in a direction beyond what can be dealt with here – is Rousseau's account of what is seen by spectators of spectators feeling pity, a perspective emphasized throughout these passages, in which we are told that "one observes daily the repugnance of horses," one "sees with pleasure" Mandeville forced to confess natural pity, "one sees, moved and crying," spectators at the theater, and natural man "is always seen heedlessly yielding to the first feeling of humanity" (SD 3:36–37; OC 3:154–156). Already in the *Second Discourse* Rousseau seems well aware of the phenomenon of the spectator of the spectacle – a second-order standpoint that will in time become crucial to the eventual operations of developed pity. Nanine Charbonnel calls helpful attention to the relation of pity to spectacle in the *Second Discourse* in *Logiques du Naturel*, vol. 3 of *Philosophie de Rousseau* (Aréopage: Lons-le-Saunier, 2006), 230.

19 See, e.g., Griswold, who regards Rousseauan pity as "minimally cognitive" ["Smith and Rousseau in Dialogue: Sympathy, Pitié, Spectatorship and Narrative," in *The Philosophy of Adam Smith*, ed. Vivienne Brown and Samuel Fleischacker (London: Routledge, 2009), 63]; and Michael Frazer, *The Enlightenment of Sympathy* (Oxford: Oxford University Press, 2010), 42, 48, 97, 123, 150, 170; though cf. Derrida, *Of Grammatology*, trans. Gayatri Spivak (Baltimore, MD: Johns Hopkins University Press, 1998), esp. 177, 182. In contemporary terms, my sense is that Rousseau's theory of pity would be better classed within cognitive sentimentalism rather than simple emotivism.

20 The French is interestingly ambiguous here: *C'est la raison qui engendre l'amour propre, et c'est la réflexion qui le fortifie; C'est elle qui replie l'homme sur lui-meme; c'est elle qui le sépare de tout ce qui le gêne et l'afflige* (OC 3:156). I provide a literal translation, though most translators (Masters included) take *elle* to refer to "*la raison*" in both instances. But it also seems consistent grammatically and substantively for *elle* to refer to either *la réflexion* or to some sort of compound of *la réflexion* and *la raison* taken together. I am indebted to John Scott for confirming my suspicions on this front.

21 Cf. the explicit treatment of this question in Audi, *Rousseau: une philosophie de l'âme* (Paris: Verdier, 2008), 107, 110–111, 125–126, 129–130; and in David Marshall, *The Surprising Effects of Sympathy: Marivaux, Diderot, Rousseau, and Mary Shelley* (Chicago: University of Chicago Press, 1988), 148–149, 151.

22 For fuller treatments of Rousseau's conception of the differences between animals and human beings, see esp. Aaron Garrett, "Human Nature," in *The Cambridge History of Eighteenth-Century Philosophy*, ed. Knud Haakonssen (Cambridge: Cambridge University Press, 2006), vol. 1, pp. 177–181; and Robert Wokler, "Perfectible Apes in Decadent

Cultures: Rousseau's Anthropology Revisited," in *Rousseau, the Age of Enlightenment, and Their Legacies*, ed. Bryan Garsten (Princeton, NJ: Princeton University Press, 2012), 1–28.

23 For an overview of this debate, see, e.g., Catherine Larrère, "Adam Smith et Jean-Jacques Rousseau: Sympathie et Pitié," *Kairos* 20 (2002): 73–74. Especially helpful on this front is the response to this debate given by John Scott; see esp. his claims that despite the "apparent contradiction," when more closely examined "there is no substantial contradiction between the two works" ["Introduction" to *The Collected Works of Rousseau*, ed. Christopher Kelly and Roger Masters (Lebanon, NH: University Press of New England, 1998), vol. 7, xxviii–xxix; cf. Scott, "Rousseau and the Melodious Language of Freedom," *Journal of Politics* 59 (1997): 809]. Scott's resolution proceeds on the grounds that while the sentiment of pity is indeed given by nature in the *Second Discourse*, this is not inconsistent with its lying dormant until the moment at which it comes to be the first sentiment "activated" in the natural course of our development, as suggested in the *Essay*.

24 In this respect, what follows develops Goldschmidt's suggestion that the two later accounts aim to provide "a more intellectual conception of pity" (as cited in Audi, *Rousseau*, 110). In a similar vein, see Dent's distinction between "sentiment" and "notion" accounts of pity in *Emile* 4 (*Rousseau*, 127ff); Morgenstern's discussion of the place of pity in Rousseau's "interconnected system of affective and cognitive structures" (*Rousseau and the Politics of Ambiguity*, 55); and Stilz's discussion of how pity contributes to a "cognitively based identification with one another" (*Liberal Loyalty*, 125–126).

25 Cf. David Marshall's description of the self-transport presented in this passage as a kind of "self-forgetting" or "self-annihilation" (*Surprising Effects of Sympathy*, 147–149).

26 See, e.g., Scott, "Rousseau and the Melodious Language," 809.

27 See, e.g., Roger Masters, *The Political Philosophy of Rousseau* (Princeton, NJ: Princeton University Press, 1960), 48. See also Orwin, who notes that "whatever may have been the basis of compassion in the state of nature, in society it depends upon the proper education of our sentiments by means of both reason and imagination" ("Rousseau and the Discovery," 301); and Morgenstern, *Rousseau and the Politics of Ambiguity*, esp. 57 and 67. Boyd similarly notes that "pity and compassion towards others can bear fruit only once the process of human development has begun. We must first acquire [] moral liberty, self-consciousness, imagination, and reason" ("Pity's Pathologies Portrayed," 522). Marks likewise notes that "developed compassion is always compassion guided by reason" ("Rousseau's Discriminating Defense," 736–737), as does Zev Trachtenberg, who notes that pity in EL and E "both depend on human cognitive development, specifically the growth of the capacities of imagination and reason that attends social life" ["Civic Fanaticism and the Dynamics of Pity," in *Rousseau and l'infame: Religion, Toleration, and Fanaticism in the Age of Enlightenment*, ed. Ourida Mostefai and John Scott (Amsterdam: Rodopi, 2009), 217]. See also Neuhouser, *Rousseau's Theodicy of Self-Love*, 176; Joshua Cohen, *Rousseau: A Free*

Community of Equals (Oxford: Oxford University Press, 2010), 107; and Audi, *Rousseau*, 108–109, 127, 421–433 (Audi is also one of the few interpreters to call explicit attention to the notion of "acquired knowledge"; see 113–114). Compare these to Derrida: "Pity does not awaken with reason but with imagination which wrenches it from its slumbering inactuality. Not only does Rousseau take for granted the distinction between imagination and reason, but he makes this difference the strength of his entire thought" (*Of Grammatology*, 182).

28 Here and later in this chapter my account parallels the helpful treatment of the relationship of pity to judgment recently offered in Schaeffer, *Rousseau on Education, Freedom, and Judgment*, 85–106; see also Derrida, *Of Grammatology*, 171ff.

29 See here again Scott, "Rousseau and the Melodious Language," 809.

30 See Masters, *Political Philosophy of Rousseau*, 42–46; Derrida, *Of Grammatology*, 174; Marshall, *Surprising Effects of Sympathy*, 149–150; Scott, "Rousseau and the Melodious Language," 810–812, 818, 823; Orwin, "Rousseau and the Discovery," 299, 305–306; Boyd, "Pity's Pathologies Portrayed," 523–524; Marks, "Rousseau's Discriminating Defense," 728; Neuhouser, *Rousseau's Theodicy of Self-Love*, 174; and Audi, *Rousseau*, 118–121.

31 In this vein see also Rousseau's claim that "to pity another's misfortune one doubtless needs to know it, but one does not need to feel it" (E 13:382; OC 4:514). As several interpreters have rightly noted, the actual experience of another's pain, so far from augmenting one's experience of developed pity, in fact may threaten it; see, e.g., Boyd, "Pity's Pathologies Portrayed," 528–530; Derrida, *Of Grammatology*, 190 (which also helpfully and explicitly calls attention to the place of both reflection and judgment in pity); and Audi's very helpful distinction between "*souffrir-avec*" and "*souffrir-comme*" (*Rousseau*, 429).

32 Elsewhere I have sought to disaggregate the developments here described and explain how and when and why they are cultivated; see "Rousseau's Virtue Epistemology," esp. 246–254.

33 On inflamed *amour-propre*, see esp. Dent, *Rousseau*, 56–59, 64–67; and Neuhouser, *Rousseau's Theodicy of Self-Love*, esp. 90–116. Neuhouser's book is valuable for its development of "*amour propre*'s positive potential" (*Rousseau's Theodicy of Self-Love*, 16; see also 29, 37, 84–85, 155ff.); on this front see also Stilz, *Liberal Loyalty*, 120–123.

34 Compare this to Derrida: "If pity moderates 'the violence of love of self,' it is perhaps less by opposing itself to it than by expressing it in an indirect way ..." (*Of Grammatology*, 174–175). Also helpful here is Charbonnel's account of how Rousseau's discussion of pity here develops "en termes de force expansive du *coeur*, de dilation, d'extension *de soi*" (*Logiques du Naturel*, 227).

35 See also Stilz, *Liberal Loyalty*, 124–125.

36 Schaeffer offers an especially helpful reading of the role of judgment in the third maxim; see *Rousseau on Education, Freedom, and Judgment*, 91–93; as well as Morgenstern, *Rousseau and the Politics of Ambiguity*, 67.

37 Humanity is a strikingly ubiquitous virtue in Rousseau's canon (see, e.g., SD
    3:18; OC 3:131; and E 13:481; OC 4:634; and LF 8:262; OC 4:1136). Yet
    humanity rarely receives explicit attention in its own right. For important
    exceptions, see Terence Marshall, "Poetry and Praxis in Rousseau's *Emile*,"
    in *Modern Enlightenment and the Rule of Reason*, ed. John C. McCarthy
    (Washington, DC: Catholic University Press, 1998), esp. 202–203, which
    emphasizes its association with egalitarianism; and Jason Neidleman,
    "Rousseau's Rediscovered *Communion des Coeurs*: Cosmopolitanism in the
    Reveries of the Solitary Walker," *Political Studies* 60 (2012): 76–94 (esp. 79
    and 87). Neidleman's study is especially valuable for its observation that "for
    Rousseau the most important political choice was not between patriotism
    and cosmopolitanism; it was rather between love of self in conjunction with
    others and love of self at the expense of others" (82).
38 Masters in this vein calls attention to the need for "the replacement of an
    impotent, humanitarian virtue by civic virtue" (*Political Philosophy of
    Rousseau*, 51). Especially helpful on this front is Boyd's emphasis on the
    ways in which pity privileges the experience of its own "sweetness" above
    the relief of suffering; see "Pity's Pathologies Portrayed," 524–526. On pity's
    weakness as it widens, see esp. Trachtenberg, "Civic Fanaticism," 217–218;
    Morgenstern, *Rousseau and the Politics of Ambiguity*, 71; and Manent,
    World beyond Politics, 189–190. Marks offers a response that argues pity's
    weakness is in fact a strength insofar as it offers a comparatively safe way for
    the individual to extend his being; see "Rousseau's Discriminating Defense of
    Compassion," esp. 728–729.
39 See, e.g., May, *Love: A History*, 158.
40 On pity's role in civic enthusiasm, see esp. Trachtenberg, "Civic Fanaticism,"
    214–215 and 219–220; and Masters, *Political Philosophy of Rousseau*, 24–25.
41 Orwin, "Rousseau and the Discovery," 298 and 303.
42 On pity's affinity to liberal aims, see esp. Boyd, "Pity's Pathologies
    Portrayed," 537.
43 The quote is from Cladis, "Redeeming Love," 223; see also his helpful dis-
    aggregation of the relationship between *amour-propre*, *amour de soi*, and
    charity at 222 and 227–229. Cladis revisits and presents a somewhat more
    tempered view of the equivalency of pity and charity in *Public Vision, Private
    Lives: Rousseau, Religion, and 21st Century Democracy* (Oxford: Oxford
    University Press, 2003), 61–63. On the tensions with Christian ethics, see
    esp. Orwin, "Rousseau and the Discovery," 296; Bloom, "Introduction," in
    Emile, trans. Bloom (New York: Basic Books, 1979), 14, 18, and Bloom,
    Love and Friendship, 51 and 63; and Richard White, "Rousseau and the
    Education of Compassion," *Journal of the Philosophy of Education* 42
    (2008): 40. Manent interestingly calls attention to the "religious character"
    of humanity; see *World beyond Politics*, 124.
44 In this vein, see esp. Singer's claim that in *Emile*, "the love of humanity seems
    to reduce to an invidious love of self" (*Nature of Love, vol. 2: Courtly and
    Romantic*, 338); Boyd's claim that "pity collapses back into self-preservation"
    ("Pity's Pathologies Portrayed," 521; see also 529–530); and Manent, *World*

beyond Politics, 205; though cf. Larrère, "Sympathie et Pitié," 80-81, which resists this conclusion.

45 Familiarity, Rousseau knows well, breeds contempt, for "long struck by the same sights, we no longer feel their impressions," and indeed "what we see too much, we no longer imagine," leading us to become in some sense "pitiless" (E 13:384; OC 4:517). Cf. Dent, *Rousseau*, 143.

46 See esp. Orwin: "in a society whose typical inhabitant Rousseau describes as 'nothing,' compassion, with its appeal to a new and distinctly modern or post-Christian sensibility, furnishes a moral strategy that is somewhat better than nothing" ("Rousseau and the Discovery," 309).

4

Smith on Sympathy

Adam Smith's renown once rested almost exclusively on his contributions to the defense of modern commercial society. But if this had been his sole concern he would hardly merit a chapter in a book dedicated to critical responses to selfishness in modern commercial society. As several generations of revisionist scholars have demonstrated, Smith was hardly an uncritical apologist for commercial society.[1] In fact, Smith was conspicuously troubled by the egocentrism that commercial society seemed to encourage, and his moral philosophy, centered as it is on the concepts of virtue and sympathy, contains much that pushes back against egocentrism. Indeed ever since his friend Hume called the agreeableness of sympathy "the hinge" upon which his ethics turned (CAS 36), Smith has been often regarded as a champion of sympathy rather than simply an apologist for self-interest, and on such grounds he merits our study here.

But Smith also deserves our attention insofar as he has also been regarded, especially recently, as a critic of love. What follows examines how these three sides of his thought – his concerns about egocentrism, his skepticism toward love, and his enthusiasm for sympathy – cohere. In so doing it particularly argues that Smith's concern to mitigate the egocentrism exacerbated by modern commercial society led him to consider both love and sympathy as possible remedies. Yet ultimately Smith judges sympathy superior to love on this front; what follows particularly argues that his preference for sympathy emerges directly out of and is indeed decisively shaped by his critique of love. Yet seeing this requires reconsidering precisely what Smith understood love to be, as well as precisely what he understood sympathy to be.

With regard to love, several recent studies have presented Smith as a critic of love, and indeed of two quite specific types of love: namely the classical conceptions of *eros* and *philia* that we have already had occasion to mention earlier. These have done much to clarify the nature and depth of Smith's engagement with Platonic and Aristotelian conceptions in particular.[2] At the same time, in focusing exclusively on *eros* and *philia* such studies have hardly exhausted the whole of Smith's engagement with love. For as I hope to show, the concepts of love with which Smith engages in *The Theory of Moral Sentiments* are not only Platonic and Aristotelian but also Christian. By extending our attention beyond his views on *eros* and *philia* to his quite conscious if less appreciated treatment of *agape*, we not only better position ourselves to account for certain central if overlooked elements of the text, but also allow Smith to emerge as a more sophisticated theorist of love, indeed one capable of discriminating between its vicious and virtuous sides.

With regard to sympathy, recent scholarship has tended to regard Smith's conception of sympathy as part of a larger project in *The Theory of Moral Sentiments* to offer a positivist or descriptive account of the "social origin" of moral judgment rather than a normative account of what is properly valued and why.[3] Again this has been helpful; such studies have done much to illuminate the degree to which Smith regarded sympathy as a social rather than a static process. Yet exclusive focus on this side of his account can blind us to the breadth and depth of his theory of sympathy. Thus what follows also argues that Smith's theory of the social role of sympathy in judgment hardly precluded his recognition of sympathy as a normatively valuable principle in its own right and as a central principle of agent motivation, as has been recently and convincingly argued.[4]

The central claim for which I argue in what follows emerges directly from these two reconsiderations. It is founded on the recognition that Smith's theory of love is not simply a critique of *eros* for its particularity, but also incorporates an appreciation of the attractions of the universality of *agape*. Yet, as I will also argue, Smith ultimately judges *agape* insufficient as a remedy for *eros*, for however admirable its scope and ambitions may be, the realization of its ambitions, Smith thinks, is compromised by our natural epistemic limits. It is this recognition, I want to argue – and not only his reservations toward *eros* – that leads Smith to regard sympathy as a central principle of motivation, and to embrace it as the best available means of replicating the practical benefits of universal charity within the confines of our epistemic limits.

By so doing I hope to illuminate the full extent of the role that Smith himself envisioned for sympathy. Previous scholars of Smithean sympathy have found in it the answers to a striking range of discrete questions, including questions about the relationship of cognition to affect in deliberations concerning justice, the processes by which groups establish norms through spontaneous intersubjective transactions, and the nature of the incentives that lead citizens of modern commercial societies to pursue the bettering of their condition.[5] Each of these questions is indeed central to Smith's vision for sympathy. At the same time, they hardly exhaust the full range of questions to which he envisioned sympathy as a response. For in addition to these concerns, *The Theory of Moral Sentiments* also presents sympathy as a key element in Smith's core project as a normative ethicist: namely to provide individual agents with resources to overcome natural self-partiality and the destructive egocentrism that follows from it.[6] Smith himself calls this the "hardest of all the lessons of morality" (TMS 3.3.8) – namely the learning of the illegitimacy of that "unjust preference" that leads one afflicted by it to forget that in fact "he is no better than his neighbour" (TMS 3.3.6) and is in truth "but one of the multitude, in no respect better than any other in it" (TMS 3.3.4; see also 2.2.2.1, 6.2.2.2). In so insisting on the need to overcome self-preference and to realize our essential equality with others, Smith clearly reveals his allegiance to the practical project described by the Enlightenment thinkers profiled in the body of this book, as well as the contemporary theorists of love examined in its introductory chapter. Our challenge in the present chapter is to demonstrate the way in which Smith specifically presents sympathy as the best available means for advancing this practical project in the absence of recourse to the traditional concept of other-directed love grounded in transcendence.

SMITH'S CRITIQUE OF *EROS*: PARTICULARITY AND UNIVERSALITY

Smith's "critique" of love is a prominent element of his ethics. We put "critique" in scare quotes from the start because, as will become clear, his theory of love contains in it several positive elements as well as several more conventionally critical elements. But that these critical elements are central to his views on love is beyond doubt. They are especially prominent in *The Theory of Moral Sentiments* but are in fact evident across his corpus – beginning with his very first publication, the 1756 *Letter to the Edinburgh Review.* The *Letter* has been recently rediscovered as a valuable window onto Smith's early engagement with Rousseau and French sources more generally.[7] Yet the *Letter* also sets the tone for much of his later treatment of love. Thus in the course of commending the *Encyclopédie* of Diderot and d'Alembert – whose fifth volume had recently been published and for which Smith otherwise had only praise – the *Letter* cautions that not all its contributions were "equal," as its editors "seem to have inserted some articles which might have been left out, and of which the insertion can serve only to throw a ridicule upon a work calculated for the propagation of every sort of useful knowledge."[8] Smith in fact names only one such article: the Abbé Yvon's "AMOUR," which, he says, "will tend little to the edification either of the learned or unlearned reader, and might, one should think, have been omitted" and replaced by pieces of "more consequence" (LER 7). In fact "AMOUR" was generally recognized in its time as quite significant, and its treatment of love parallels several of Smith's own claims.[9] Yet Smith nevertheless singles it out, and his decision to do so is important insofar as it signals a broader pattern that would emerge in his later ethics. For here too Smith often describes love as out of place in both the world in which he lives and the world his moral theory envisions; thus in a set of condemnatory observations he insists expressions of love "appear ridiculous," are "always laughed at," are characterized by "grossness," and always strike us as "indecent" (TMS 1.2.2.1–2 and 1.2.1.2; cf. LJA iii.21 and LJB 103).

But what exactly is wrong with love – if we can even speak that way – on Smith's view? Several conjectural explanations for his seeming hostility might be ventured, ranging from his attitudes to masculinity and effeminacy to his skepticism toward the value of the classical ideal of erotic philosophical excellence.[10] Grounds for psychobiographical conjectures are also not wanting; the thin records of Smith's seemingly celibate life would seem to testify to a singularly unerotic existence, and his paean to his deceased mother – "a person who certainly loved me more than any other person ever did or ever will love me; and whom I certainly loved and respected more than I ever shall either love or respect any other person" (CAS 237) – are easy fodder for cynics.[11] But for all this there is yet an important substantive claim at the heart of Smith's critique of love. It is specifically that love – and especially erotic and romantic love – privileges the particular over the universal.

The main focus of Smith's treatment of *eros* is the fact that it is grounded in the particular. Smith begins his critique of *eros* on this front by distinguishing his own view from a familiar claim from which he means to distance himself: namely that the indecency of sexuality owes to the fact that its are "the passions which we share in common with the brutes," and which, lacking "the characteristical qualities of human nature," are "upon that account beneath its dignity." Smith associates this claim with "some ancient philosophers" and dismisses it, suggesting that the reason for "our aversion for all the appetites which take their origin from the body" in fact lies elsewhere. After all, he insists (anticipating, as he often does, later discoveries in evolutionary biology and experimental economics) that in fact several passions "which we share in common with the brutes, such as resentment, natural affection, even gratitude ... do not, upon that account, appear to be so brutal."[12] What makes *eros* problematic then is not its brutishness but its exclusivity: "the true cause of the peculiar disgust which we conceive for the appetites of the body when we see them in other men, is that we cannot enter into them" (TMS 1.2.1.3). As Smith makes clear, it is precisely from the perspective of "a third person" that love is laughable; however enthralling love may be for lovers, to those who stand outside and "cannot enter into it," it is "ridiculous" at best and repugnant at worst (TMS 1.2.2.1).[13]

Now, that Smith's critique of *eros* is founded upon the claim that it privileges the particular over the universal has been well established by those who have called attention to his "heavy emphasis on the epistemic and moral priority of particulars and individuals" and its uneasy relation to "the tendency towards 'universalism' " that is also to be found in his account.[14] Such studies have also helpfully noted his concerns regarding "the danger of excluding impartial spectators," and especially his fear that such exclusions distinguish *eros* as "outside the social web, inaccessible to sympathy, perhaps even antisocial."[15] In so doing, these studies have helpfully brought to the foreground the crucial tension between the partiality inherent in love and the impartiality necessary for judgment. But at least three other points can, I think, usefully be added here. The first concerns what we mean when we say that it is the "particularity" of *eros* that renders it problematic. Smith comes to his study of *eros* with a set of assumptions that stand in diametric opposition to the promise that Diotima means to extend to us. Where Diotima envisions an ascent from particular beautiful bodies to the beautiful itself, Smith seems to assume that *eros* is and must always be limited to the first stage, that of focus on a particular individual. Further, *eros* is doubly particular in Smith's account: first, *eros* is particular insofar as it is necessarily experienced by a single particular individual (that is, it is *felt by a particular agent* whose feelings cannot be replicated or recreated by a spectator); second, *eros* is particular insofar as it is necessarily directed to a single particular individual (that is, it is *felt for a particular individual* for whom a spectator cannot replicate or recreate such a feeling). Clarifying these two senses of "particularity" thus helps to establish both what Smith finds so troubling in *eros*, as well as what he hopes to find elsewhere. In short, where *eros* is necessarily felt *by one and for one*, what Smith seeks is a sentiment that can be felt *by all and for all*.

A second element of Smith's focus on particularity that deserves further attention concerns the *reasons* for his privileging the particular over the universal. These lie in his epistemological commitments and their implications for his ethics. Two accounts of these commitments and their implications are familiar today. One suggests that Smith's skepticism toward universal benevolence is the product of our epistemic and psychological predilection to privilege the local over the distant.[16] A second emphasizes the role of Humean association in Smith's epistemology, arguing for the centrality of the imagination in both practical and philosophical life.[17] Each of these views is of course in some crucial sense clearly right. Yet neither captures the whole of Smith's conception of epistemology's relations to ethics. To see this, it is necessary to examine Smith's conception of sensation and perception – an aspect of his system that remains surprisingly understudied given his ubiquitous use of the terminology of sensation and perception and the fact that Smith dedicated one of his few properly "philosophical" essays entirely to this question.[18] Space doesn't permit an investigation of this here, except to say that emphasis on particularity is hardly an idiosyncratic element of Smith's views on love and affection, but rather is central to an epistemology of sensation that privileges "immediate" over "remote" effects and the intensity of primary over "secondary" passions (TMS 1.2.3.4, 1.2.2.4).

A third element of Smith's focus on particularity that deserves attention is how he proposes to *remedy* this privileging of particularity. Smith's claims on this front come in his shift from "the passions which take their origin from the body" (TMS 1.2.1) to those "which take their origin from a particular turn or habit of the imagination" (TMS 1.2.2). In so doing, Smith shifts his focus to two types of love of greater accessibility to third parties: familial love and romantic love as portrayed in both dramatic and literary works. Each of these is felt more by the imagination than by the body, and it is this, he insists, that renders them accessible to and inclusive of spectators. Smith makes this clear in his account of why "though we do not properly enter into the attachment of the lover, we readily go along with those expectations of romantic happiness which he derives from it":

> Though we feel no proper sympathy with an attachment of this kind, though we never approach even in imagination towards conceiving a passion for that particular person, yet as we either have conceived, or may be disposed to conceive, passions of the same kind, we readily enter into those high hopes of happiness which are proposed from its gratification, as well as into that exquisite distress which is feared from its disappointment. It interests us not as a passion, but as a situation that gives occasion to other passions which interest us. (TMS 1.2.2.2)

Contextualizing love – that is, adding a narrative that connects discrete expressions and objects of love to universal human concerns – translates love into a language intelligible to the imagination. This shifts the focus from particulars to generals, thereby providing a point of entry for sympathetic spectators who would otherwise be excluded. Setting such passions on the stage and the page is an especially useful means of allowing the spectator to access them; hence Smith's repeated praises of various love poets and romance novelists and playwrights (praises that would be very odd indeed were Smith merely a critic of love).[19] And these are not the only sites for the translation of love into sympathy; Smith is of course acutely sensitive to the theatricality of everyday life, and even when he describes such a commonplace as the happy family, his account gives prominent emphasis to how we feel when we see such: "With what pleasure do we look upon a family, through the whole of which reign mutual love and esteem ... How uneasy are we made when we go into a house in which jarring contention sets one half of those who dwell in it against the other"? (TMS 1.2.4.2)

In this sense, romantic and familial love aim to remedy the particularity and exclusivity of strictly physical *eros*. But that this remedy is insufficient as a means of fully overcoming partiality is clear; Smith himself insists that "even of the passions derived from the imagination, those which take their origin from a peculiar turn or habit it has acquired, though they may be acknowledged to be perfectly natural, are, however, but little sympathized with" (TMS 1.2.2.1). While imagination can help move us beyond particularity, insofar as the imagination is itself shaped by its own "peculiar turn or habit," it yet retains a particularity that awaits a fuller and very different resolution.

FROM *EROS* TO *AGAPE*: SMITH ON
CHRISTIAN LOVE

Smith's account of *eros* thus defines a problem. *Eros* establishes power-ful bonds between particular individuals, yet such bonds are by nature exclusionary; the erotic bond that connects one to another necessarily shuts out all others. As a theorist of both moral psychology and political order, Smith's task is then to define some substitute capable of retaining the benefits of that *eros* that connects selves to others, while also mitigat-ing the exclusionary propensities seemingly endemic to *eros* itself.[20]

   It is tempting at this point to turn to Smith's account of sympathy. As others have shown, Smith's turn to sympathy is itself the consequence of his project to find a "demotic" alternative to the particularity and exclu-sivity of *eros*.[21] Yet we do Smith a disservice, I think, if we turn directly to sympathy at this point. For Smith himself entertained another, dif-ferent alternative to the particularity of *eros*: namely the universal love of Christian charity. Unfortunately, Smith's engagement with charity has been almost wholly neglected.[22] Yet it demands our attention for two reasons: first for what it reveals of Smith's views on religion; and second for the light it sheds on how he understood the specific questions that sympathy is meant to answer.

   Our treatment of Smith's conception of Christian love begins with a crucial, though so far as I know heretofore unnoticed fact: namely that every one of Smith's explicit references to Christianity in *The Theory of Moral Sentiments* focuses on love. To be sure: in several other passages Smith comments quite critically on aspects of various confessional tradi-tions from Quakerism to Catholicism, and he is also often taken to allude to various Christian dogmas at certain places. Yet however this may be, we can say with certainty that in *The Theory of Moral Sentiments* Smith's explicit engagement with Christianity is limited to three passages, the stated aim of each of which is to present the "great law" or core "pre-cept" of Christianity in the terms of the Sermon on the Mount. Thus in his first and best-known reference, Smith notes that "as to love our neigh-bour as we love ourselves is the great law of Christianity, so it is the great precept of nature to love ourselves only as we love our neighbour, or what comes to the same thing, as our neighbour is capable of loving us" (TMS 1.1.5.5). In his second reference he argues "that the sense of duty should be the sole principle of our conduct, is no where the precept of Christianity," Christianity being rather "a religion in which, as it is the first precept to love the Lord our God with all our heart, with all our soul, and with all our strength, so it is the second to love our neighbour as we love ourselves" (TMS 3.6.1). In his third reference Smith describes the position "much esteemed by many ancient fathers of the Christian church" and also embraced by numerous post-Reformation divines: namely that "benevolence or love was the sole principle of action" of God, and that it is "by actions of charity and love only that we could imitate, as became us, the conduct of God" (TMS 7.2.3.2–3).

Smith's texts have been repeatedly flogged for insights into what they might reveal of the place of religion in his theory as well as for what they might reveal of his own religion or irreligion.[23] Yet one wonders whether such readings might not sometimes miss the forest for the trees. It is hard not to be struck by the fact that neither studies of Smith's religion nor studies of his views on love have noted that all three passages on Christianity in *The Theory of Moral Sentiments* are solely and exclusively concerned with love. Appreciating this fact and its larger implication – namely that Smith consistently viewed religion through the lens of morality[24] – may do much to move discussions of his religion beyond now familiar debates over his thoughts on providence and atonement, and also do much to recenter our focus on what is genuinely novel and philosophically significant in his treatment of religion – namely his theory of the "natural principles of religion" (TMS 3.5.13). Saving this for another occasion, I want to focus here on a second benefit of attending to Smith's engagement with Christian love: namely that doing so can help clarify exactly what he thought could and could not be expected from sympathy.

We begin on this front with the third of the three passages cited previously. The passage is to be found in the chapter dedicated to "those systems which make virtue consist in Benevolence" (TMS 7.2.3). As in the two other chapters dedicated to the question of 'wherein virtue consists' (see TMS 7.1.2), Smith examines both modern systems – here represented by the Cambridge Platonists and his teacher Hutcheson – and ancient systems – here represented by "those philosophers who, about and after the age of Augustus, called themselves Eclectics, who pretended to follow chiefly the opinions of Plato and Pythagoras," and who "upon that account are commonly known by the name of the later Platonists" (TMS 7.2.3.1). A number of conjectures have been put forth concerning exactly who Smith had in mind here.[25] Yet it seems evident that in referencing the Eclectics, he had in mind the Alexandrine school from Potamon to Hypatia that flourished from the first to the fourth century AD, and that was the explicit subject of several prominent eighteenth-century studies of Eclecticism, including those to be found in the *Encyclopédie* and in

Hutcheson's brief history of philosophy (each of which were likely well known to Smith).[26] In any case, our difficulties at identifying Smith's target may explain why the substantive significance of his treatment of the Eclectics has been underemphasized – a treatment that focuses precisely on their concept of love.

Smith's treatment of Eclecticism begins with a statement of its foundational claims: first, "in the divine nature, according to these authors, benevolence or love was the sole principle of action, and directed the exertion of all the other attributes," and second, "the whole perfection and virtue of the human mind consisted in some resemblance or participation of the divine perfections, and, consequently, in being filled with the same principle of benevolence and love which influenced all the actions of the Deity." With this in place Smith lays out the key claim of the Eclectics with regard to the nature and value of love:

The actions of men which flowed from this motive were alone truly praise-worthy, or could claim any merit in the sight of the Deity. It was by actions of charity and love only that we could imitate, as became us, the conduct of God, that we could express our humble and devout admiration of his infinite perfections, that by fostering in our own minds the same divine principle, we could bring our own affections to a greater resemblance with his holy attributes, and thereby become more proper objects of his love and esteem; till at last we arrived at that immediate converse and communication with the Deity to which it was the great object of this philosophy to raise us. (TMS 7.2.3.2)

Several aspects of this account are immediately striking. The first, noted already, is its focus on love (and indeed the ease with which Smith moves back and forth here between "love" and "benevolence").[27] A second striking element concerns Smith's understanding of the relationship between metaphysics and morality. His point of departure here is clearly an ontological claim concerning the nature of the divine – recognizable as *Deus caritas est* – yet Smith's focus here as elsewhere is moral rather than metaphysical. Smith indeed is willing to grant the ontological point without objection or elaboration; in a later line he simply concedes that "benevolence may, perhaps, be the sole principle of action in the Deity," and that "there are several, not improbable, arguments which tend to persuade us that it is so" (TMS 7.2.3.18). Yet the key point is that Smith's aim is not to evaluate the legitimacy of the metaphysical claim but to specify the ethical teaching that follows from it: in this case, that virtue consists in imitating divine benevolence. But perhaps the most striking element of the passage concerns its agreements with positions Smith elsewhere advances in his own name. On several fronts, Smith works along paths blazed, on his own account, by the Eclectics themselves: thus his claim that the Eclectics chiefly sought to define the "truly praise-worthy" and the "proper objects of love and esteem" deserves to be read along-side Smith's own accounts of merit (esp. TMS 2.1) and praiseworthiness (esp. TMS 3.2), and his insistence that the Eclectics aimed principally to encourage our "imitation" of God's "infinite perfections" can be usefully read alongside Smith's accounts of our efforts to imitate "absolute perfection" (see esp. TMS 1.1.5.9–10 and 6.3.23–25).

Yet for all these resonances between Smith's account of the Eclectic position and his own positions, it is their differences that most demand our attention. Two are especially important. The first concerns the "rigorism" of the Eclectics, to which Smith calls attention in his reminders that the Eclectics considered virtue to consist "only" in love "alone." In so doing, Smith suggests that the Eclectics suffer from the same reductive propensity as Mandeville, albeit from the other side (see TMS 7.2.4). But Smith's second concern is more crucial for our purposes. This concerns their differing views on the limits of our capacities and the implications of such limits on our capacity for transcendence. The key claim of Eclectic ethics, as presented by Smith, is that the "perfection and virtue of the human mind" consists "in some resemblance or participation of the divine perfections." But this is a claim Smith himself cannot support. Smith hardly denies that it is beneficial for us and perhaps even necessary for us to *pursue* perfection.[28] But where he and the Eclectics differ is that the Eclectics believe human beings are in fact capable of achieving perfection in practice – a perfection that consists specifically in a self-transcendence that affords access to a higher realm dedicated to "that immediate converse and communication with the Deity to which it was the great object of this philosophy to raise us" (TMS 7.2.3.2). Smith, however, doubts that transcendence of this sort is either possible or desirable. His strident castigations in *The Theory of Moral Sentiments* of the vanity and insanity of Caesar, Alexander, and Socrates – all of whom are explicitly described as having believed themselves to have been in direct communication with the divine (TMS 6.3.28) – clearly attest to his skepticism on this front. And herein lies Smith's key objection to Eclectic ethics. Like Caesar, Alexander, and Socrates, the Eclectics err in confusing our duty to strive to "approximate" perfection with the mistaken belief that such transcendent perfection can be attained in practice.[29]

The Eclectic conception of love thus poses a specific challenge for Smith: for all its substantive attractions, ultimately it strikes him as epistemically illegitimate insofar as it requires access to a transcendent realm beyond our capacity to enter directly. This becomes even more evident in what follows. After finishing with the Eclectics, Smith turns to "many ancient fathers of the Christian church" and "several divines of the most eminent piety and learning" who further developed the Eclectic position, naming Ralph Cudworth, Henry More, and John Smith (TMS 7.2.3.3). That Smith identifies these Cambridge Platonists as the preeminent modern theorists of love and benevolence is of interest in itself; at the very least it suggests that his own engagement with the Cambridge Platonists was directed less to the texts for which they are remembered today than to such largely forgotten texts as More's *Essay on Disinterested Love* (which Smith likely knew through its publication in Glasgow by the Foulis Press in 1756) and John Smith's *Select Discourses* (esp. 5.2–4).[30] Yet for the present purposes, Smith's engagement with the Cambridge Platonists is less crucial than his more substantive and extended engagement with Hutcheson, the thinker he calls "undoubtedly, beyond all comparison, the most acute, the most distinct, the most philosophical" of the champions of love and benevolence (TMS 7.2.3.3).[31]

Smith's treatment of Hutcheson follows the same route as his treatment of Eclecticism: namely sympathy toward his insistence on the primacy of benevolence and skepticism toward the epistemic assumptions on which his argument for this primacy is founded. Smith himself attests to his agreement with Hutcheson on the former front, reminding us at the start of 7.2.3.4 that he himself "observed already" in his own name that benevolence pleases by "a double sympathy" (e.g., TMS 1.2.4.1, 2.1.5.2–3); that it is always the "proper object of reward" (e.g., TMS 2.1.1.1, 2.1.4.2); and that even its weaknesses are agreeable and forgivable (e.g., TMS 1.2.4.3). But most importantly, Smith describes Hutcheson as believing that

> In directing all our actions to promote the greatest possible good, in submitting all inferior affections to the desire of the general happiness of mankind, in regarding one's self but as one of the many, whose prosperity was to be pursued no further than it was consistent with, or conducive to that of the whole, consisted the perfection of virtue. (TMS 7.2.3.11)

Smith's sympathy with this claim is to some degree suggested in his own language; his thrice-repeated claim, as quoted in the introductory section of this chapter, that we must come to regard ourselves as "but one of the multitude" (TMS 2.2.2.1, 3.3.4, 6.2.2.2), seems to be directly drawn from the terms of his overview of Hutcheson's ethics – an overview that goes on to emphasize our need to "check the injustice of self-love" and also "nourish and support in the human heart the noblest and the most agreeable of all affections" (TMS 7.2.3.14).

Yet even if Smith shares Hutcheson's concern to check selfishness, he cannot bring himself to approve of Hutcheson's route to such ends. First, like the Eclectics, Hutcheson suffers from a fatal rigorism, evident in his claim that virtue consists in pure, disinterested benevolence "alone," without corruption by any "baser alloy" (TMS 7.2.3.6).[32] Second, and again like the Eclectics, Hutcheson's justification of this claim rests on grounds Smith rejects. In particular, Hutcheson takes as foundational our desire for "the general happiness of mankind" and the "prosperity of the whole." Smith himself, however, is prone to insist that man is "so imperfect a creature," one who often acts on the basis of "many other motives" (TMS 7.2.3.18). While Hutcheson's vision of universal charity may be substantively attractive, Smith counters that it is better suited to the infinite capacities of divine beings rather than limited men.

Smith's treatments of the theories of agapic love set forth by the Eclectics and by Hutcheson both come to the same conclusion: admiration for their vision of love, and skepticism toward the human capacity to realize the transcendence that such a love would require. Smith, we might say, seems divided between his admiration for this vision of the ethical ideal and his sober realization of the limits of our practical capacity to realize it. This same orientation characterizes another of his treatments of love elsewhere that likewise deserves more careful attention than it has received. The passage has hardly been overlooked; indeed it is often marshaled as evidence of Smith's seeming preference for negative justice over benevolence as a foundational social principle.[33] But Smith's intentions here are more complex, and are perhaps fully intelligible only when we examine them in light of his attitudes toward *agape* as developed in the passages on the Eclectics and on Hutcheson examined earlier.

The passage in question begins with a portrait of the best society:

Man, who can subsist only in society, was fitted by nature to that situation for which he was made. All the members of human society stand in need of each others assistance, and are likewise exposed to mutual injuries. Where the necessary assistance is reciprocally afforded from love, from gratitude, from friendship, and esteem, the society flourishes and is happy. All the different members of it are bound together by the agreeable bands of love and affection, and are, as it were, drawn to one common centre of mutual good offices. (TMS 2.2.3.1)

Three aspects of this portrait deserve notice: first, Smith's aim here is to present his vision of the best society (or in his words the society that "flourishes and is happy"); second, the happiness and flourishing of such a society is guaranteed chiefly by its capacity to "bind together" its members; and third, the vehicle for these bonds is "love and affection," and indeed a decidedly universal love and affection that binds "all the different members" of a society to "one common centre." This third point itself replicates a point that Smith elsewhere makes in his own name: namely that "the affections which tend to unite men in society" are "humanity, kindness, natural affection, friendship, esteem," which are to be distinguished from those "affections which drive men from each other, and which tend, as it were, to break the bands of human society" (TMS 6.3.15–16). But compare this to the alternative that Smith describes in the next paragraph:

> But though the necessary assistance should not be afforded from such generous and disinterested motives, though among the different members of the society there should be no mutual love and affection, the society, though less happy and agreeable, will not necessarily be dissolved. Society may subsist among different men, as among different merchants, from a sense of its utility, without any mutual love or affection; and though no man in it should owe any obligation, or be bound in gratitude to any other, it may still be upheld by a mercenary exchange of good offices according to an agreed valuation. (TMS 2.2.3.2)

Here too three aspects demand immediate notice: first, that the society in which there is "no mutual love and affection" will be "less happy and agreeable"; second, the aim of such a society is considerably more utilitarian – in Smith's words, merely to "subsist" or be "upheld"; and third, the conditions of its subsistence are not social bonds but the mere "mercenary exchange of good offices."

Now, the challenge is to determine Smith's intentions in setting forth this contrast in the precise way he has. Until now it has largely been assumed that Smith's aim is to call for a wholesale shift from the loving to the merely just society; in this sense, the contrast is meant as a shift from starry idealism to hard-headed realism. But I want to propose a quite different reading: namely that Smith is making a much more limited claim here, and meant this contrast not as a call for a shift from love to justice but rather as a call for the improvement of the just or second-best society in a manner that replicates what is best in the genuinely flourishing and happy society, a society that he genuinely admires and values in the same way that he admires and values the love described by Hutcheson and the Eclectics. Put in the context of the modern theorists of love examined in this book's introduction, Smith's concern in this passage is not simply to jettison love for justice, but rather to point to a way by which justice and love might be reconciled via recovery of a kind of love capable of preempting the degeneration of liberal society into an order of merely atomistic and mercenary producers and exchangers.

The chief evidence for the conventional reading – that is, the view that Smith privileges negative justice over love – consists in the recognition of the congruence between his comments on the second-best society, built on a "mercenary exchange of good offices," and the society of the *Wealth of Nations* that is of course built on a system of market exchange to secure "those good offices which we stand in need of" (WN 1.2.2). This parallel is crucial and undeniable; Smith makes clear in his drafts of the passage in both his *Lectures on Jurisprudence* and an early draft of the *Wealth of Nations* that this society is itself built on bonds forged by a form of exchange for which "mere love is not sufficient" (LJA vi.44–45; ED 22–24). At the same time, this point demands caution on two fronts.

First, Smith's contrast between the ideal society and the second best society needs to be read in the context of his discussions of the relationship of the real and ideal that we have already had occasion to mention. In these, Smith's aim is not to call for any jettisoning of the concept of perfection. Instead his claim is that genuine improvement requires our concerted efforts to "approximate" the realization of the ideal through an improvement of the real in such a way that even if our efforts fall short of "absolute perfection" – and indeed must fall short – they yet constitute "a much nearer approximation towards perfection" than that which we may otherwise have achieved (TMS 1.1.5.8–10).[34] Smith seems to be developing a quite similar sort of argument here, and indeed the deflationary tone of his sketch of the second-best society coupled with the celebratory tone of his sketch of the best society suggests his deep awareness of the costs inherent in jettisoning the ideal for the real; the two, for Smith, are bound in a complex dialectic in which one demands the continually recognized presence of the other.

A second reason for caution emerges in Smith's development of these claims in the remainder of the chapter. Smith tends to be read as affirming the distinction, first set forth by Kames, concerning the "stricter obligation" we have to justice than to benevolence (TMS 2.2.1.5). Yet this time-honored reading demands caution. In the first place, Smith's aim here seems to be limited to a relatively noncontroversial insistence that all societies must take justice as a first principle insofar as no society can subsist without it. We thus do Smith a disservice if we take his emphasis on the lexical priority of justice given its simple indispensability to social order as a claim concerning its relative value as a moral principle. In addition, far from reaffirming Kames' distinction, Smith also challenges it in a subtle way by introducing an often-overlooked but crucial qualification. Kames' position, as restated by Smith, is that beneficence cannot be "extorted by force" among "equals" (TMS 2.2.1.7). But as we are then explicitly told, the state of equality to which Smith here refers is that which exists "naturally, and antecedent to the institution of civil government" – the state of nature, not civil society (TMS 2.2.1.7, 9). This has a radical if underappreciated implication: it is that however illegitimate commanding mutual good offices may be in a natural state of perfect equality, on Smith's view it may be entirely legitimate – even necessary – to do so in civil society, in which "a superior" may, "with universal approbation, oblige those under his jurisdiction to behave, in this respect, with a certain degree of propriety to one another." This has important implications for the recent debate over the nature of the role Smith envisions for that "civil magistrate" charged with the duty to "command mutual good offices to a certain degree" (TMS 2.2.1.8).[35] But for our purposes it is enough that this passage merely points away from a vision of Smith as a defender of crude selfishness, and gives us reason to take him at his word when he says nature "formed men for that mutual kindness, so necessary for their happiness" (TMS 6.2.1.19), and that even (perhaps especially) in liberal societies based on justice, Smith envisioned an important role for something like benevolence or love.

Taken collectively, Smith's several passages on Christianity, on the Eclectics, on Hutcheson, and on the flourishing society, attest to a sustained engagement with the Christian conception of love across *The Theory of Moral Sentiments*. In particular they attest to Smith's recognition of the benefits of this conception of love conceived as a means of mitigating the challenges posed by self-love. Furthermore, Smith finds this conception of love attractive insofar as it also provides a remedy for the specific shortcomings of *eros*. For where *eros* is necessarily felt *by one and for one*, the love described in the passages examined earlier is a love felt *by all and for all*. Yet for all these genuine attractions, Smith is hesitant to endorse this love in his own name. *Agape*, however substantively attractive it may be, simply asks more of us than our limited epistemic capacities allow us to achieve. In this sense, Smith's critique of *eros* and his consideration and ultimate rejection of *agape* together not only set the stage for sympathy but also define the two specific fronts on which sympathy must prove itself: first, as capable of extending to all and being experienced by all; and second, as suited to our epistemic capacities and limits.

FROM *EROS* AND *AGAPE* TO SYMPATHY

And with this we come to Smith's theory of sympathy. Smithean sympathy, as we have already had occasion to note, plays several discrete roles in his system. But for our purposes, two roles are especially important. First, sympathy provides the foundations for the universal social bond that *agape* also sought to establish, yet does so independently of *agape*'s extensive epistemic demands. Second, sympathy seeks to gratify certain longings of the self – longings not dissimilar to those that lie at the heart of *eros*. Taken together, in aspiring to fulfill these two aims, sympathy aims to remedy the shortcomings of *eros* and *agape* alike.

We begin with the first task, namely sympathy's role in promoting social bonds. Sympathy's utility on this front is presented in the course of one of Smith's most direct comparisons of sympathy and love. In concluding the chapter that begins with his comparison, examined earlier, of the society built on love and the society built on justice, Smith explicitly differentiates between "the general fellow-feeling which we have with every man merely because he is our fellow-creature" and "those exquisite sentiments which are commonly called love, esteem, and affection, by which we distinguish our particular friends and acquaintance" (TMS 2.2.3.10). At least two distinctions are at work here. First, sympathy seems to be felt much less intensely than love; one is a merely "general" feeling where the other is "exquisite." Second, love is limited to "particular" others with whom we have certain proximate connections, whereas sympathy is something "we have with every man" as a simple consequence of a recognition of our similarities as species members. Sympathy thus achieves a universality that other forms of love lack. But even more importantly, sympathy is universal not only in the sense that it is felt *for* every man, but also in the sense that it is felt *by* every man; hence Smith's repeated insistence that sympathy is felt by "every impartial spectator" and "every indifferent by-stander" and "every human heart" and "every reasonable man" and "every body who knows of it" (TMS 2.1.2.2–3). Sympathy's utility thus lies precisely in the fact that it is in principle capable of both universal extension and universal accessibility, in direct contrast to the particularity and exclusivity characteristic of *eros*.

Sympathy's contrast with *eros* is thus clear. But sympathy also has a second advantage, one that specifically contrasts with *agape*. For not only is sympathy, as we have seen, available to all, it is also freely available without any of the epistemic costs of *agape*. As Smith's foundational account of sympathy makes clear, sympathy is available to all those capable of both sensation and imagination – that is to say, to everyone (see, e.g., TMS 1.1.1.2). The advantages of a concept based on such minimal requirements become clear when compared to the more extensive requirements of love and universal benevolence. As Smith makes clear, "universal benevolence, how noble and generous soever, can be the source of no solid happiness to any man who is not thoroughly convinced that all the inhabitants of the universe...are under the immediate care and protection of that great, benevolent, and all-wise Being" (TMS 6.2.3.2). In the terms of our inquiry, an embrace of universal benevolence requires acceptance of theism, just as the Hutchesonian or Eclectic conception of agapic love is founded on acceptance of theism. Smith himself, in contrast, consistently resists efforts to ground his foundational conceptions in theological or cosmological commitments. His preference for sympathy over love, like other of his foundational concepts, is thus founded precisely on his belief that it is "much more suitable to the weakness of his powers, and to the narrowness of his comprehension" (TMS 6.2.3.6).

Sympathy's advantages over traditional conceptions of love thus consist in its greater universality and in its greater accessibility. But what exactly does sympathy get us? In short: sympathy establishes a foundation for a social bond that minimizes and manages self-love without requiring *agape*'s extensive commitments. And here the contrast with *agape* is crucial in a second way as well. It is tempting to want to find in sympathy, insofar as it specifically works to mitigate our egocentrism and to encourage greater sensitivity to the conditions of others, the foundation for a thick social bond – a bond that might enable otherwise discrete individuals and groups to transcend their deepest differences and the social divides that separate them. If so, sympathy would in fact constitute a remarkable resource in the effort to transcend the social costs of group prejudices and the class divisions that material inequality tends to reify in advanced societies. Yet on this front, what demands notice is that Smith not only conspicuously fails to endorse sympathy as a means to such ends, but also, and in sharp contrast, emphasizes sympathy's manifest incapacity on this front.

In presenting this side of sympathy, Smith makes clear the degree to which *agape* and sympathy differ. Central to *agape* is of course love for the poor; thus not only does Jesus in the Gospels repeatedly invoke our specific duties to the poor but also proclaims that "as ye have done it unto one of the least of these my brethren, ye have done it unto me" – in the terms of our inquiry, love of the poor simply *is* love of the divine.[36] But sympathy encourages a quite different, indeed diametrically opposed, attitude toward the poor. Far from encouraging active relief of their misery, or even a basic identification with their suffering, sympathy does little to mitigate the propensity of ordinary agents in fact to "despise, or, at least, to neglect persons of poor and mean condition" (TMS 1.3.3.1). Smith further develops this idea in one of his most striking set pieces, namely the comparison of our attitudes to the rich man and the poor man that he deploys to account for "the origin of ambition" and "the distinction of ranks" (TMS 1.3.2). The rich man, it is here explained, expects that his riches will "naturally draw upon him the attention of the world," and that the sympathetic will always be "disposed to go along with him in all those agreeable emotions" that his comfortable circumstances afford. The poor man, however, can feel only shame when he thinks of how others see him, knowing that he can expect "scarce any fellow-feeling with the misery and distress which he suffers," and that "if the extremity of his distress forces them to look at him, it is only to spurn so disagreeable an object from among them" (TMS 1.3.2.1). All of this serves to reaffirm Smith's fundamental suspicion that in fact "men, though naturally sympathetic, feel so little for another, with whom they have no particular connexion, in comparison of what they feel for themselves" (TMS 2.2.3.4). Far from the champion of our natural and intimate sensitivity to the plights of others, Smith thus presents himself here rather as a phenomenologist of our "dull sensibility to the afflictions of others" (TMS 1.3.1.13).

What are we to make of this? It would be tragically wrong to suggest on the basis of such remarks that Smith was somehow indifferent to the plight of the poor; as we now appreciate better than ever, thanks to much excellent recent scholarship, the normative impetus behind Smith's political economy is a concern for alleviating the conditions of the least well-off.[37] What we should rather take from these claims about the relationship of sympathy to poverty is that sympathy is not the remedy that Smith envisions to narrow the emotional divide of the rich from the poor and enable individuals occupying such differing social positions to better identify with each other. If anything, sympathy exacerbates this gap insofar as it leads those in the middle to avert their gaze from the poor and to focus their attention instead on the rich. In this sense, sympathy, so far from promoting the project of *agape*, seems to work at cross-purposes with it. But what then does sympathy in fact do, and how and why ought it be regarded as a "moral sentiment" – and indeed the foundation of a "theory of moral sentiments" – if its proper function is not in fact to create social bonds that transcend the divides of inequality?

Herein lies our core claim. Sympathy does play a key social role for Smith. But this role consists not in serving as a foundation for the sorts of thick bonds of one to another that were central to the traditional conception of love, but rather in ensuring that the rather minimal bonds that hold a liberal society together are not, as Smith says, "broke asunder" (TMS 2.2.3.3). In this sense, sympathy's chief social purpose is to mitigate the main threat to these minimal bonds – a threat that Smith himself squarely identifies as self-love. In this vein, Smith begins his key discussion of sympathy's relationship to justice by calling attention to what he sees as the chief threat to the security and stability of the just society: namely "the natural preference which every man has for his happiness above that of other people." In so insisting, it is clearly not Smith's aim to pass judgment on this disposition; as is elsewhere made clear, a natural propensity to prefer self to others, when properly moderated and regulated, is the legitimate foundation of a well-functioning economic order. In contrast, what Smith means to show here is that the same disposition that can work to such obvious material benefit can also serve as a source of both moral corruption and political destabilization if left unregulated. Thus while it might be true

that every individual, in his own breast, naturally prefers himself to all mankind, yet he dares not look mankind in the face, and avow that he acts according to this principle. He feels that in this preference they can never go along with him, and that how natural soever it may be to him, it must always appear excessive and extravagant to them. When he views himself in the light in which he is conscious that others will view him, he sees that to them he is but one of the multitude in no respect better than any other in it. If he would act so as that the impartial specta-tor may enter into the principles of his conduct, which is what of all things he has the greatest desire to do, he must, upon this, as upon all other occasions, humble the arrogance of his self-love, and bring it down to something which other men can go along with. (TMS 2.2.2.1)

Smith here outlines a primary ethical task for the citizen of a liberal soci-ety: namely the mitigation of the natural propensity to self-preference that so often blinds us to our essential equality with others. But Smith here also explains the means by which this end is to be reached: namely by the self-loving agent's willing decision to bring down his self-love "to something which other men can go along with." And with this, we can see Smith's hope for sympathy: namely that the natural desire for the esteem and approval of others inherent to sympathetic beings will encourage them to strive to overcome their natural self-preference. In this sense, sympathy plays a key role in mitigating self-love and thereby advancing the project defined by an otherwise unavailable *agape*.[38]

Sympathy's social task, we might thus conclude, is not to establish the thick bonds of identification characteristic of active love, but to achieve something more minimal and manageable: namely the mitigation of self-love in such a way that we render our natural self-preference non-threatening to others. Put differently – and hopefully in a way authentic to both Smith's intentions as well as to the basic terms of the contemporary debate – sympathy properly understood leads us not to love or beneficence but to justice. In this sense, the social force of sympathy lies in the fact that the "sympathetic resentment" and "sympathetic indignation" that we feel when we see innocent others suffering at the hands of the guilty leads us to endorse their efforts to punish such offenders and thereby restore conditions of both equity and social stability (see, e.g., TMS 2.1.2.5 and 2.1.5.6).[39]

Sympathy thus plays a key role in helping us to overcome our natural self-preference and to establish a set of indispensible, if minimal, bonds with others. At the same time, sympathy's utility is not merely social. In addition to remedying the social challenges posed by self-love, sympathy also seeks to gratify a more personal need. Now, that Smith conceived of human beings as decidedly needy is well known to students of his economics; the entire departure point of the *Wealth of Nations* is of course Smith's insistence that we are dependent on others beyond ourselves for the production of those goods necessary for our physical survival (WN 1.1.11, 1.2.2). But Smith's insistence on our neediness also has another dimension. On his account of human nature, the external goods necessary for our physical survival are only one sort of need among many. Beyond these material needs, Smith calls attention to our love needs; hence his frequent insistences that "man naturally desires, not only to be loved, but to be lovely; or to be that thing which is the natural and proper object of love," that "there is a satisfaction in the consciousness of being loved, which, to a person of delicacy and sensibility, is of more importance to happiness, than all the advantage which he can expect to derive from it," that "the chief part of human happiness arises from the consciousness of being beloved," that foremost among "all those sentiments for which we have by nature the strongest desire" is in fact "the love, the gratitude, the admiration of mankind," and that "the great object of our ambition" is "to be beloved by our brethren" (TMS 3.2.1, 1.2.4.1, 1.2.5.1, 3.4.7, 6.2.1.19; cf. 3.1.7). Smith's striking reiterations of this claim suggest that so far from thinking that we can somehow do without love, he in fact regarded our love-needs as a principal source of motivation.

And herein lies the crux of the issue on this front. Earlier we suggested that Smith regarded the traditional conception of love as in some sense unavailable to us in light of both our epistemic limits and the conditions of our society, and especially its propensity to privilege mercenary exchange of useful goods over free exchange of love. Yet if so, we would seem to be in a bind, caught between our natural needs and the limits of both our epistemic natures and the society in which we find ourselves. How then are we to bridge this divide? It is here that sympathy plays one of its most important roles. A central feature of Smith's account of sympathy concerns its role in the promotion and preservation of our tranquility; thus his prominent emphasis on "the healing consolation of sympathy" which in our "greatest and most dreadful distress" afford us the "most healing balsam" (TMS 1.1.2.5, 2.2.2.3, 3.2.17). In this sense sympathy plays a role akin to that envisioned by Aristophanes in *Symposium* for love: sympathy, that is, heals the wounds characteristic of what Smith calls our "human" side and consciously distinguishes from our "divine" side (TMS 3.2.32).[40] Put slightly differently, the sympathy of spectators is something for which a person principally concerned "passionately desires" and indeed "longs," and it is only the actual and conscious possession of such sympathy that can satisfy our natural and anxious desires for such (TMS 1.1.4.7). And in this respect Smith goes farther than he is sometimes taken to have gone. In his excellent study of Smith's ethics, Gilbert Harman notes that "for Smith the key point is that sympathy is desirable. Not only do spectators want to be able to sympathize with agents, but agents also want the sympathy of spectators."[41] Yet Smith in truth goes even further. Sympathy is not merely desirable, but needful; sympathy is not merely a supererogatory concern but rather reflective of our deepest needs and longings.

This key fact leads us to a final observation: namely that our deep need for sympathy in turn serves as a powerful motivating force of our action. This capacity of sympathy to serve as a principle of agent motivation has been recently restated as a challenge to a general scholarly consensus.[42] For some time, and at least since its presentation by the editors of the Glasgow edition, sympathy has tended to be seen as an element of Smith's theory of judgment rather than an other-directed sentiment akin to pity or compassion or benevolence.[43] Now, as a response to *Das Adam Smith Problem* – as it was when this claim was proposed by Walther Eckstein in the textual apparatus of his 1926 German translation – this view is quite beneficial and indeed has done much to recover the sophistication of Smith's account of judgment. Yet the claim seems to have outlived its usefulness at this point, and further reiterating it in an effort to tack away from now-discredited errors may well encourage a different error, namely obscuring Smith's emphasis on sympathy's actual motivational force. This motivational force has been recently shown to be an integral element of Smith's account of commercial activity, especially evident in Smith's claim that our efforts to better our conditions are driven by our desire "to be taken notice of with sympathy, complacency and approba-tion," and that it is "of such mighty importance" for men to "stand in that situation which sets them most in view of general sympathy and atten-tion" (TMS 1.3.2.1, 1.3.2.8–9).[44] But in light of the role of sympathy in helping to overcome our self-love, and the role of sympathetic resentment in helping us to establish justice, it is clear that Smith regarded sympathy not merely as a motivating source in commercial pursuits but also in our most important activities as moral and political agents.

SYMPATHY: BENEFITS AND CHALLENGES

Smith himself understood that the shift from love to sympathy that this chapter has traced came with both specific benefits and potential limits. The benefits are by now mostly clear. To restate only two: on the level of the moral psychology of the individual, sympathy provides spectators with a relatively low-cost method of assuaging their own love needs and those of others. On a more specifically political level, sympathy offers a means by which a shared framework of social concern might arise, and specifically one capable of mitigating the destructive forms of self-concern without the extensive epistemic demands of traditional *agape*. As Smith would be the first to insist, these are remarkable advantages. Yet here, as elsewhere, Smith was characteristically sober, and forthrightly acknowledged both sympathy's specific limits, and indeed the challenges that this very shift from love to sympathy brings. We conclude by point-ing out two of these challenges.

The first concerns the implications of this shift for our moral psychol-ogy. As we have seen, a chief reason for Smith's admiration of sympathy is its simultaneous universal accessibility and its universal extension; sym-pathy, that is, can be felt by every human being and felt for every human being. At the same time, Smith knows that what is felt by "every" person is not always felt by any one of them "entirely." In explicating this claim,

Smith calls frequent and conspicuous attention to the gap in intensity between the sympathetic feeling of the spectator and the sentiment of the person principally concerned; hence his claim that a spectator's sympathy is always "weaker in degree" than what the person principally concerned feels (TMS 1.1.1.2), that "mankind, though naturally sympathetic, never conceive, for what has befallen another, that degree of passion which naturally animates the person principally concerned" (TMS 1.1.4.7), that our sympathy with pains "falls greatly short of what is naturally felt by the sufferer" (TMS 1.3.1.3), and that our sympathy with sorrow "always falls much more short" (TMS 1.3.1.8; cf. TMS 1.3.1.12).

These passages attest to Smith's sensitivity to a distinction between primary or "original" and secondary or "reflected" impressions derived from the senses, and his related claim that "all sympathetic passions" are "inferior to the original ones" owing to "general causes" (TMS 6.2.1.1, 1.2.3.1). But however valuable these claims may be for the insight they provide into Smith's epistemic commitments, they also have crucial implications for the shift from love to sympathy that we have sought to trace. One is especially important: it is that Smith himself recognizes that sympathy is not enough to fulfill with any degree of completeness the love needs that he takes to be natural to the human person. Thus however blithely Smith may at times insist that this sympathy shortfall is in fact of little concern because "all that is wanted and required" is merely that degree of sympathy sufficient for "the harmony of society," his equally forthright admission that a sufferer "longs for that relief which nothing can afford him but the entire concord of the affections of the spectator with his own" suggests that our sympathy needs are at once quite genuine and profoundly greater than that minimal degree of sympathy necessary for the preservation of social order as well as the minimal sympathy that spectators are capable of giving (TMS 1.1.4.7).

Sympathy thus seems to go an important part of the way toward helping us satisfy what Smith takes to be our natural love-needs. Yet in a crucial sense, it alone isn't enough. We are thus left wondering: what might we need to add to sympathy to get us all the way there? A similar question arises on a second front. As we have seen, sympathy's utility, in Smith's eyes, consists not simply in its capacity to gratify some degree of our love-needs, but also in its capacity to establish a foundation for social bonds capable of mitigating the socially destructive tendencies of excessive self-love. But here too we wonder: is sympathy alone sufficient to get us there?

Some insight is provided in one of the most important lines of the book. In the passage containing his first invocation of Christianity as a religion founded on love of neighbor, Smith observes,

> And hence it is, that to feel much for others and little for ourselves, that to restrain our selfish, and to indulge our benevolent affections, constitutes the perfection of human nature; and can alone produce among mankind that harmony of sentiments and passions in which consists their whole grace and propriety. As to love our neighbour as we love ourselves is the great law of Christianity, so it is the great precept of nature to love ourselves only as we love our neighbour, or what comes to the same thing, as our neighbour is capable of loving us. (TMS 1.1.5.5)

There is much in this passage that is striking; among its most striking (if least noted) claims is that the "perfection of human nature" is what "alone can produce among mankind that harmony of sentiments": a claim that would seem to call into question a consensus view that Smith's views on social order can and ought to be understood independently of his views on ethical self-perfection.[45] But leaving this for a separate occasion, what interests us here is Smith's claim that the perfection of our nature requires two specific and distinct operations: first we must come to "restrain our selfish" affections, and then we must "indulge our benevolent affections." What then enables us to fulfill these two tasks? Sympathy clearly plays a key role – but perhaps not the role that we might have assumed. As argued earlier, sympathy's aim is not to encourage us to "indulge our benevolent affections"; as Smith's account of our ordinary disposition toward the poor makes clear, we can expect little from sympathy on this front. Sympathy's contribution instead lies on the other side of the ledger – that is to say, in helping us "restrain our selfish" affections, by leading us to temper the pitch of our self-preference to the degree that others can enter into it.

Sympathy is thus responsible for half of the project of promoting perfection and thereby achieving social harmony, though not the half we might have expected. This leads to a question. If sympathy's main job is to restrain self-love, what, if not sympathy, will enable us to realize our benevolent affections? For this task, Smith suggests, we must go beyond sympathy and embrace the "virtue" that is described in the next paragraph as associated with "something uncommonly great and beautiful" (TMS 1.1.5.6). Now, what this virtue is would be the subject of a different project. For our purposes, sympathy, we can simply conclude, is in some radical sense not enough for Smith, insofar as it can neither fully satisfy our individual love needs, nor can it alone guarantee the perfection of human nature necessary for the harmony of society. And if that is correct, the effort to substitute sympathy for love may need to give way to an effort to demonstrate how the latter might be joined to the former.

NOTES

1 Particularly helpful recent studies on this front include Charles L. Griswold, Jr., *Adam Smith and the Virtues of Enlightenment* (Cambridge: Cambridge University Press, 1999); and Dennis Rasmussen, *The Problems and Promise of Commercial Society: Adam Smith's Response to Rousseau* (University Park: Penn State University Press, 2009). I have also sought to explore these issues in *Adam Smith and the Character of Virtue* (Cambridge: Cambridge University Press, 2009).

2 See especially Martha Nussbaum, *Love's Knowledge: Essays on Philosophy and Literature* (Oxford: Oxford University Press, 1990), 338–347; Douglas J. Den Uyl and Charles L. Griswold, Jr., "Adam Smith on Friendship and Love," *Review of Metaphysics* 49 (1996): 609–637; and Lauren Brubaker, "'A Particular Turn or Habit of the Imagination': Adam Smith on Love, Friendship, and Philosophy," in *Love and Friendship: Rethinking Politics and Affection in Modern Times*, ed. Eduardo Velasquez (Lanham, MD: Rowman and Littlefield, 2003), 229–262.

3 See, e.g., D. D. Raphael, *The Impartial Spectator: Adam Smith's Moral Philosophy* (Oxford: Clarendon Press, 2007), 134–135 (quote at 135); and Fonna Forman-Barzilai, *Adam Smith and the Circles of Sympathy* (Cambridge: Cambridge University Press, 2010), 12–14.

4 See especially Leonidas Montes, "*Das Adam Smith Problem*: Its Origins, The Stages of the Current Debate, and One Implication for Our Understanding of Sympathy," *Journal of the History of Economic Thought* 25 (2003): esp. 82–85, and Montes, *Adam Smith in Context* (London: Palgrave Macmillan, 2004), 45–55; see also Eric Schliesser's review of Montes and Raphael in *Ethics* 118 (2008): 569–575; and the response in Ian S. Ross, *The Life of Adam Smith*, 2nd ed. (Oxford: Oxford University Press, 2010), 478n.

5 For key studies of the role of Smithean sympathy in each of these processes, see respectively Michael Frazer, *The Enlightenment of Sympathy: Justice and the Moral Sentiments in the Eighteenth Century* (Oxford: Oxford University Press, 2010), 89–111; James Otteson, *Adam Smith's Marketplace of Life* (Cambridge: Cambridge University Press, 2002), esp. 13–64; and Pierre Force, *Self-Interest Before Adam Smith: A Genealogy of Economic Science* (Cambridge: Cambridge University Press, 2003), 42–47.

6 This chapter gives less attention to its subject's theory of self-love and ego-centrism than do the other three exegetical chapters of this work so as not to repeat claims I have made at length elsewhere (esp. *Adam Smith and the Character of Virtue*, 146–150, 187–201, and "Adam Smith on Living a Life," in *Adam Smith: His Life, Thought, and Legacy*, ed. Ryan Patrick Hanley (Princeton, NJ: Princeton University Press, 2016), 123–137.

7   On the aims of the *Letter*, see esp. Jeffrey Lomonaco, "Adam Smith's 'Letter to the Authors of the Edinburgh Review'," *Journal of the History of Ideas* 63 (2002): 659–676. Smith's debts to and engagement with Rousseau have been of interest to many recently; see, e.g., Rasmussen, *Problems and Promise of Commercial Society*; Hanley, *Smith and the Character of Virtue*, 24–52; and Charles L. Griswold, Jr., "Smith and Rousseau in Dialogue: Sympathy, *Pitié*, Spectatorship and Narrative," in *The Philosophy of Adam Smith*, ed. Vivienne Brown and Samuel Fleischacker (London: Routledge, 2010), 59–84.

8   On Smith's engagement with the *Encyclopédie*, see Robert Mankin, "Pins and Needles: Adam Smith and the Sources of the *Encyclopédie*," *Adam Smith Review* 4 (2008): 181–205; Neven Leddy, "Adam Smith's Critique of Enlightenment Epicureanism," in *Epicurus in the Enlightenment*, ed. Leddy and Avi S. Lifschitz (Oxford: Voltaire Foundation, 2009), 183–205; and Hanley, "Adam Smith and the *Encyclopédie*," *Adam Smith Review* 9 (2016).

9   These begin with the opening line of the entry: "*il entre ordinairement beaucoup de sympathie dans l'amour*" (*Encyclopédie* 1:367; at http://artflsrvo2 .uchicago.edu/cgi-bin/philologic/getobject.pl?c.o:1672.encyclopedie0513). Smith's decision to focus on "AMOUR" also places him within a larger related discourse; see esp. Leddy, "Smith's Critique of Enlightenment Epicureanism," 184.

10 On Smith's stances toward masculinity and femininity, see, e.g., Stewart Justman, *The Autonomous Male of Adam Smith* (Norman, OK: University of Oklahoma Press, 1993), esp. 14–15, 26; on his skepticism toward ancient philosophical excellence, see Den Uyl and Griswold, "Smith on Friendship and Love," 631–637.

11 On Smith's likely celibacy, see Ross, *Life of Adam Smith*, 227–228, 432; and Nicholas Phillipson, *Adam Smith: An Enlightened Life* (New Haven, CT: Yale University Press, 2010), 136.

12 For recent research in experimental economics that focuses on Smith's treatment of resentment and its significance as a wellspring of civilized social orders, see, for example, Vernon L. Smith, "Adam Smith and Experimental Economics: *Sentiments* to *Wealth*," in *Adam Smith: His Life, Thought, and Legacy*, ed. Ryan Patrcik Hanley, 262–280.

13 My analysis here parallels those of both Nussbaum and Brubaker; see Nussbaum, *Love's Knowledge*, 340–341; and *Upheavals of Thought: The Intelligence of Emotions* (Cambridge: Cambridge University Press, 2003), 464–465; and Brubaker, "'Particular Turn or Habit'," 234–235.

14 Den Uyl and Griswold, "Smith on Friendship and Love," 635. See also Nussbaum's helpful related claim that for Smith, "love is an intense response to perceptions of the particularity, and the particular high value, of another person's body and mind," in *Upheavals of Thought*, 465; see also *Love's Knowledge*, 342; and Brubaker, "'Particular Turn or Habit'," 235–236.

15 Brubaker, "'Particular Turn or Habit'," 242; and Den Uyl and Griswold, "Smith on Friendship and Love," 630; see cf. their claims that *eros* is "destructive of social concord" and "antisocial" insofar as it is "closed off to the spectator," and that love that "cancels the need for sympathy of a

spectator is inherently dangerous politically" insofar as it "privileges the perspective of the actor over that of the spectator, and thereby loses perspective
altogether," as opposed to "healthy or 'respectable' love" which "incorporates spectating" (629–632); and Nussbaum's claims that for Smith, "love's
exclusive character … makes him think it inimical to general social concern"
(*Upheavals of Thought*, 466), and that love's "mysteriousness and exclusivity" place it outside of the "network of mutual concern" necessary for morality (*Love's Knowledge*, 344–345).

16 See, e.g., Forman-Barzilai, *Smith and the Circles of Sympathy*, esp. 137–151.
17 See esp. Griswold, "Imagination: Morals, Science and Arts," in *The
Cambridge Companion to Adam Smith*, ed. Knud Haakonssen (Cambridge:
Cambridge University Press, 2006), 22–56. I examine this claim in greater
detail in "Scepticism and Naturalism in Adam Smith," in *Philosophy of
Adam Smith*, ed. Vivienne Brown and Samuel Fleischacker, 198–212.
18 For a recent and welcome attempt to begin to connect Smith's theories of
sensation and perception to his theories of sympathy and judgment, see Brian
Glenney, "Perception by Sympathy: Connecting Smith's *External Senses* to
his *Sentiments*," *Adam Smith Review* 8 (2015): 241–255.
19 Smith's poetic tastes lead him consistently to prefer the pastoral and tran-
quilizing; thus his celebrations of both Tibullus and Gray (TMS 1.2.2.2),
each consistent with his preference for serenity and quiet and the common
state of mind (LRBL 2.96 and 1.139), and perhaps also his emphasis on the
appropriateness of the diminutive in expressing love (LRBL 2.104). More
generally on the ways in which Smith thinks literature draws in the spectator
in "a kind of sympathetic reason-giving that is highly characteristic of morality," see Nussbaum, *Love's Knowledge*, 345–346.
20 In this sense, the shortcomings of *eros* are only fully seen from a specifically political perspective, if indeed expressions of *eros* are in fact capable of
regulation by spectatorial processes (as importantly argued by Brubaker; see
"'Particular Turn or Habit'," 260n13).
21 Den Uyl and Griswold begin their essay by calling attention to the fact that
"the centrality of sympathy to Adam Smith's *Theory of Moral Sentiments*
points to the centrality of love in the book," and later call attention to
"the 'demotic' view of sympathy that drives the theory" and the "tendency
towards universalism in the sense of the lowest common denominator"
("Smith on Friendship and Love," 609, 627–628).
22 See, e.g., Den Uyl and Griswold's representative claim that "Smith is virtu-
ally silent about Christian love," perhaps owing to his ostensible "hostility
to Christian theology and virtue theory" ("Smith on Friendship and Love,"
611n6).
23 The literature on Smith and religion is large and growing, but for an important
recent contribution which argues for the sincerity of Smith's religiosity, see
Chad Flanders, "Hume's Death and Smith's Philosophy," in *New Essays on
Adam Smith's Moral Philosophy* (Rochester, NY: RIT Press, 2012), 195–210.
I provide a reading of Smith's treatment of the moral psychology of religious
belief in "Adam Smith on the 'Natural Principles of Religion'," *Journal of
Scottish Philosophy* 13 (2015): 37–53.

24 See esp. Schliesser's discussion of Smith's "Spinozistic" approach to religion in his *Ethics* review (574–575).

25 I provide a fuller discussion of this issue in "Smith and the *Encyclopédie*," 224–226. For various attempts to identify the Eclectics, see, e.g., the editorial notes in the Glasgow Edition of TMS (300n1), in Haakonssen's edition (354n51); and in the impressive French translation of Michaël Biziou et al. (402n). Leddy also calls attention to Smith's likely familiarity with "ECLECTISME" ("Smith's Critique of Enlightenment Epicureanism," 184).

26 Diderot, "ECLECTISME," in *Encyclopédie*, vol. 5 (Paris, 1755); Hutcheson, "Dissertation on the Origin of Philosophy," in *Logic, Metaphysics, and the Natural Sociability of Mankind*, ed. James Moore and Michael Silverthorne (Indianapolis, IN: Liberty Fund, 2006), 7–8.

27 Smith tends to equate benevolence with good-will, in accord with its Latin roots (e.g., TMS 7.2.3.1). Smith does not, however, provide a direct account of the nature of the relationship of benevolence to love of the sort that, for example, Kant later does in his discussions of *Wohlwollen*, as examined in Chapter 5.

28 The question of the substantive role played by Smith's frequent invocations of the concept of perfection have much occupied recent scholars; I present my claims on the nature and significance of these invocations in "Smith and Virtue," in *The Oxford Handbook of Adam Smith*, ed. Christopher Berry, Maria Pia Paganelli, and Craig Smith (Oxford: Oxford University Press, 2013).

29 In this context, see especially the claim that "Adam Smith's error was the error, and the glory, of the Enlightenment, trying to liberate us from transcendence," and specifically from "transcendent love" [Deirdre McCloskey, "Adam Smith, The Last of the Former Virtue Ethicists," *History of Political Economy* 40 (2008): 65–68; quote at 68].

30 Indeed in each of these texts one finds substantive claims that closely parallel claims made in TMS; see esp. More's comments on the rigorism of Stillingfleet which "resolves all love into selflove" [*Essay on Disinterested Love* (Glasgow, 1756), 1–2, 5, 24]; and John Smith's accounts of the relationship of divine perfection to human imperfection [*Select Discourses* (Edinburgh, 1756), 106–107], and the relationship between metaphysics and morals (*Select Discourses*, 114).

31 This is not the only place Smith would profess his admiration for Hutcheson; Smith's reference at TMS 1.3.1.1 to that "late ingenious and subtile philosopher" is almost certainly to Hutcheson and not Butler, as the Glasgow edition suggests.

32 Smith, it should be said, is not entirely fair in ascribing to Hutcheson the position that "self-love was a principle which could never be virtuous in any degree or in any direction" (TMS 7.2.3.12–13).

33 Representative of several such arguments is the claim that for Smith "it is justice, above all, that now makes social life possible. Bonds between people in commercial society are not those of passion or affection but those of either contract or mutual enablement. Benevolence is too flimsy a passion on which to rely for the necessaries of life; nor is it sufficiently intense or constant to

keep society bound together. But the division of labour is enough to perform both these tasks" [Lisa Hill and Peter McCarthy, "On Friendship and *necessitudo* in Adam Smith," *History of the Human Sciences* 17 (2004): 11].

34 While not our focus here, this statement also bears centrally on the question of Smith's relative allegiances to preservation of social order and promotion of individual perfection. Smith has sometimes been taken to privilege the former over the latter (see esp. Den Uyl and Griswold, "Smith on Friendship and Love," 615–616, 626; Forman-Barzilai, *Smith and the Circles of Sympathy*, 106–134). Smith himself though clearly regards the two concepts as standing in a both/and rather than either/or relation; see, e.g., his explicit insistence that it is precisely "the perfection of human nature" that "can alone produce among mankind that harmony of sentiments and passions in which consists their whole grace and propriety" (TMS 1.1.5.5).

35 Compare, e.g., Fleischacker, *On Adam Smith's Wealth of Nations: A Philosophical Companion* (Princeton, NJ: Princeton University Press, 2004), 212; and Craig Smith, "Adam Smith: Left or Right?" *Political Studies* 61 (2015): 784–798, which, like my account in what follows, emphasizes the degree to which this claim is "ring-fenced and qualified" by Smith himself (794). I offer a fuller treatment of this question in "The 'Wisdom of the State': Adam Smith on China and Tartary," *American Political Science Review* 108 (2014): 371–382 (see esp. 381).

36 Matthew 25:40 (KJV).

37 A classic study is Istvan Hont and Michael Ignatieff, "Needs and Justice in the *Wealth of Nations*: An Introductory Essay," in *Wealth and Virtue: The Shaping of Political Economy in the Scottish Enlightenment* (Cambridge: Cambridge University Press, 1983), 1–44; numerous additional studies are listed at *Adam Smith and the Character of Virtue*, 15n1.

38 When Smith returns to this theme in Part 3, he punctuates his central account of what enables us to overcome self-preference with two pointed "it is nots": "it is not the love of our neighbour," and "it is not the soft power of humanity" that enables us to transcend egoistic self-preference (TMS 3.3.4). In the terms of our study, neither *agape* nor humanity (itself, as we saw in Chapter 2, Hume's substitute for *agape*), is sufficient.

39 For a helpful study of this side of Smith's system, see especially Spencer Pack and Eric Schliesser, "Smith's Humean Criticism of Hume's Account of the Origin of Justice," *Journal of the History of Philosophy* 44 (2006): 47–63.

40 The comparison may be less far-fetched than it may at first appear. Putting *Symposium* next to Smith has the particular benefit of clarifying that for Smith it is not philosophy but the ordinary events of human life that heal our human wounds – not in transcendence of the ordinary, but in the such civilized pursuits as sharing a taste for literature, conversation, and mirth in company. These, Smith insists, are "the most powerful remedies for restoring the mind to its tranquility" (TMS 1.1.4.9–10; cf. 1.1.5.2, 7.4.17), and as such demand to be set next to Smith's account of the role of philosophy in relieving anxiety in HA. Of course even in TMS our "instinctive sympathy" only reaches its full potential when it is translated into "a curiosity to inquire" into the situation of another (TMS 1.1.1.9).

41 Harman, "Moral Agent and Impartial Spectator," *The Lindley Lecture* (Lawrence: University of Kansas Press, 1986), 8.

42 In this vein, see especially Montes' claim that "sympathy entails a motivational force that is shaped by a continuous process of transformation inherent in human interaction" ("*Das Adam Smith Problem*," 84) and Brubaker's claim that "sympathetic fellow feeling directly motivates actions helpful to others, the Christian charity of Smith's conclusion" ("'Particular Turn or Habit'," 231).

43 As Montes shows, this view was first set forth by Eckstein in his notes as a response to *Das Adam Smith Problem*, and then further developed by Raphael and Macfie [Montes, "*Das Adam Smith Problem*," 78; for the original claim, see Eckstein, "*Einleitung des Herausgebers*," in *Theorie der ethischen Gefühle*, trans. Eckstein (Hamburg: Felix Meiner Verlag, 2004 [1926]), lx–lxi. For recent restatements, see, e.g., Hill and McCarthy, "On Friendship and *necessitudo*," 5; and Forman-Barzilai, *Smith and the Circles of Sympathy*, 12–13.

44 For an important treatment of these passages and the status of sympathy in commercial activity – and indeed its relationship to vanity and amour-propre, see esp. Force, *Self-Interest before Smith*, as cited in n5 in this chapter.

45 See again the sources noted at n34.

5

Kant on Love

RETHINKING KANT VIA KANT'S RETHINKING

Turning to Kant for insight on love would seem, on its face, to be an exercise in futility, the quintessence of looking for love in all the wrong places. What after all could we hope to learn about love from one who notoriously derides romantic love as pathological, who reduces sex to reciprocal usage of genitalia, who reserves his highest praises for benefactors with cold rather than warm hearts, and who admires the stoicism of one who, when he sees others suffering whom he cannot help, says "what is that to me"?[1] Given the prominence of these passages and the attention they have received, small wonder that we tend to regard Kant today as one of love's most hostile critics.

Yet to write off Kant's views on love is, I think, a grave mistake.[2] For not only is Kant *not* a critic of love, but he in fact deserves to be regarded as one of the truly preeminent modern theorists of other-directed love for two specific reasons. First, Kant offers what is arguably the most comprehensive contemporary critique of the sentimental other-directedness that the eighteenth century sought to introduce as an alternative to traditional theistic conceptions of love of others. Second, Kant not only details the shortcomings of the sentimentalist conception, but he also develops a new conception of love in his own right, one that specifically aims to move us past sentimentalist theories of humanity, sympathy, and compassion without leading back to theological conceptions of *agape* or *caritas*.

In what follows I aim to trace out the constitutive elements of Kant's theory of love, and specifically to show his efforts to ground the love of others in a rational extension of self-love forms the foundational core of his alternative to both theistic and sentimentalist conceptions. Kant, in so doing, represents a crucial extension of Rousseau. Like Rousseau, Kant believes that the extension of self-love to others is the necessary core of any legitimate other-directedness in a world in which a love grounded on the transcendent is unavailable. But Kant takes Rousseau's insight a considerable step further in explaining that this extension is justifiable by reason, and indeed is mandated by reason itself. In so doing, Kant offers a revaluation of the key sentimentalist insight set forth by Rousseau, and demonstrates specifically how this insight, suitably grounded in reason, can lead beyond sentimentalism without leading back to theism.

Kant, I thus hope to show, marks a key turning point in the history of the idea of other-directedness. Where his Enlightenment predecessors turned to sentiment to confront the new challenges posed by liberated self-love, Kant sought to challenge the sufficiency of their sentimentalist response. In this sense his conception of love of others represents at once an endorsement of the concern about self-love that he shared with his eighteenth-century predecessors as well as the beginnings of a new way of confronting this challenge. Kant himself understood his conception of love to be superior to the alternatives on offer not only on the grounds of the legitimacy of its foundations, but also on the grounds that, in contrast to other eighteenth-century theories of other-directedness, his theory is at once practically efficacious, capable of being extended universally, and supportive of rather than inimical to our duty to recognize the dignity of others. For all of these reasons Kant's theory of love is of significant interest to those interested in the history of the idea of love. Yet it is also deserving of the attention of more specialized students of his thought. Thus what follows also argues that Kant's efforts to define an alternative foundation for love of others is a principal concern in his practical ethics, indeed one that binds his earliest contributions to practical ethics in the precritical period to his mature concerns in the *Doctrine of Virtue*.

SYMPATHY AND SELF-LOVE IN THE PRECRITICAL KANT

Kant's precritical ethics have recently begun to receive considerable critical attention. Yet these writings still tend to be regarded through the lenses established by the categories of Kant's later aesthetics and anthropology.[3] And for good reason: Kant himself presents his fundamental text of his precritical period, *Observations on the Feeling of the Beautiful and Sublime*, as an inquiry into the aesthetic categories of the third *Critique*, and the most striking claims of the *Observations*, namely those on race and gender, are anthropological claims in keeping with the sort of inquiry Kant would later develop in the *Anthropology* itself. But we do a disservice to Kant's precritical texts if we fail to note their foundational significance for his critical ethics. Thus the claim for which I argue here: namely that in his precritical ethics, Kant not only defines a key problem that he will address in his critical ethics, but also goes strikingly far toward laying the foundation for his critical solution to this problem.

This key problem can be easily stated: by what means can self-love be best restrained so that we can establish right relationships with others?[4] This problem takes center stage in two remarkable precritical passages. Each tells a story, and specifically a story of the transformation of an egocentric individual into one who comes to value others. The first comes early in the *Observations* and recounts the story of Carazan's dream, a story Kant knew from its recent reprinting in a literary periodical.[5] It is a story important to Kant for several reasons; not only does it introduce his treatment of the sublime in the *Observations* by affording "an example of the noble dread" that solitude inspires (O 25n; AA 2:209n), but also its critique of futile attempts to substitute "religious devotions" for performance of genuine moral duty anticipates the foundational contrast Kant would draw in his later religious writings between "*religion of rogation*" and "*moral religion*" (e.g., RWL 95; AA 6:51 and RWL 137; AA 6:103 and RWL 122; AA 6:84 and RWL 190; AA 6:170–171).[6] But for our purposes, the story's chief import lies in its depiction of the relationship of self-love to the love of others. Carazan himself is initially presented as through and through egocentric and indifferent to others; thus in our introduction to him we are told that "the more his riches had grown, the more did this miserly rich man bar his heart to compassion (*Mitleiden*) and the love of others (*der Liebe gegen jeden andern*)." In this sense, the figure of Carazan is clearly meant to depict commercial modernity's encouragement of self-concern and inhibition of love for others – what Kant calls "*Menschenliebe*."[7] Indeed it is on these grounds that, in Carazan's dream, the angel of death bars Carazan from heaven and sentences him to eternal solitude: "You have closed your heart to the love of humankind (*Menschenliebe*), and held on to your treasures with an iron hand. You have lived only for yourself."[8] Carazan's punishment is meant to fit his crime; having lived only for himself, he is condemned to die and live alone in "a fearful realm of eternal silence, solitude and darkness" – a sentence that elicits "unspeakable dread" and "mortal terrors" and "bewilderment" and "unbearable anguish." But at the very moment this anguish is greatest, Carazan awakens to tell us that he has "been instructed to esteem human beings (*Menschen hochzuschätzen*); for even the least of them, whom in the pride of my good fortune I had turned from my door, would have been far more welcome to me in that terrifying desert than all the treasures of Golconda" (O 25n; AA 2:209–210n).

Carazan's story is clearly a conversion narrative, and specifically a narrative of conversion from self-love to love of others. And this particular sort of conversion was hardly a matter of idle interest to Kant, but rather one that touched his deepest philosophical and personal concerns in the precritical period.[9] Indeed a second and clearly parallel conversion story dates to this same period – but this time it tells the story not of a fictional character, but of Kant himself. This comes in what is likely his most important autobiographical reflection of the 1760s:

> I myself am a researcher by inclination. I feel the entire thirst for cognition and the eager restlessness to proceed further in it, as well as the satisfaction at every acquisition. There was a time when I believed this alone could constitute the honor of humankind, and I despised the rabble who knows nothing. *Rousseau* has set me right. This blinding prejudice vanishes, I learn to honor human beings, and I would feel by far less useful than the common laborer if I did not believe that this consideration could impart a value to all others in order to establish the rights of humanity. (R 96; AA 20:44)

Kant's remark – certainly the best known of all of the "Remarks" to be found in his personal copy of the *Observations* – has been cited by multiple scholars, often in the specific context of assessing his profound debts to Rousseau.[10] But for our purposes, what matters is less the light this remark sheds on his philosophical development in the precritical period than the light it sheds on the way in which Kant conceived of both the substance and resolution of the tension between self-love and the love of others. And indeed what is especially striking here is that Kant describes his own struggle and its resolution in precisely those terms in which he described Carazan's struggle and resolution: that is, a dramatic and sudden shock out of a life defined by love of self and contempt for others, and an emergence into a new life centered less on personal honor than on concern to "honor human beings."

Kant's and Carazan's conversion narratives thus each tell the same story: the reorientation of the selfish from self to others. Yet for all their similarity, the stories are radically incomplete insofar as neither explains how this transformation occurs. This was hardly a task that Kant shied away from, however; as I hope to show, much of Kant's energy in both the precritical and critical periods was in fact dedicated to defining the mechanism that makes a transformation of self-love into love of others possible.

In the precritical texts, Kant begins his account by surveying the answers of the eighteenth-century sentimentalist tradition: sympathy, pity, and compassion. In several crucial respects Kant is sympathetic to this tradition. First, he agrees that we are by nature possessed of other-directed sentiments resistant to self-interest; thus in lines that closely parallel both Rousseau's treatment of natural pity and Smith's treatment of sympathy, Kant asks, in his early ethics lectures, "do I have, not merely a self-interested feeling, but also a disinterested feeling of concern for others (*ein uneigen-gemeinnütziges Gefühl*)?" "Yes," he answers: "the weal and woe of another touches us directly: the mere happiness of another pleases us in the telling: even that of fictional persons whose tale we know of, or in distant ages – this common concern is so great that it collides with the self-interested (*eigennützigen*) feeling" (LE 3; AA 27:3). In continuing, he also explains that this other-directed feeling is not only natural, but "a noble feeling," indeed one "nobler than the self-interested one," owing partly to its provenance as a gift from God (LE 3; AA 27:3). And such praises of the nobility and naturalness of the other-directed sentiments were hardly limited to Kant's lectures. The *Observations* emphasizes these as well; thus, in a key passage on theatrical spectatorship, Kant emphasizes the degree to which we are moved by "magnanimous sacrifice for the well-being of another," and the degree to which "the misfortune of others stirs sympathetic sentiments in the bosom of the onlooker and allows his magnanimous heart to beat for the need of others" (O 27; AA 2:212). On such grounds Kant suggests sympathy deserves to be classified among those "good moral qualities that are loveable and beautiful," and which, to the extent that they work with virtue, "may also be regarded as noble" – hence his claim that "a certain tenderheartedness that is easily led into a warm feeling of sympathy (*ein warmes Gefühl des Mitleidens*) is beautiful and loveable, for it indicates a kindly participation in the fate of other people, to which principles of virtue likewise lead" (O 29–30; AA 2:215). And Kant finds this desirable: "sympathy and complaisance (*Mitleiden und Gefälligkeit*) are grounds for beautiful actions that would perhaps all be suffocated by the preponderance of a cruder self-interest (*Eigennutzes*)" (O 31; AA 2:217); sympathy, in short, "is a great antidote against selfishness (*Eigennutz*)" (R 72; AA 20:9–10).

Kant thus clearly finds much to admire in sentimentalized other-directedness insofar as it is at once natural, noble, and aspires to the useful end of mitigating self-interest. At the same time, Kant clearly recognized the limitations of this sentiment in a way that challenges the defenses of sentimentalized other-directedness offered by Hume and Smith and Rousseau. These limits are particularly emphasized in the "Remarks." Here Kant notes that for all its seeming nobility, the sentimental other-directedness that previous eighteenth-century thinkers had championed was deeply problematic, thus "the universal love of humankind (*die allgemeine Menschenliebe*) has something high and noble in it, but in a human being it is chimerical. If one aims for it one gets used to deceiving oneself with longings and idle wishes" (R 83; AA 20:25). Sentimental other-directedness is a chimera partly because human beings are incapable of realizing it given limits of their nature that prevent them from being able to sustain it or to extend it universally. But it is also chimerical insofar as it fails to enable us to realize in practice the noble ends it encourages us to imagine; thus his claim that "compassion (*Mitleiden*) is an *affect* of benevolence toward the needy, according to which we imagine that we would do what is in our power to help them; it is thus for the most part a chimera, because it is neither always in our power nor in our will" (R 157; AA 20:134–135), and his claim elsewhere that "the sympathetic sentiment is true if it is equal to the altruistic powers, otherwise it is chimerical" (R 185–186; AA 20:173). All of this points to Kant's conclusion that good-doing is to be preferred to mere good-feeling – in his words, that compassion "must never rule, but must be *subordinated* to the capacity and reasonable desire to *do* good" (R 103; AA 20:56).[11]

Of particular interest here is the association of compassion and imagination, an association that Kant further develops in his broader differentiation between the sorts of other-directed sentiments experienced by those living in the state of nature and those living in advanced civilized societies. The former, Kant explains, will aid suffering others when their help is needed, whereas the developed imaginations of the latter inhibit real practical action; thus "with opulence the fantasy of the love of humanity (*die Phantasie der Menschenliebe*) *cultivates* itself and the capacity and appetite reduces itself," while "the simple human being attends to no other except to him he can help" (R 157; AA 20:135). "Good-heartedness," Kant concludes, "arises through the *culture* of moral but inactive sentiments and is a moral delusion," the mere conceit of those who live "in a state of opulence" and have "imaginary needs" and are "selfish (*eigennützig*)" – a far cry from the man of the state of nature "more capable of altruistic and active sentiments (*mehrer gemeinnützigen und tätigen Empfindungen fähig*)" (R 185–186; AA 20:173). In this sense, sentimentalized other-directedness is largely a symptom of the corrupted imaginations and inflamed self-love endemic to opulent, comfortable conditions, an affect that privileges the feeling of well-wishing so pleasant to its possessor to the necessarily uncomfortable work of actual good-doing. And Kant is explicit that sentimentalized other-directedness has more than a little of the selfish in it; hence his conclusion that "the affectionate instincts of compassion and sympathy (*die teilnehmende Instinkte des Mitleidens und der Wohlgewogenheit*)" are "merely great strivings to mitigate the ills of others, taken from the self-approval of the soul" (R 163; AA 20:144).

Kant brings this line of critique to a head in his ethics lectures in a gloss on an unnamed Rousseau. He begins this critique by insisting on the basic insufficiency of pity in modern society, a state in which "the needy have multiplied," and "civilized man is much constrained by self-serving (*eigennützige*) artificial desires" (LE 25; AA 27:58). Thus the thought-experiment Kant sets before his students: "Transfer a man of nature (not a man of the woods, who is perhaps a chimera, but a simple man) into the midst of artificial society." What would happen? As one "whose love is *real*" he "loves *in a more limited way*, and his love cannot be extended to *everyone*." Instead he works to help those he can help, and does not much bother himself with those outside of his circle of influence: "as soon as they are too much for his powers, wishings and pityings strike him as too foolish" (LE 30: AA 27:64–65). Compare this to civil man:

In present-day civil society, since the needs multiply, the *objects of pity* mount up; the capacity of men itself declines, since in part *really*, and in part though illusion, they are weak and thus miserable; for the evils of illusion, which make me *in imagination*, and a thousand others *in reality* similar, are on the increase. What must *human love* (Menschenliebe) be *here*? A *topsoil*, an imagined human love, a yearning of the fancy, is the natural consequence. So it now spreads abroad, and corrupts *the heart*. Since, through morality, the fanciful love of humanity (*Phantastische Menschenliebe*) is so widely diffused in people by instruction, it remains a matter of speculation everywhere in life, a topic of romances, such as Fielding's etc., that has no effect, since (1) it is too exalted, and (2) does not get rid of the obstacles. (LE 30; AA 27:65).[12]

Kant here outlines a crucial problem: the conditions of the modern world render urgent the need for us to provide active assistance to others, yet these very same conditions have led us to prefer the enjoyment of pleasing feelings of humanity to the unpleasant exertions that our neighbors need and which natural man was able and willing to perform. Our pleasing sentiments of compassion are thus bought at the cost of being able to act for others, and hence Kant's insistence that our "merely *yearning* or *wishful* love" is simply "not good, since it is (1) *useless*; (2) *deceptive*, in that it squanders time and actually impedes practical love; for the love that is *too little practical* has the love that is all-too-greatly *fanciful* as its cause" (LE 29; AA 27:64; cf. R 103; AA 20:56).

What solution to this problem can Kant provide? In his lectures, he suggests education: "our education, and mutual education, must be such that our sympathies do not become *fanciful*, but remain confined to the *practical*. I must be *upright*, and attend to my obligations; but the exalted pretension of wanting to love the whole of mankind is a fraud. He who loves the Tartar, loves not his neighbour. Loving *all*, we love *none*, and our love is therefore less" (LE 32; AA 27:67; cf. O 35; AA 2:222). But this must lead us to wonder: exactly what does it mean to "educate" our concern for others so that it is capable of responding to the practical challenge of human need? It is to this question that Kant addresses what is perhaps the crucial passage on the question of sentimental other-directedness in the *Observations*, namely the passage that continues his discussion of sympathy, quoted earlier. Having established that sympathy is "beautiful and loveable" insofar as it works to the same ends as virtue, Kant goes on to explain:

But this kindly passion is nevertheless weak and is always blind. For suppose that this sentiment moves you to help someone in need with your expenditure, but you are indebted to someone else and by this means you make it impossible for yourself to fulfill the strict duty of justice; then obviously the action cannot arise from any virtuous resolution, for that could not possibly entice you into sacrificing a higher obligation to this blind enchantment. If, by contrast, general affection (*allgemeine Wohlgewogenheit*) towards humankind has become your principle, to which you always subject your actions, then your love towards the one in need remains, but it is now, from a higher standpoint, placed in its proper relationship to your duty as a whole. The universal affection is a ground for participating in his ill-fortune, but at the same time it is also a ground of justice, in accordance with whose precept you must now forbear this action. Now as soon as this feeling is raised to its proper universality, it is sublime, but also colder. For it is not possible that our bosom should swell with tenderness on behalf of every human being and swim in melancholy for everyone else's need, otherwise the virtuous person, like Heraclitus constantly melting into sympathetic tears, with all this goodheartedness would nevertheless become nothing more than a tenderhearted idler. (O 30; AA 2:215–216)

This passage does important work. First and foremost, Kant here lays out the sort of education that ennobles or elevates merely sentimental other-directedness from the level of mere affect to genuine virtue. And in so doing, Kant further lays out the key components of his critique of other-directed sentiment as well as the key components of his critical solution to this problem.

On the former front, Kant in this passage clearly develops three key critiques of sentimentalized other-directedness. First, as he says, it is "weak" – that is, and in keeping with criticisms that we have seen him make elsewhere, it is largely a mere good feeling incapable of sustaining beneficent action in practice; as he says later, sympathy is simply "not enough to drive indolent human nature to actions for the common weal" (O 32; AA 2:218). Second, it is "blind" – that is, it is indiscriminate insofar as it lacks a capacity to differentiate between those who deserve and those who do not deserve our commiseration; as he says later, sympathy and benevolence are "very much subject to the change of circumstances," and thus "readily take[] on different shapes as the objects display one aspect or another" (O 33; AA 2:219), and hence his claim that this "blind pity" itself "brings justice into disorder" (R 131; AA 20:97). And third, and again in keeping with his other criticisms, it is "not possible" – that is, it simply asks more of us than our limited energies can sustain, and indeed aspiring to follow it must necessarily reduce one to a mere "tenderhearted idler."

Kant's critique thus runs deep. But his assessment here is not only meant to be critical; indeed in this passage Kant also lays out the fundamental elements of the alterative solution to the problem of self-love and love of others that he will develop in his mature ethics. Here too the elements are threefold. First, Kant here explains that the key shift that the agent needs to make is the conversion of mere sentiment to "principle," and indeed a principle to which the subject will "always subject your actions." Second, Kant insists that we must reach a point where we come to feel not only compassion or even love for others, but that we come to regard our love in the context of our "duty as a whole." And third, Kant insists that we aspire to raise our immediate affections to the level of what he here calls "proper universality." Each of these moves is key, for it is from these specific three elements – principle, duty, and universality – that Kant will build the core of his alternative to sentimental other-directedness.

Kant's emphasis on principle here is especially crucial. Much of his critical ethics of course rests on the distinction between inclination and principle, and it is striking to note the degree to which the foundations for this position have already been laid in the *Observations*, which frequently insists on the "quality of principles in comparison to emotions" (O 34; AA 2:221), judging principles superior to emotions insofar as principles, unlike emotions, enable us to resist momentary inclinations (e.g., O 31; 2:217 and O 35; AA 2:222) – hence Kant's consistent identification in the *Observations* of the peak of virtue, the melancholy man, as one who "subordinates his sentiments to principles" (O 33; AA 2:220; cf. O 35; AA 2:222). Kant makes the significance of principles especially clear in his key passage on the relationship of principles to virtue:

> Thus true virtue can only be grafted upon principles, and it will become the more sublime and noble the more general they are. These principles are not speculative rules, but the consciousness of a feeling that lives in every human breast and that extends much further than to the special grounds of sympathy (*Mitleidens*) and complaisance. I believe that I can bring all this together if I say that it is the feeling of the beauty and the dignity of human nature. The first is a ground of universal affection (*allgemeinen Wohlgewogenheit*), the second of universal respect (*allgemeinen Achtung*), and if this feeling had the greatest perfection in any human heart then this human being would certainly love and value even himself, but only insofar as he is one among all to whom his widespread and noble feeling extends itself. Only when one subordinates one's particular inclination to such an enlarged one can our kindly drives be proportionately applied and bring about the noble attitude that is the beauty of virtue. (O 31; AA 2:217)

This passage has received considerable attention, especially recently, for the degree to which it seems to anticipate Kant's formulation of the categorical imperative even in the 1760s.[13] But the passage also deserves attention from the perspective of our concern with love and sentiment. In this respect the passage is important for two reasons. First, Kant here reiterates the necessity of grounding concern for others in principle rather than sentiment, and the need to render this concern "universal" as well; here and elsewhere Kant reserves his admiration for that higher disposition distinguished by "its inalterability as well as the universality of its application" (O 34; AA 2:221). But there is also something more at work here – something that Kant has not yet made explicit but which emerges directly from his concerns noted above about sentimentalized other-directedness. As we have seen, Kant is sensitive to the propensity of sentimental feelings to elevate their possessor and indeed to augment rather than mitigate egocentrism. It is with this in mind that he thus comes, in this passage and elsewhere, to add a new element to the project – namely, what he here calls "universal respect."

What then is this "universal respect," and why does Kant think it necessary to join it to "universal affection"? The answer seems to be that Kant worries that mere affection for others devoid of an associated respect for others can easily degenerate into a form of inequality that is both unstable and unjust. It is for this reason that Kant even in these early remarks frequently insists on joining together "love and respect" (R 68; AA 20:5; cf. R 101; AA 20:52 and R 146; AA 20:120), and even goes so far as to say that "this composite sentiment is the greatest impression that can ever befall the human heart" (R 65; AA 20:3; cf. O 45; AA 2:235). These claims are important for two reasons. First, Kant's explicit and consistent efforts to join love and respect throughout his texts of the 1760s directly anticipates the joining of love and respect that, as we shall see, is the foundation on which he builds his theory of love in the *Metaphysics of Morals* – a fact that suggests not only that this concept was evident to Kant three decades earlier than often emphasized, but also that his very concern to join respect to love was itself the product of his concerns regarding the specific tension of self-love and love of others.[14]

This in turn suggests a second, more substantive significance of his effort to join respect to love. In so doing Kant aims to address what he takes to be one of the most pernicious shortcomings of sentimentalized other-directedness. Kant worries in several places that the sympathy of the civilized often inflames egocentrism and thereby further reifies an inequality that defines the relationship of the sympathetic to the human objects of their feelings. This is troubling to Kant insofar as he is of course committed to the notion that equality is the precondition for any adequate theory of virtue or right relations with others. In the earlier passage, this emerges in his insistence that when "one subordinates one's own particular inclination to such an enlarged one," he then will "love and value even himself, but only in so far as he is one among all to whom his widespread and noble feeling extends itself." This idea also manifests itself in his contemporary insistence that "true love" is precisely the same as "rectitude" – "it is the love we have by nature, the fundamental love, for it is founded upon a living feeling of *equality*" (LE 30; AA 27:65).[15] Kant's effort here and elsewhere to join respect to love is itself perhaps best understood then as an effort to overcome the propensity of the sentimentally other-directed at once to overvalue themselves and to undervalue others, and thereby to reestablish, within the context of modern civil society, a recovery of what is best in our natural condition: namely the capacity to love others in a way that preserves their dignity and supports rather than undermines equality. Any adequate theory of other-directedness, that is, must preserve the recognition that "one human being counts as much as another" (R 91; AA 20:36).

Taken altogether then, Kant's precritical writings have taken three key steps: they have (1) defined the problem between self-love and the love of others; (2) defined one possible answer to this problem, that of sentimental other-directedness; and (3) defined several problems with that answer. What remains now is for Kant to develop his alternative solution out of the materials he introduced in the course of developing his critique of sentimental other-directedness in his precritical writings. In particular, Kant has yet to explain the legitimate foundations on which genuine other-directedness is to be founded, grounds neither sentimental nor theistic. As he says in the "Remarks" directly on the heels of his autobiographical note regarding Rousseau, "it is very ridiculous to say that you shall love other people, one rather must say that you have good reason (*guten Grund*) to love your neighbor" (R 96; AA 20:45) – a claim repeated in the early ethics lectures in which Kant insists that one "cannot say, as an absolute injunction, Thou shalt love! This love is that of wishing well, or of pleasing well" (LE 24; AA 27:53). With respect to love then, the key challenge of the critical writings is to define these alternative grounds.

THE CRITICAL SOLUTION: THE *GROUNDWORK* AND THE SECOND *CRITIQUE*

Kant's precritical treatment of other-directedness thus defines the problem that his critical theory of other-directedness will need to answer: namely, on what grounds can we legitimately found love for others, if not sentiment? But in addition to defining these grounds, Kant's substantive theory of other-directedness will need to remedy several specific shortcomings of the sentimental theory. As we have seen, the principal shortcomings of sentimentalized other-directedness are threefold: (1) it is inefficacious insofar as it privileges subjective good-feeling over practical good-doing; (2) it is indiscriminate insofar as it is idiosyncratic to circumstance rather than universal; and (3) it reifies inequality between the compassionate and the objects of their compassion. Kant thus has a tall order ahead: not only must he define grounds for other-directedness that are both non-sentimental and nontheistic, but he must also define a form of other-directedness that (1) is capable of effecting practical action toward others; (2) is capable of being felt to all others, universally; and (3) serves to augment rather than undermine conditions of rightful equality between individuals in a way that promotes rather than inhibits recognition of their dignity.

As I hope to show in what follows, it is to these questions that Kant's theory of other-directedness as developed in his two chief contributions to practical ethics in the 1780s – the *Groundwork* and the second *Critique* – are dedicated. These texts, in keeping with the general framework established in the precritical ethics, take as one of their chief aims the establishing of a morality that is capable of transcending self-love. This is not the place to attempt to provide a comprehensive survey of the critical ethics, but it is important, given the theme of the present inquiry, to note the degree to which this concern with transcending self-love animates Kant's practical ethics in this period. In this vein Kant presents the *Groundwork* as an effort to offer an account of the supreme principle of morality in such a way that we can see with maximum clarity a moral worth independent of all concerns of self-love; indeed "to behold virtue in her proper form is nothing other than to present morality stripped of any admixture of the sensible and of any spurious adornments of reward or self-love (*Selbstliebe*)" (G 77n; AA 4:426n). This concern is even more pronounced in the second *Critique*; here he insists that "the direct opposite of the principle of morality is the principle of *one's own* happiness made the determining ground of the will" (CPrR 168; AA 5:35); indeed "so distinctly and sharply drawn are the boundaries of morality and self-love (*Selbstliebe*)" that they are evident to all (CPrR 169; AA 5:36; cf. LE 184; AA 27:422 and RWL 90–91; AA 6:45 and A 264–265; AA 7:153).[16] By self-love, Kant here seems to refer to all inclination; thus his claim in the second *Critique* that "all material practical principles as such are, without exception, of one and the same kind and come under the general principle of self-love or one's own happiness (*Selbstliebe oder eigenen Glückseligkeit*)" (CPrR 155; AA 5:22; cf. LE 48–49; AA 27:253). These, at any rate, are of course the grounds on which Kant builds a foundational claim of his critical ethics: namely that insofar as the rendering of one's own subjective happiness the determining ground of the will is the direct inverse of moral worth, worth must necessarily be wholly independent of all inclination and consist solely in the direct determination of the will by the moral law, and all moral actions must thus be performed not merely in conformity with the law but for the sake of the law (e.g., G 45; AA 4:390 and G 49; AA 4:393 and CPrR 159–160; AA 5:26 and CPrR 198–199; AA 5:72 and CPrR 267; AA 5:159).[17]

Kant's critical ethics thus clearly aims to awaken our suspicions of self-love. At the same time, Kant neither regards self-love as a static monolith, nor is he prone to regard all forms of self-love as equally pernicious. To this end, in several places Kant draws a distinction between different types of self-love, and aims to establish the difference between its legitimate and more subversive forms (see, e.g., LE 17–18; AA 27:41

and LE 24; AA 27:53 and RWL 90–91n; AA 6:45–46n and LE 129–130; AA 27:348–350 and LE 363–364; AA 27:620–622).[18] But of all of these discussions, the most important for our present purposes is that in the second *Critique*:

All the inclinations together (which can be brought into a tolerable system and the satisfaction of which is then called one's own happiness) constitute *regard for oneself* (*Selbstsucht*) (*solipsismus*). This is either the self-regard of *love for one-self* (*Selbstliebe*), a predominant *benevolence* toward oneself (*Wohlwollens gegen sich selbst*) (*Philautia*), or that of *satisfaction with oneself* (*Wohlgefallens an sich selbst*) (*Arrogantia*). The former is called, in particular, *self-love* (*Eigenliebe*), the latter, *self-conceit* (*Eigendünkel*). Pure practical reason merely *infringes upon* self-love, inasmuch as it only restricts it, as natural and active in us even prior to the moral law, to the condition of agreement with this law, and then it is called *rational self-love* (*vernünftige Selbstliebe*). But it *strikes down* self-conceit alto-gether, since all claims to esteem for oneself that precede accord with the moral law are null and quite unwarranted...Now, the propensity to self-esteem, so long as it rests only on sensibility, belongs with the inclinations which the moral law infringes upon. So the moral law strikes down self-conceit. (CPrR 199; AA 5:73; cf. LE 135–137; AA 27:357–360)

Kant's distinction of two types of self-love is crucial for several reasons that concern his theory of other-directed love.[19] His key claim here is that the sort of self-love that is characteristic of what is here called self-conceit, or *Eigendünkel*, and which – not unlike Rousseau's *amour-propre* – often leads us to focus on our relative worth compared to others, is pernicious insofar as it promotes a false sense of superiority to others, and hence needs to be "struck down."[20] This of course is precisely the sort of perni-cious self-preference that Kant thinks endemic to the agent's assessment of relative positioning with regard to the objects of his compassionate feelings. It is this same self-conceit that Kant has in mind in suggest-ing that self-love is opposed to morality insofar as it is the source of that destructive "propensity to make oneself as having subjective deter-mining grounds of choice into the objective determining ground of the will in general" (CPrR 200; AA 5:74).[21] Herein also lies the seed of the "radical evil" that worries Kant, itself the product of that excessive self-preference that leads one to prefer one's inclinations and private hap-piness not only to that of others but to the demands of the moral law itself.[22] Yet Kant differentiates this pernicious self-love from another self-love, *Eigenliebe*. This self-love consists not in self-preference in matters of comparison, but in "benevolence toward oneself." In addition, Kant also thinks that this self-love is capable of being brought under the restrictions of reason, resulting in what is here called "rational self-love (*vernünftige*

Selbstliebe)" (cf. RWL 90–91n; AA 6:45–46n). Both claims are essential not only to Kant's theory of self-love, but also to his theory of other-directed love. For as he goes on to show, it is precisely the bringing of *Eigenliebe*, dedicated to fostering benevolence toward the self and promoting regard for our ends, under the control of reason, that furnishes what Kant takes to be the only defensible ground for love of others.

Now, to some degree, this claim must necessarily seem odd on its face. That Kant would attempt to save benevolence toward others on the grounds of self-love would seem to violate on two fronts the basic principle of Kant's critical ethics: that only that action done from duty – that is, done solely on account of respect for the law and independent of all inclination or concern for outcomes – can be considered genuinely moral (e.g., G 54–56; AA 4:399–401 and G 64–66; AA 4:410–413 and CPrR 205–206; AA 5:81–82). So to suggest that a love for others founded on a particular form of self-love is in fact moral would seem to challenge the foundation on which Kant bases his critique of the corruption of morality by empirical inducements and the concomitant necessity of locating moral worth in the will determined by reason. Furthermore, Kant's most notorious descriptions of benefaction in the *Groundwork* seem to reinforce our sense that morality and self-love must never meet. Hence his particularly notorious account of the genuine "philanthropist" (*Menschenfreund*):

> To be beneficent where one can is a duty, and besides there are many souls so sympathetically attuned that, without any other motive of vanity or self-interest they find an inner satisfaction in spreading joy around them and can take delight in the satisfaction of others so far as it is their own work. But I assert that in such a case an action of this kind, however it may conform with duty and however amiable it may be, has nevertheless no true moral worth but is on the same footing with other inclinations, for example, the inclination to honor, which, if it fortunately lights upon what is in fact in the common interest and in conformity with duty and hence honorable, deserves praise and encouragement but not esteem; for the maxim lacks moral content, namely that of doing such actions not from inclination but *from duty*. (G 53; AA 4:398)

It is this line of argument, of course, that has given rise to the popular image of Kant as champion of the idea that the only morally worthy benefaction is that done with cold heart and gritted teeth – that of one who is "beneficent not from inclination but from duty" and who is "by temperament cold and indifferent to the sufferings of others" (G 53–54; AA 4:398–399). As a result of these claims, many have wondered about the extent of Kant's seeming praises of cold-heartedness.[23] But like others,

it seems to me that such a reading misconstrues the intentions of the
Groundwork – a work of course meant less as a handbook of normative
practical ethics than as an attempt to reveal with maximum clarity the
constitutive principles of moral worth, principles that can be brought
into relief more readily by way of certain types of examples.[24] But I am
less concerned to argue this here than to treat the substantive question
to which these formulations give rise: namely, what ought to prompt us
to other-directed actions if not sentiment? Put slightly differently, and in
the context of Kant's idiom, if indeed "it is very beautiful to do good to
human beings from love for them and from sympathetic benevolence,"
but "this is not yet the genuine moral maxim of our conduct," how can
we as self-loving beings "put the determining ground of our will" solely
in "the law itself and in respect for this law"? (CPrR 206; AA 5:82).

Kant's answer lies in his revaluation of love itself. To this point, Kant
has largely regarded love as suffering from the same shortcomings that
vitiated those sentimental forms of other-directedness for which we feel
"*immediate* inclination" (e.g., G 53; AA 4:397). But now Kant introduces
a new concept of love, and does so in a passage that is key not only to the
argument of the *Groundwork* but indeed to the central issue at the heart
of our inquiry in this book. This is the gloss he offers in the *Groundwork*
on the Gospel commandment of love of neighbor. In illustration of the
claim that proper moral worth in instances of other-directed action consists solely in these efforts to promote the happiness of others "not from
inclination but from duty," Kant explains:

It is undoubtedly in this way, again, that we are to understand the passages from
scripture in which we are commanded to love our neighbor, even our enemy.
For, love as an inclination cannot be commanded, but beneficence from duty
(*Wohltun aus Pflicht*) – even though no inclination impels us to it and, indeed,
natural and unconquerable aversion opposes it – is *practical* and not *pathological* love, which lies in the will and not in the propensity of feeling, in principles
of action and not in melting sympathy (*schmelzender Teilnehmung*); and it alone
can be commanded. (G 54–55; AA 4:399)[25]

Kant's commentary on the second commandment is key for several reasons. First, and with great clarity, he here sets forth his rejection of previous conceptions of other-directedness. In keeping with his earlier critique,
Kant clearly here rejects the "melting sympathy" that is evidence of the
heteronomy that comes from privileging the "propensity of feeling."
Second, Kant also here rejects the theistic grounding for love; his articulation of the second commandment of love of others is clearly meant
to stand independently of the first commandment of love of God – a

commandment that here and elsewhere (though not in all places, as we will have reason to note in what follows) is conspicuously absent from Kant's commentary on the Gospel command. Thus Kant's dual rejection of both theism and sentiment as the grounds for our love of others – a rejection in keeping with his explicit claims elsewhere that any form of morality that is founded either "on incentives" or which "derives morality from a divine, all-perfect will" ultimately reduces to a form of unwarranted heteronomy (G 90–91; AA 4:442–443; cf. CPrR 191–192; AA 5:64 and CPrR 243–244; AA 5:129 and LE 68; AA 2:277). Against these notions of a love for others that is prompted either by the inclinations of sentiment or the commands of God, Kant means to propose the alternative of a love for others conceived solely as a command arising from the will, and hence a duty (though cf. LE 177; AA 27:413).

Kant's intended alternative grounds are thus clear. But how can he square this circle? On what grounds can he reasonably claim that we have a duty to love others that emerges strictly from pure reason, purged of all dependence on theism or sentimentalism? The answer to this lies in Kant's distinction between different forms of self-love and his call for transformation of proper self-love via extension by reason. In this sense, Kant applies to the concept of love the move that provides the impetus for the categorical imperative. Here again a full review of this fundamental concept lies beyond our scope; for our purposes, what is crucial is that Kant consistently introduces the categorical imperative, in all its forms, as a means by which the subjective maxims that guide our individual actions might be brought into conformity with universal law (e.g., G 56–57; AA 4:402–403 and G 72–73; AA 4:420–421 and CPrR 192; AA 5:64–65). And it is precisely this that Kant aims to apply to love itself in his attempt to generate a defensible theory of practical love superior to indefensible pathological love. In brief – and in a way that hopefully captures the heart of Kant's intention even if it will require further explication – practical love is best understood as proper self-love (*Eigenliebe*) extended by reason to others in a way that can meet the universalizing test of the categorical imperative.[26]

To understand better what is at stake here, we may do best to follow Kant's own approach in the *Groundwork* in which he develops this claim less through any direct explication than through examples. Kant famously offers four examples of how the categorical imperative's universalizability test applies in cases of perfect duties to self, imperfect duties to self, perfect duties to others, and imperfect duties to others. In each of these examples, the animating tension is that between self-love and its capacity to be universalized; hence the first example, which concerns suicide, comes down to "whether this principle of self-love (*Princip der Selbstliebe*) could become a universal law of nature," and the second example, which concerns keeping of promises, reduces to whether "this principle of self-love or personal advantage" is not just consistent with our future welfare but also "right" (G 74; AA 4:422). And this tension also lies at the heart of the key example for present purposes, namely that of the reluctant would-be benefactor who, on seeing suffering others whom it is in his power to help thinks, "what is it to me?" His maxim is non-malfeasance: "let each be as happy as heaven wills or as he can make himself; I shall take nothing from him nor even envy him; only I do not care to contribute anything to his welfare or to his assistance in need!" (cf. LE 183; AA 27:421 and LoP 477; AA 9:490). But in offering his commentary on this maxim, Kant makes clear why it is insufficient:

> Now, if such a way of thinking were to become a universal law the human race could admittedly very well subsist, no doubt even better than when everyone prates about sympathy and benevolence (*Teilnehmung und Wohlwollen*) and even exerts himself to practice them occasionally, but on the other hand also cheats where he can, sells the right of human beings or otherwise infringes upon it. But although it is possible that a universal law of nature could very well subsist in accordance with such a maxim, it is still impossible to will that such a principle hold everywhere as a law of nature. For, a will that decided this would conflict with itself, since many cases could occur in which one would need the love and sympathy of others and in which, by such a law of nature arisen from his own will, he would rob himself of all hope of the assistance he wishes for himself. (G 75; AA 4:423)

Here Kant explains the proper relationship between self-love and the love of others, and explains why it is impossible to have one without the other. His formal claim here is that our love of others is properly founded on self-love. Put differently, love of others is the necessary consequence or the mandated duty that emerges from the subjecting of self-love to the categorical imperative's universalizability test. As that test makes clear, not only is the bad self-love of self-esteem culminating in excessive self-preference clearly illegitimate – the superiority sought by self-preference is of course a zero-sum good and hence clearly nonuniversalizable – but the good and natural self-love of benevolent concern for one's own ends is defensible before the categorical imperative only if it is extended to a similarly benevolent concern for the ends and happiness of others. In this way, Kant derives love of others from reason's extension of self-love rather than sentiment or divine command – an innovation that distinguishes his concept of love from other concepts traditional and contemporary. Without depending on either sentiment or on God, Kant uses reason to establish a means of mitigating self-preference and thereby bring our subjective self-love in accord with that of others.

The key category here is the subject's recognition of a very specific element of his nature: his neediness. The human being, Kant explains, continually exists in a condition of need, a condition that itself gives rise to our own natural self-love. But it is our reasoned reflection on this inescapable neediness, Kant further insists, that necessarily leads us to the duty to love others. This side of his argument, present already in the *Groundwork* in its reference to the possibility that "many cases could occur in which one would need the love and sympathy of others" takes center stage in the account of love set forth in the second *Critique*. This account begins with the anthropological claim that "to be happy is necessarily the demand of every rational but finite being." At the same time, "satisfaction with one's whole existence is not, as it were, an original possession," but rather "is instead a problem imposed on him by his finite nature itself, because he is needy and this need is directed to the matter of his faculty of desire, that is, something related to a subjective feeling of pleasure or displeasure underlying it by which is determined what he needs in order to be satisfied with his condition." The problem is that this subjective experience of need cannot be regarded as law, "since a law, as objective, must contain the *very same determining ground* of the will in all cases and for all rational beings" (CPrR 159; AA 5:25). The only way by which we can resolve this subjective necessity and bring it into harmony with the dictates of universal law is to extend it to others:

Let the matter be, for example, my own happiness. This, if I attribute it to each (as, in the case of finite beings, I may in fact do) can become an *objective* practical law only if I include in it the happiness of others. Thus the law to promote the happiness of others arises not from the presupposition that this is an object of everyone's choice but merely from this: that the form of universality, which reason requires as the condition of giving to a maxim of self-love (*Selbstliebe*) the objective validity of a law, becomes the determining ground of the will; and so the object (the happiness of others) was not the determining ground of the pure will; this was, instead, the mere lawful form alone, by which I limited my maxim based on inclination in order to afford it the universality of a law and in this way to make it suitable for pure practical reason; only from this limitation, and not from the addition of an external incentive, could there arise the concept of *obligation* to extend the maxim of my self-love to the happiness of others as well. (CPrR 167–168; AA 5:34–35)[27]

Self-love, in short, is at once the precondition for as well as the target
of the love of others. It is a precondition for love of others insofar as it
defines the legitimate self-love of *Eigenliebe* or benevolent concern with
our own ends which it is our duty to extend to embrace others as well so
that our "maxim of self-love" might be raised to the "objective validity of
a law." In the contemporary ethics lectures (Collins), Kant sums this up
in explaining that, "if we wish to be loved, we must also display a love
for mankind. Hence we must do to others what we demand they should
do to us" (LE 173; AA 27:407). But equally importantly, self-love is the
target of the love of others insofar as the recognition of our duties of love
to others necessarily humbles the illegitimate self-love of *Eigendünkel*,
the egocentric propensity to prefer self to others and to seek superiority
over them.

A final element of the treatment of love of others in the second *Critique*
also demands notice. As we have seen, one of Kant's chief concerns is to
define a form of love of others that is independent of both theistic as well
as sentimental foundations – that is, in keeping with our triangle metaphor, a love of others that depends only on the love of self rather than
the love of God. Kant's regrounding of love of others in self-love and the
neediness it prompts takes us a long way toward this end. But if indeed
love of neighbor can be defended without recourse to a lexically prior
love of God, how then ought the dual commands of the Sermon on the
Mount – which of course seem to require precisely this – be read? Kant
has an answer:

The possibility of such a commandment as *Love God above all, and your neighbor as yourself* agrees with this very well. For, as a commandment it requires
respect (*Achtung*) for a law that *commands love* and does not leave it to one's
discretionary choice to make this one's principle. But love for God as inclination
(pathological love) is impossible, for he is not an object of the senses. The same
thing toward human beings is indeed possible but cannot be commanded, for it is
not within the power of any human being to love someone merely on command.
It is, therefore, only *practical love* that is understood in that kernel of all laws.
To love God means, in this sense, to do what He commands *gladly*; to love one's
neighbor means to practice all duties toward him *gladly*. (CPrR 207; AA 5:83)

Two aspects of this striking reformulation of the first command deserve
particular notice. First, Kant here is reinterpreting the first command to
suggest that what the Christian religion calls love of God is equivalent
to his conception of cheerfulness in the consciousness of our doing our
duty (cf. LE 65; AA 27:274 and LE 90–91; AA 27:300 and LE 108; AA
27:322 and LE 118; AA 27:335 and LE 442–444; AA 27:720–22 and

RWL 200; AA 6:182).²⁸ Second, in invoking the love of God in precisely this way, Kant means to strike down our self-esteem in a very particular sense of striking down the self-esteem of those proud of their compassion; thus his insistence that the cognizance of the sublimity of the moral law represented by the love of God serves specifically "to check, or where possible, prevent, a *merely moral* enthusiasm which infects many people" and which produces that "moral enthusiasm and exaggerated self-conceit (*moralische Schwärmerei und Steigerung des Eigendünkels*)" characteristic of "a frivolous, high-flown, fantastic cast of mind" which flatters itself "with a spontaneous goodness of heart that needs neither spur nor bridle" (CPrR 208; AA 5:84–85).²⁹ Indeed there is no passion more than compassion that encourages its possessor "to rove among fancied moral perfections," and hence the necessity of duty to "set limits of humility (i.e., self-knowledge) to self-conceit as well as to self-love" (CPrR 209; AA 5:86).

LOVE AND RESPECT IN THE *METAPHYSICS* OF MORALS

Kant's practical writings of the 1780s, as we have seen, inaugurate a crucial revaluation of the concept of other-directed love. This theory, grounded as it is in the extension of self-love by reason, is regarded by Kant as an advance beyond traditional theistic and contemporary sentimentalist conceptions, each of which he thinks to be vulnerable to accusations of heteronomy. Furthermore, Kant's explicit distinction of the legitimate self-love of *Eigenliebe* from the corrupt self-love of *Eigendünkel* allows him not only to show how the love of others can be grounded in resources natural to us (unlike theistic other-directedness) but also allows him to show how his concept of love can restrain the sorts of egocentrism inimical to equality (unlike sentimental other-directedness). This represents a remarkable advance in the idea of charity in modernity. But Kant was hardly finished. The idea of other-directed love continued to occupy him to the end of his philosophical career, and is particularly prominent in his major practical text of the 1790s, the *Metaphysics of Morals*, as well as his contemporary ethics lectures.³⁰ Here Kant sets forth his most developed account of love, drawing upon and further extending the foundational principle of his critical-period theory of other-directedness, namely the insistence on extending proper self-love via reason to a benevolent concern for the ends of others. Yet he also presents several new elements of his theory of love in these texts – elements either not central to or wholly absent from the precritical and critical theories, but which are central to his larger project of defining a concept of love that promotes efficacious and practical benefaction and which serves to encourage rather than impede the recognition of others' claims to equal dignity. It is to these ends, I want to argue, that the theory of love that Kant develops in the *Metaphysics of Morals* particularly emphasizes respect for others and respect for the law as indispensible to love itself.

We begin with what is common to the *Metaphysics of Morals* theory of love and the earlier theory of love. This consists principally in the claim that practical love can only be founded on reason's extension of self-love to others. This indeed is the core claim of his principal discussions of love in the *Metaphysics of Morals*, which come in the *Doctrine of Virtue*, or *Tugendlehre*, dedicated to defining the principles of virtue – that is to say, those duties for which only we ourselves can give ourselves the law and are thus the product of internal freedom, as opposed to those duties of right, surveyed in the *Doctrine of Right*, or *Rechtslehre*, which concern the conditions of external freedom (see, e.g., MM 512–513; AA 6:379–380). As such, virtue is concerned not with external formal conditions, but with ends that are "objectively necessary" – "that is, an end that, as far as human beings are concerned, it is a duty to have" (MM 513; AA 6:380). As is well known, Kant goes on to insist that there are two ends that are at once duties: "they are *one's own perfection* and *the happiness of others*" (MM 517; AA 6:385). For our purposes, it is the second of these ends that are also duties that must be our principal concern, for it is here that Kant presents his core account of proper other-directedness – an account that builds upon and further develops his earlier theory of love. Thus in his first account in the *Tugendlehre* of "the happiness of others as an end that is also a duty," Kant explains

> *Benevolence* (*Wohlwollen*) can be unlimited, since nothing need be done with it. But it is more difficult to *do good* (*Wohltun*), especially if it is to be done not from affection (love) for others but from duty, at the cost of forgoing the satisfaction of concupiscence and of active injury to it in many cases. – The reason that it is a duty to be beneficent is this: since our self-love (*Selbstliebe*) cannot be separated from our need to be loved (helped in case of need) by others as well, we therefore make ourselves an end for others; and the only way this maxim can be binding is through its qualification as a universal law, hence through our will to make others our ends as well. The happiness of others is therefore an end that is also a duty. (MM 524; AA 6:393)

Kant here reiterates several claims familiar from both his earlier treatments of love and his claims elsewhere in the *Tugendlehre*, including especially the superiority of duty to affection, the requirement that our subjective maxims conform to universal law, and the superiority of good-doing to well-wishing (cf. LE 353; AA 27:607). But what is (somewhat) new here is the way in which he regards self-love. As before, the principal claim is that our self-loving concern with our own ends can only be legitimized if we extend our concern so that it embraces the ends of others as well. But to this is added another suggestion: namely that in our neediness we not only depend on others for practical assistance, but demand that these others recognize *us* as ends in ourselves. This, at any rate, seems to be what lies behind the claim that our needs lead us to "make ourselves an end for others." What is key here is that even as this process replicates the earlier extension of our concern for our own ends to include others' ends, now this process of how we ought to regard others rests on a subjective awareness of how we are asking them to regard us, and specifically how we are asking them to regard us in our time of greatest need. And this demand that others not merely help us but recognize us as ends in ourselves in turn serves as the foundation of Kant's main claim with regard to love in what follows: specifically that practical love of others ultimately needs to be founded not in our feelings for others, or even our recognition of their dignity, but in our self-awareness of the demands on others that our own self-love prompts.

This is a striking claim. In the first place, as has been noted by Allen Wood, the only place that Kant in fact employs the universalizability test in the *Metaphysics of Morals* is in the context of this discussion of our duties of beneficence to others.[31] Further, not only is legitimate love of others independent of affection for others, but it also seems to be independent of any assessment of what we owe them on account of their intrinsic dignity, either as beings created in the image of God (i.e., dignity in the Christian sense), or as autonomous ends in themselves (dignity in the Kantian sense). Kant returns to this in a key passage on love of others in the *Tugendlehre*. He introduces this account by ringing changes on a set of now-familiar themes: that true love consists neither in "feeling" nor "delight" in others but in "the maxim of *benevolence* (practical love), which results in beneficence" (MM 569; AA 6:449), that "the duty of love for one's neighbor (*die Pflicht der Nächstenliebe*)" consists in "the duty to make others' *ends* my own" (MM 569; AA 6:450), and that a genuine philanthropist takes satisfaction "when things go well for every other" (MM 570; AA 6:450). And the key passage follows:

In accordance with the ethical law of perfection "love your neighbor as yourself," the maxim of benevolence (practical love of human beings) (*praktische Menschenliebe*) is a duty of all human beings toward one another, whether or not one finds them worthy of love. – For, every morally practical relation to human beings is a relation among them represented by pure reason, that is, a relation of free actions in accordance with maxims that qualify for a giving of universal law and so cannot be selfish (*ex solipsismo prodeuntes*). I want everyone else to be benevolent towards me (*benevolentiam*); hence I ought also to be benevolent toward everyone else. But since all *others* with the exception of myself would not be *all*, so that the maxim would not have within it the universality of a law, which is still necessary for imposing obligation, the law making benevolence a duty will include myself, as an object of benevolence, in the command of practical reason. This does not mean that I am thereby under obligation to love myself (for this happens unavoidably, apart from any command, so there is no obligation to it); it means instead that lawgiving reason, which includes the whole species (and so myself as well) in its idea of humanity as such, includes me as giving universal law along with all others in the duty of mutual benevolence, in accordance with the principle of equality, and *permits* you to be benevolent to yourself on the condition of your being benevolent to every other as well; for it is only in this way that your maxim (of beneficence) qualifies for the giving of universal law, the principle on which every law of duty is based. (MM 570; AA 6:450–451; cf. RWL 182; AA 6:160–161 and MM 530–531; AA 6:402)

This passage is significant in part for the ways in which it brings together several fundamental claims that Kant has already set forth. But in addition to synthesizing several discrete claims already made, this passage also adds several new elements – or at least makes explicit several points seemingly implicit in the earlier accounts. First, as its first line makes clear, the entirety of the "ethical law of perfection" is to be found in the second commandment, and this commandment can be "represented by pure reason" wholly independently of any reference to the first commandment (cf. MM 531; AA 6:402). This is consistent not only with the discrete argument made here but with Kant's ethics more generally, which, as he explains in the conclusion of the *Metaphysics of Morals*, regards duties to God as "entirely beyond the bounds of purely philosophic ethics" (MM 599; AA 6:488); indeed "the question of what sort of moral relation holds between God and the human being goes completely beyond the bounds of ethics and is altogether incomprehensible for us" (MM 602; AA 6:491). Second, this opening line also makes clear that we have a duty to love others wholly independent of any consideration of whether they are "worthy of love": a view that distinguishes Kant's position from the theistic position but also seems to distance it from his own arguments for moral worth and human dignity. Third, Kant suggests that his concern is not to establish simply the duty of an individual subject to love others, but what he here calls "the duty of mutual benevolence." This should not be overstated; as he makes clear, "the benevolence present in love for all human beings is indeed the greatest in its *extent*, but the smallest in its *degree*; and when I say that I take an interest in this human being's well-being only out of my love for all human beings, the interest I take is as slight as an interest can be. I am only not indifferent with regard to him" (MM 570–571; AA 6:451).[32] Much like Hume and Rousseau and Smith, Kant means to defend his conception of other-directedness on the precise grounds of its weakness and its wideness. But there is also something more at work here – namely the shift of the discussion back to Kant's principal concern in the defining duties of love in the *Metaphysics of Morals*: namely the issue of "equality."

The significance of this final point is reiterated in Kant's final discussion of the love of others in the *Tugendlehre*. Here he explains why being beneficent and indeed working "to promote according to one's means the happiness of others in need, without hoping for something in return, is everyone's duty":

> For everyone who finds himself in need wishes to be helped by others. But if he lets his maxim of being unwilling to assist others in turn when they are in need become public, that is, makes this a universal permissive law, then everyone would likewise deny him assistance when he himself is in need, or at least would be authorized to deny it. Hence the maxim of self-interest would conflict with itself if it were made a universal law, that is, it is contrary to duty. Consequently the maxim of common interest, of beneficence toward those in need, is a universal duty of human beings, just because they are to be considered fellow human beings, that is, rational beings with needs, united by nature in one dwelling place so that they can help one another. (MM 572; AA 6:453)

Two points here again demand notice. First, Kant very explicitly insists that we owe others our love simply insofar as they are human beings, but again, by this he means not that they are human beings created in the divine image or human beings that are possessed of dignity, but because they are human beings with needs. Second, what is especially remarkable here is that these needs are mutual and universal, and that indeed it is the mutual effort to satisfy mutual needs that not only makes love itself necessary, but is what animates and explains human society.

To now, Kant's account of love in the *Metaphysics of Morals* has focused on further developing several elements of the account of love present in earlier texts. Yet his argument here also presents several new elements, each of which demands our attention insofar as it plays a key role in the efforts of Kant to provide a theory of love that remedies certain discrete problems endemic to the sentimental view of love. Three of these new elements deserve particular attention: first, Kant's explicit distinction between benevolence and beneficence, which seeks to buttress his aims of rendering love of others practical and efficacious in the world; second, his efforts to recover respect for others alongside love of others, intended to contribute to the mitigation of potential inequality between benefactors and recipients of their love and charity; and third, Kant's recovery of respect for law, intended to recover one side of the concern for transcendence central to the traditional conception of love.

Kant presents his core claim with regard to the first of these new elements in the course of his account of beneficence as the first division of duties of love. Here he explains, "benevolence is satisfaction in the happiness (well-being) of others; but beneficence is the maxim of making others' happiness one's end, and the duty to it consists in the subject's being constrained by his reason to adopt this maxim as a universal law" (MM 571; AA 6:452). Kant's own concern is clearly with beneficence insofar as it and it alone is practical, both in the familiar sense that it can in fact give rise to actions in the world, and in the technical Kantian sense that it can serve as a determining ground of the will. On this second front, Kant repeatedly notes that our feelings of benevolence toward others can never be considered a duty insofar as such feelings are "natural predispositions of the mind" that have been given as Kant says "originally" to "every human being" (MM 528–529; AA 6:399–400); such sensible feelings given to us by nature simply cannot be commanded as an object of freedom, and hence cannot be considered moral (MM 574–575; AA 6:456–457). At most they can be considered "*subjective* conditions of receptiveness to the concept of duty," and our obligations with regard to such feelings are limited to the imperfect duty "only to *cultivate* it and to strengthen it through wonder at its inscrutable source" (MM 528–529; AA 6:399–400), and indeed to encourage such feelings to the extent that they constitute "impulses that nature has implanted in us to do what the representation of duty alone might not accomplish" (MM 576; AA 6:457). Sympathy and compassion and pity are then not to be shunned insofar as they afford the stop-gap or second-best solution on which we can fall back when practical love is lacking; thus Kant suggests that "the wisdom of nature has planted in us the predisposition to compassion in order to handle the reins *provisionally*, until reason has achieved the necessary strength" (A 355; AA 7:253), and that we have "an indirect duty to cultivate the compassionate natural (aesthetic) feelings (*die mitleidige natürliche (ästhetische) Gefühle*) in us, and to make use of them as so many means to sympathy based on moral principles and the feeling appropriate to them" (MM 575; AA 6:457; cf. LE 178; AA 27:414–415).[33] But this is hardly an about-face on Kant's part; even here, the indirect duty to cultivate other-directed sentiments is circumscribed by the specific question of whether such sentiments in fact serve to promote practically efficacious beneficent activity. Thus the caveat: "when another suffers and, although I cannot help him, I let myself be infected by his pain (through my imagination), then two of us suffer, though the trouble really (in nature) affects only *one*." And this, he insists, is absurd: "there cannot possibly be a duty to increase the ills in the world" (MM 575; AA 6:547).[34] Kant here seems to extend further his earlier observation in the second *Critique* that in fact the "feeling of compassion and tender sympathy" must itself seem "burdensome to right-thinking persons," insofar as it "brings their considered maxims into confusion, and produces the wish to be freed from them and subject to lawgiving reason alone" (CPrR 235; AA 5:118). All told, even as Kant seeks to recover good-feeling here, it is not good-feeling in itself that he values but only that good-feeling that helps our phenomenal selves to realize and fulfill our duties to good-doing.

Kant's critique of compassion in this passage introduces a second important element of his final theory of love, namely its relationship to respect. In this vein the passage quoted previously goes on to explain that not only can there not be any duty to compassion (*Mitleid*), but further that this sort of sentimental other-directedness is in fact a threat to human dignity itself. And here Kant makes fully explicit the claim that has been implicit in his critique of sentimental other-directedness going back to the precritical period: namely that this would be "an insulting kind of beneficence, since it expresses the kind of benevolence one has towards someone unworthy, called *pity* (*Barmherzigkeit*); and this has no place in people's relations with one another" (MM 575; AA 6:457).[35] Here lies the core of Kant's most damning criticism of sentimental other-directedness: namely that so far from promoting a recognition of the worth and dignity of others, it subverts it – and indeed in two ways. First, the good feeling enjoyed by sentimental benefactors leads them to consider themselves morally superior to others. Second, insofar as the recipients of his benefactions are dependent on him for their well-being, they are necessarily humbled – if not simply humiliated – before him by their dependence. This, on Kant's terms, is necessarily the worst of all worlds: so far from restraining self-love, such a love only reifies the inequalities born of egocentrism and dependence. Sentimental other-directedness is thus doubly problematic insofar as it at once inflames our own bad self-love and subverts the good self-love of others.

The remedy to this lies not simply in a redefinition of love that establishes the grounds on which we ought to help others, but also in our cultivation of a self-aware understanding of *how* we ought to fulfill our duties of love to others. That is, insofar as putting others under obligation necessarily lowers their self-esteem and "humbles the other in his own eyes" at the same time that it heightens a benefactor's self-esteem and offers him an opportunity for "reveling in moral feelings" (MM 572; AA 6:453), the challenge is to develop a new means by which these benefactions can be delivered.[36] On this front Kant suggests that "since the favor we do implies that his well-being depends on our generosity, and this humbles him, it is our duty to behave as if our help (*Wohltätigkeit*) is either merely what is due him or but a slight service of love, and to spare him humiliation and maintain his respect for himself (*seine Achtung für sich selbst*)" (MM 568; AA 6:448–449). The best means by which this can be done, Kant suggests, is for the benefactor to "practice his beneficence in complete secrecy" (MM 572; AA 6:453). But this is not the only – or even the most practical – approach. On the contrary, the most effective means of ensuring that the dignity of the recipients of benefaction lies the concept of respect, understood as "the *maxim* of limiting our self-esteem (*Selbstschätzung*) by the dignity of humanity in another person, and so as respect in the practical sense" (MM 569; AA 6:449).

It is for this reason then that Kant binds the duties of love to duties of respect in his mature formulation. Many of course have noticed the importance of the duty of respect in the *Metaphysics of Morals*, and in particular Kant's claims that we are "under obligation to acknowledge, in a practical way, the dignity of humanity in every other human being," and that respect consists in the "recognition of a *dignity* (*dignitas*) in other human beings, that is, of a worth that has no price, no equivalent for which the object evaluated (*aestimii*) could be exchanged" (MM 579; AA 6:462). But what interests us here, beyond the mere rhetorical force of these calls, is the fact that it is precisely Kant's theory of the duties of love for others that makes his theory of the duty of respect for others necessary. Respect for others, that is, is necessary in order to temper the propensities to inequality in even the best forms of love. In this sense, respect plays a key role beyond its oft-noticed role in preserving proper distance between human beings. Kant's "analogy with the physical world" on this front has particularly attracted notice, and especially his claim that "*attraction* and *repulsion* bind together rational beings (on earth). The principle of *mutual love* (*Wechselliebe*) admonishes them constantly to *come closer* to one another; that of the *respect* (*Achtung*) they owe one another, to keep themselves *at a distance* from one another" (MM 568–569; AA 6:449; cf. MM 585; AA 6:470). Kant's Newtonian metaphor naturally invites a visual-spatial image of human beings as striving for an appropriate equilibrium, preserving proper space in their relations among each other.[37] But there is another side here, for not only does Kant think that the joining together of respect and love is necessary to preserve an equilibrium on the horizontal plane, but also, as importantly, on the vertical axis of moral worth. Love without respect necessarily forces each party to higher and lower positions on this axis, whereas the addition of respect for others guarantees or preserves equality or equilibrium to the maximum degree possible. It is for this reason that Kant defines the peak figure of his ethics not as a lover of human beings but as a friend of human beings – defined specifically as the one who feels not just love but love and respect:

A *friend of human beings* (*Menschenfreund*) as such (i.e., of the whole race) is one who takes an effective interest in the well-being of all human beings (rejoices with them) and will never disturb it without heartfelt regret. Yet the expression 'a *friend* of human beings' is somewhat narrower in its meaning than 'one who merely loves human beings' (*des blos Menschenliebenden*) (a *philanthropist*). For the former includes, as well, thought and consideration for the *equality* among them, and hence the idea that in putting others under obligation by his benefi-cence he is himself under obligation, as if all were brothers under one *father* who wills the happiness of all. (MM 587; AA 6:472–473)

The true friend of human beings thus overcomes "arrogance," the first of the vices that "violate duties of respect for human beings," a vice that further "demands from others a respect it denies them" (MM 581; AA 6:465).[38] Recognizing instead that "universal love of one's neighbor can and must be based on equality of duties" (MM 576; AA 6:548), and indeed that "taking to heart the duty of being benevolent as a friend of human beings (a necessary humbling of oneself) serves to guard against the pride that usually comes over those fortunate enough to have the means for beneficence" (MM 587–588; AA 6:473), his love enables him to fulfill his duties of love without violating duties to recognize the dig-nity of others.[39]

Yet in addition to respect for others, there is a final form of form of respect that also plays a central role in Kant's mature conception of love, namely respect for the law. This moral feeling, as others have noted, occupies a unique place in Kant's project; insofar as it is the result of the consciousness of having acted in accord with the law, it is the only true intellectual feeling, and hence the only one that can find a legitimate place in a moral system (see esp. CPrR 201–203; AA 5:76–78; cf. CPrR 234; AA 5:117).⁴⁰ For present purposes though, one aspect of this feeling is particularly important. Throughout our larger study of love in this book, the relationship of the love of others to both self-love and to the love of the transcendent has been a main focus. Kant's conception of respect for the law plays a crucial role in both his own ethics and in this larger project. Wood captures much of the significance of this in Kant's system in describing "the uncanny combination of abasement and exaltation that Kant calls 'respect'," which "combines the pain of our humiliated self-conceit with our awe and wonderment at the dignity and sublime vocation we have as rational beings."⁴¹ In terms of our larger argument in this book, respect for the law serves at once to restrain pernicious self-love and reopens the question of whether and how it might be possible for us to experience transcendence. Kant's account of the experience of beholding the law indeed explicitly reopens the question of what relationship there may be between the overcoming of egoism and the experience of self-transcendence. In this vein Kant explains that the experience of respect for the law at once "noticeably reduces our self-conceit (*unseren Eigendünkel*)" and induces "humiliation" and "the lowering of pretensions to moral self-esteem (*moralischen Selbstschätzung*) – that is, humiliation on the sensible side," itself "an elevation of the moral – that is, practical – esteem for the law itself on the intellectual side" (CPrR 203–204; AA 5:79). The upshot of this is clearly "striking down self-conceit (*den Eigendünkel niederschlägt*)" (CPrR 210; AA 5:87). Yet importantly, not only does the experience of respect restrain our bad self-love, but it also lifts us beyond ourselves: "once one has laid self-conceit aside and allowed practical influence to that respect, one can in turn never get enough of contemplating the majesty of this law, and the soul believes itself elevated in proportion as it sees the holy elevated above itself and its frail nature" (CPrR 203; AA 5:77). Indeed to truly experience this respect that emerges from our self-aware capacity to behold the moral law is not merely to liberate us from the natural laws of animal nature, but to offer us "a view into a higher, immutable order of things in which we already are and in which we can henceforth be directed, by determinate precepts, to carry on our existence in accordance with the highest vocation of reason" (CPrR 226; AA 5:107–108). Even in a secular age it may be that transcendence is not absolutely beyond our grasp.

NOTES

1 See, respectively, G 54–55; AA 4:399 and MM 426–427; AA 6:277 and G 53–54; AA 4:398–399 and G 75; AA 4:423. The third and fourth of these cases are examined in what follows; the first and second I discuss in "Kant's Sexual Contract," *Journal of Politics* 76 (2014): 914–927.

2 Happily I am not alone in so thinking; recent treatments of Kant's theory of love which likewise find his theory valuable (even if for reasons different from those I develop subsequently) include Marcia Baron, "Love and Respect in the *Doctrine of Virtue*," in *Kant's Metaphysics of Morals: Interpretive Essays*, ed. Mark Timmons (Oxford: Oxford University Press, 2002); Marguerite La Caze, "Love, That Indispensible Supplement: Irigaray and Kant on Love and Respect," *Hypatia* 20 (2005): 92–114; Martin Moors, "Kant on: 'Love God Above All, and Your Neighbor as Yourself'," in *The Concept of Love in 17th and 18th Century Philosophy*, ed. Gábor Boros, Herman de Dijn, and Moors (Leuven: Leuven University Press, 2007); Christoph Horn, "The Concept of Love in Kant's Virtue Ethics," in *Kant's Ethics of Virtue*, ed. Monika Betzler (Berlin: Walter de Gruyter, 2008); Marcia Baron and Melissa Seymour Fahmy, "Beneficence and Other Duties of Love in *The Metaphysics of Morals*," in *The Blackwell Guide to Kant's Ethics*, ed. Thomas E. Hill, Jr. (London: Wiley-Blackwell, 2009); Fahmy, "Kantian Practical Love," *Pacific Philosophical Quarterly* 91 (2010): 313–331; and Christine Swanton, "Kant's Impartial Duties of Love," in *Perfecting Virtue: New Essays on Kantian Ethics and Virtue Ethics*, ed. Lawrence Jost and Julian Wuerth (Cambridge: Cambridge University Press, 2011).

3 There are welcome signs of recent change on this front; see esp. the essays collected in Susan Shell and Richard Velkley, eds., *Kant's Observations and Remarks: A Critical Guide* (Cambridge: Cambridge University Press, 2012).

4 Kant's largely neglected contextual engagement with the eighteenth-century self-love debate has been recently and very helpfully surveyed in Eric Entrican Wilson, "Kant and the Selfish Hypothesis," *Social Theory and Practice* 41 (2015): 377–402.

5 The version of the story known to Kant was that published as "Carazans Traum" in the *Bremisches Magazin zur Ausbreitung der Wissenschaften, Künste und Tugend* 4 (1761): 539–546 – itself a quite literal translation of an English story that had originally appeared in *The Adventurer* 132 (1754): 226–232, and was reprinted with light emendations in *The Gentleman's Magazine* for February 1754, pp. 76–78.

6 For further key treatment of Carazan's dream, see esp. Shell, *Kant and the Limits of Autonomy* (Cambridge, MA: Harvard University Press, 2009), 36–38.

7 Kant's version of the story differs in a substantively important way from the original here in its silence on divine love. Thus the English original speaks not only of compassion and what Kant here calls "the love of humankind" but also of "that devotion which arises from the love of God, and necessarily includes the love of man"; in this it is closely followed by the German

translation from which Kant drew his account: "*diejenige Andacht, welche aus der Liebe Gottes entstehet, und die Liebe des Nächsten notwendig auch mit einschließet*" ("Carazans Traum," 540).

8   Here too Kant's transcription omits the emphasis on divine love in the original (see "Carazans Traum," 543), which emphasizes that Carazan's devotion falls short "because it was not prompted by love of God" ("*denn die Liebe Gottes hat ihn nicht angefachet*"). Kant's version, in sharp contrast to the original, clearly and consciously aims to decouple the love of others from divine love.

9   And indeed beyond: for an important and stimulating discussion of the degree to which the *Groundwork* itself deserves to be read as a "conversion narrative," see Shalini Satkunanandan, "The Extraordinary Categorical Imperative," *Political Theory* 39 (2011): 234–260.

10 I treat this question and the associated scholarship at length in my "Rethinking Kant's Debts to Rousseau," *Archiv für Geschichte der Philosophie* (forthcoming). In the context of the present work, deserving particular mention here is Kant's related though lesser-known observation that "only the doctrine of Mr. *Rousseau* can bring it about that even the most learned philosopher, with his knowledge, earnestly regards himself, without help from religion, as no better than the common man" (R 187–188; AA 20:176), as well as his claim that "*humility* is therefore not a *monkish* virtue, as Hume believes, but already needful even in natural morality" (LE 16; AA 27:39).

11 The *Lectures on Pedagogy* – a posthumously published text collated from Kant's notes and which thus cannot be taken as necessarily representative of Kant's views – contains a parallel passage: "Children must be prevented from any yearning, languishing sympathizing (*Teilnehmung*). Sympathizing is actually sensitivity; it agrees only with a character that is sensitive. It is still different from compassion and is an evil which consists merely in bemoaning a thing" (LoP 474; AA 9:487).

12 In this context see also Kant's related and Rousseauan observations that "the corruption of our time can be boiled down to this, that no one demands to be content with himself, or also good, but instead to appear so" (R 122; AA 20:84), and that man "in a state of opulence has imaginary needs and is selfish" (R 185; AA 20:173).

13 See, e.g., Paul Guyer, "Freedom as the Foundation of Morality: Kant's Early Efforts," in *Kant's Observations and Remarks*, ed. Susan Shell and Richard Velkley, esp. 78–79.

14 That this is the case is further suggested by the Newtonian metaphor Kant uses with regard to self-interest and love in the lectures: "the disinterested feeling is like a force of attraction, and the self-interested feeling like a force of repulsion. The two of them, *in conflictu*, constitute the world" (LE 3–4; AA 27:4). Kant soon after applies this even more directly to love and respect: "Love wishes for closer union; sublimity frightens us away" (LE 14: AA 27:31). Kant of course would employ this same metaphor in the 1780s in his history essays and in the *Metaphysics of Morals* (see section three of this chapter) in order to describe the attraction and repulsion that governs social forms organized by "unsocial sociability."

15 Cf. Kant's claim on the following page with regard to the axiom that "*All men are equal to one another*": "To the savage it is a principle; but to us, who have strayed so far from it, it is a thing to be proved, and the basis of *ethics*" (LE 31; AA 27:66–67).

16 See, e.g., La Caze, "Love, That Indispensible Supplement," 96.

17 For a succinct presentation of this position, see David Cartwright, "Kant's View of the Moral Significance of Kindhearted Emotions and the Moral Insignificance of Kant's View," *Journal of Value Inquiry* 21 (1987): 295–296; for a critique of the rigid divide between pure practical philosophy and empiricism, see esp. Jeffrey Edwards, "Self-Love, Anthropology, and Universal Benevolence in Kant's Metaphysics of Morals," *Review of Metaphysics* 53 (2000): 887–914.

18 On these see also esp. Moors, "Kant on: 'Love God Above All'," 256–257.

19 Kant's key distinction between these two types of self-love has only relatively recently begun to attract significant attention; see, e.g., Edwards, "Self-Love, Anthropology, and Universal Benevolence," 902n54; Stephen Engstrom, "The *Triebfeder* of Pure Practical Reason," in *Kant's Critique of Practical Reason: A Critical Guide*, ed. Andrews Reath and Jens Timmerman (Cambridge: Cambridge University Press, 2010), 101–104; Wilson, "Kant and the Selfish Hypothesis," 387n1; and now most fully in Kate Moran, "Delusions of Virtue: Kant on Self-Conceit," *Kantian Review* 19 (2014): 419–447.

20 On *Eigendünkel* as promoting comparison and threatening inequality, see esp. Allen W. Wood, "Self-Love, Self-Benevolence, and Self-Conceit," in *Aristotle, Kant, and the Stoics: Rethinking Happiness and Duty*, ed. Stephen Engstrom and Jennifer Whiting (Cambridge: Cambridge University Press, 1996), 145–150; Moran, "Delusions of Virtue," esp. 422, 436.

21 See also the related claim by Swanton that the proud suffer from a "lack of self-love" insofar as they "are dependent for their sense of self-worth on comparisons with others" ("Kant's Impartial Duties of Love," 256).

22 On radical evil and self-conceit, see, e.g., Wood, "Self-Love, Self-Benevolence, and Self-Conceit," 154; and Wilson, "Kant and the Selfish Hypothesis," 391.

23 Wood seems right to say "probably nothing in Kant's ethical writing has earned him more hostility" than his discussion of the cold-hearted benefactor ("The Final Form of Kant's Practical Philosophy," in *Kant's Metaphysics of Morals*, ed. Mark Timmons, 15). Some of the key concerns on this front have been most prominently outlined in Michael Stocker, "The Schizophrenia of Modern Ethical Theories," in *Virtue Ethics*, ed. Roger Crisp and Michael Slote (Oxford: Oxford University Press, 1997); for important extension of these concerns, see Karen Stohr, "Virtue Ethics and Kant's Cold-Hearted Benefactor," *Journal of Value Inquiry* 32 (2002): 187–204. For an important response, see Baron, *Kantian Ethics Almost without Apology* (Ithaca, NY: Cornell University Press, 1995), chapter 6.

24 A point made especially helpfully in Michael Frazer, *The Enlightenment of Sympathy: Justice and the Moral Sentiments in the Eighteenth Century and Today* (Oxford: Oxford University Press, 2010), 114–115; see also

Wilson, "Kant and the Selfish Hypothesis," 393; and Edwards, "Self-Love, Anthropology, and Universal Benevolence," 889.

25 Fahmy offers a nuanced and insightful analysis of Kant's mature conception of *Teilnehmung* in the *Metaphysics of Morals*, and suggests that it is best understood not merely as compassion or even passive sympathy per se, but as "active sympathetic participation with others" [Fahmy, "Active Sympathetic Participation: Reconsidering Kant's Duty of Sympathy," *Kantian Review* 14 (2009): 31; cf. 34, 42–46]. At the same time, clearly Kant's earlier usage of the term here in the *Groundwork* suggests a view of *Teilnehmung* not far removed from simple *Mitleid*.

26 In making this claim I want from the outset to distinguish it from a familiar claim with which it could be easily confused: namely that Kant's theory of love is simply an extension of egoism – a time-honored view that goes back to Schopenhauer and extends through Wood's claim that for Kant "love exhibits a kind of second-order self-partiality" [Wood, *Kant's Ethical Thought* (Cambridge: Cambridge University Press, 1999), 271; cf. 274], and, more polemically, the charge that "Kant's concept of the love of God is indeed nothing but this *ego*-centric, rationally sublimated variation of *amor complacentiae* (a morally sublimated *Liebe des Wohlgefallens an sich selbst*)" [Moors, "Kant on: 'Love God Above All'," 257]. This is, I think, too reductive insofar as it fails to distinguish legitimate self-love – that is, benevolence for our own ends, which Kant indeed very much wants to extend to others – from improper self-love – that is, self-preference or self-partiality, which Kant is quite concerned to limit. For another sort of response to this view, see, e.g., Horn, "The Concept of Love in Kant's Virtue Ethics," 163. But for present purposes, what I am concerned to emphasize is the way in which Kant means to extend self-love to include the ends of others. This concern of Kant's has been all too rarely noted in the literature; the only discussion of which I am aware that points in this direction is Fahmy's insightful claim that "given that we express self-love by desiring and pursuing our own happiness, we love our neighbors *as ourselves* by making their happiness one of our ends" (Fahmy, "Kantian Practical Love," 329).

27 Cf. the discussion of this passage in Edwards, "Self-Love, Anthropology, and Universal Benevolence," 902–905, which omits the last line and hence shifts emphasis away from the rational extension of self-love to others. Closer to the position for which I argue here is Engstrom's discussion of how the moral law "infringes self-love from within, not as a mere external restraint" ("*Triebfeder* of Pure Practical Reason," 112–113; see also 106–107).

28 See Moors, "Kant on: 'Love God above All'," 249–250, 254–255; Baron, *Kantian Ethics Almost without Apology*, 206; Fahmy, "Kantian Practical Love," 317, 321.

29 See, e.g., Wilson, "Kant and the Selfish Hypothesis," 395–396.

30 On this front, see Horn's claim that the *Metaphysics of Morals* account is simply a "condensed form" of the theory of love set out in these lectures; Horn, "The Concept of Love in Kant's Virtue Ethics," 147; though cf. Moors, "Kant on: 'Love God Above All'," 260, and esp. 263–264, which particularly emphasizes the differences between the ways in which the *Tugendlehre*

account and the Vigilantius notes account conceive of the role played by divine love in *Menschenliebe*.

31 Wood, "The Final Form of Kant's Practical Philosophy," 5; cf. Horn, "The Concept of Love in Kant's Virtue Ethics," 158.

32 See in this context La Caze's helpful observation that Kant's conception of "love for all humanity is quite minimalist," and indeed is "great in extent, but small in degree" ("Love, That Indispensible Supplement," 97). Kant's development of this thought goes on to address the question of how we might square our easily universalized well-wishing with our necessarily limited and seemingly local powers of good-doing (see esp. MM 571; AA 6:451–452). This important point has been examined by several commentators (see esp. Baron and Fahmy, "Beneficence and Other Duties of Love," 222–223), but is not central to my claims here.

33 Kant's insistence in the *Metaphysics of Morals* on the indirect duty of cultivating sympathy has attracted significant attention for the degree to which it suggests a perhaps less antipathetic attitude toward emotion and affect than has been often assumed. For the more limited view that we indeed have a duty to cultivate these affective dispositions but only insofar as they help animate our phenomenal selves to better strive to perform the duties mandated by our noumenal selves, see, e.g., Wood, *Kant's Ethical Thought*, 270; Wood, "The Final Form of Kant's Practical Philosophy," 16–19; Stohr, "Virtue Ethics and Kant's Cold-Hearted Benefactor," 195–196, 201; and Baron, *Kantian Ethics Almost without Apology*, 212–222. A particularly strong version of this claim is made by Cartwright, who suggests that Kant's account of this indirect duty "is addressed to the morally developing personality who needs nonmoral aid to do that commanded by duty" ("Kant's View of the Moral Significance of Kindhearted Emotions," 293). For the view that Kant in fact believes we have a robust duty on this front and that he values this disposition not merely as instrumental but as valuable in itself, see esp. Fahmy, "Active Sympathetic Participation," esp. 31, 37–42; and, from a different perspective, Frazer, *Enlightenment of Sympathy*, esp. 113, 119–121.

34 See esp. Baron, *Kantian Ethics Almost without Apology*, 211–212.

35 Relatedly see also the treatment of "anti-paternalism and the duty of beneficence" in Baron and Fahmy, "Beneficence and Other Duties of Love," 213–214 and Frazer, *Enlightenment of Sympathy*, 126–127.

36 On this front see Baron and Fahmy's helpful comparison of Kant here to "the Aristotelian idea that acting well involves not just doing a virtuous action, but doing it in the right way, and with the right tone and gesture" ("Beneficence and Other Duties of Love," 215).

37 See esp. Baron, "Love and Respect," 391–392, 406; Swanton, "Kant's Impartial Duties of Love," 242; La Caze, "Love, That Indispensible Supplement," 95; Horn, "The Concept of Love in Kant's Virtue Ethics," 148. Swanton also helpfully goes on to explain how the joining of respect to love is necessary so that "love is not to descend into pathological forms" (244) – a view that importantly accords with the position I develop here; see also Horn, "The Concept of Love in Kant's Virtue Ethics," esp. 166. Swanton also very helpfully details both the universality of Kant's conception of

love (247–248) as well as its weakness (250); on this last point regarding its thinness or weakness, see also esp. La Caze, "Love, That Indispensible Supplement," 97; Horn, "The Concept of Love in Kant's Virtue Ethics," 165.

38 See also Baron, *Kantian Ethics Almost without Apology*, 197–198.

39 Though it remains a question whether even the most perfect practical love can overcome this inequality; on this front, see e.g., Kant's claim that "beneficence creates a debt that can never be repaid" and must necessarily subordinate the recipient to the giver (LE 199; AA 27:442–443; cf. LE 423; AA 27:696).

40 See esp. Satkunanandan, "The Extraordinary Categorical Imperative," 247–249; and Guyer, "Moral Feelings in the *Metaphysics of Morals*," in *Kant's Metaphysics of Morals: A Critical Guide*, ed. Lara Denis (Cambridge: Cambridge University Press, 2010), 130–139. For a recent reading of *Menschenliebe* itself as a parallel source of moral motivation that generates a specific disposition toward the moral law, see Dieter Schönecker, "Kant über Menschenliebe als moralische Gemütsanlage," *Archiv für Geschichte der Philosophie* 92 (2010): 133–175; this interpretation of *Menschenliebe* however rests on an emphasis on *Liebe des Wohlgefallens* somewhat removed from the concept of love of others with which I am engaged here (see esp. 137, 152, 173; see also Fahmy, "Kantian Practical Love," 325–327).

41 Wood, "Self-Love, Self-Benevolence, and Self-Conceit," 154.

Epilogue

This book has sought to chronicle the essential features of the four most well-developed versions of a remarkable conceptual innovation. The four concepts that have been our focus here – Hume's concept of humanity, Rousseau's concept of pity, Smith's concept of sympathy, and Kant's concept of love – all deserve to be regarded as sophisticated efforts to respond to one of the most significant moral and political challenges posed by modernity. In liberating self-love, modernity opens up the possibility of a world in which we all become not only strangers to but enemies of each other – a world of egocentrism at best and exploitation at its worst. Further, insofar as it denies recourse to the transcendent categories on which the traditional understanding of love had been founded, the emergence into modernity rendered it impossible for those concerned by this possibility to seek recovery of the traditional concept of neighbor love. These four innovative theories, however, offer us a means of mitigating the worst potentialities of modern liberal politics in a manner at once consistent with liberalism's minimal foundations and indeed capable of securing the significant benefits that liberalism has made possible.

At the same time, for all the sophistication and innovation of the eighteenth-century theorists profiled here, it is hard to shake the feeling that there may yet be something wanting in their proposals. Different readers will feel different versions of this unease. Some may worry that these theories of other-directedness, for all their successes at tempering self-love, yet fall short of the warm care and concern that would distinguish a truly decent society. On this view, the eighteenth-century theories do not go quite far enough. Other readers may worry that, again despite their practical successes in mitigating self-love, these theories concede the field too easily to the secular critique of transcendence. On this view, the eighteenth-century theorists go entirely too far. I confess that I share certain of these reservations. My own concern ultimately reduces to a worry that the practical success of these other-directed theories, as genuinely admirable as it is, has been bought at the expense of a recovery of the love that most of us would find more fulfilling. Put differently, the eighteenth-century vision of other-directedness is in some sense necessary but not sufficient: necessary to mitigate our worst propensities but insufficient to enable us to realize our best aspirations.

This concern is brought to a particular head by Kant's theory of love. Kant's theory, as I have sought to show, is a striking achievement. In justifying the rational extension of self-love to others, Kant provides the Enlightenment's most sophisticated response to the problem of how self-love can best be mitigated, and at the same time does so in a way that provides an alternative to both the sentimental and theistic options previously on offer. This achievement strikes me as a marvel. At the same time, it is impossible for me not to feel that there is something deeply lacking in Kant's account. And I suspect many of us feel this as soon as we compare our experiences of love to Kant's account; however much we may be impressed by its sophistication and intricacy, there is yet something in it that is seems deeply out of step with how many of us experience love – how we *feel* love – on a subjective (or what Kant might call an anthropological) level. On these grounds it is difficult not to sympathize with those who suspect that "Kant's 'practical love' is not love" insofar as its reverence for duty and antipathy to feeling mistakenly conflates "love" with "loving behaviour."[1] Put bluntly: Kant may be right to say that mitigating selfish and encouraging loving behavior is what love does. Yet we each know in our hearts that what love does is not the same – and ultimately may not even matter to us as much – as how love feels.

We are left then in an interesting position. Kant, it seems to me, provides the fullest possible account of what is necessary to restrain self-love and justify the love of others in a world skeptical of transcendence. But however useful his account may be as a solution to this problem, it leaves another problem unanswered: namely the problem of accounting for the longings that so many of us have experienced in our own capacities as lovers – longings that specifically lead us to wish to be and to be with beings who are not just unencumbered autonomous selves. What, if anything, can be done about this? Kant provides a remedy for a specific modern ill – but does his remedy itself admit of a supplement capable of rendering it not only practically useful but also genuinely fulfilling?

It is tempting at this point to look back again to *eros* and *agape*. Whatever else may be said of these loves and their many differences, they stand united as efforts to confront the question that Kant's theory of love leaves unanswered: that is, to provide a means whereby both the mitigation of what is worst within us and the embrace of what is best beyond us might be realized. The pull that these loves exert on us remains powerful and it seems clear that their attractions have yet to fade even in an age inimical to their foundational commitments. But if they are indeed unavailable to us in their original senses, then we will need an alternative if we hope to solve the problem with which Kant's theory of love leaves us. What this alternative would need to provide is a means of joining to Kant's practical solution to the problem of self-love a way of gratifying those longings that love continues to inspire in us. My sense is that many of the resources for this may be available to cultures beyond the West; indeed it seems almost beyond doubt that the attractions of many Westerners to several forms of "Eastern spirituality" consist precisely in the fact that these systems privilege universal love and self-transcendence, synthesizing these two aims in a beautiful vision of human aspiration and greatness, and indeed do so in a modality that is not recognizably theistic in a way familiar to us from the Abrahamic religions. Whether this vision can ever be fully at home in cultures far removed from those in which they originally flourished is a question that goes well beyond this book. For now, the question we are left with if we hope to preserve liberalism's practical gains and also recover love's highest promise is whether it is truly possible to have both universal love and self-transcendence without theism.

NOTE

1 Oswald Hanfling, "Loving My Neighbour, Loving Myself," *Philosophy* 68 (1993): 149; see also Allen W. Wood, "Self-Love, Self-Benevolence, and Self-Conceit," in *Aristotle, Kant, and the Stoics: Rethinking Happiness and Duty*, ed. Stephen Engstrom and Jennifer Whiting (Cambridge: Cambridge University Press, 1996), 145.

Index

CPSIA information can be obtained
at www.ICGtesting.com
Printed in the USA
LVOW11*2305301217

561237LV00005BA/57/P

9 781107 105225